AMERICAN CHEESE

AMERICAN CHEESE

AN INDULGENT ODYSSEY THROUGH THE ARTISAN CHEESE WORLD

JOE BERKOWITZ

HARPER ● PERENNIAL

NEW YORK ● LONDON ● TORONTO ● SYDNEY ● NEW DELHI ● AUCKLAND

HARPER ● PERENNIAL

HarperCollins books may be purchased for educational, business, or sales promotional use. For information, please email the Special Markets Department at SPsales@harpercollins.com.

FIRST EDITION

Designed by Jamie Lynn Kerner

Library of Congress Cataloging-in-Publication Data has been applied for.

ISBN 978-0-06-293489-5 (pbk)

20 21 22 23 24   LSC   10 9 8 7 6 5 4 3 2 1

For my grandmother, Rita Pagenkopf. This should hopefully make up for at least some of the times I didn't call.

Your body is not a temple, it's an amusement park.
Enjoy the ride.
—ANTHONY BOURDAIN

CONTENTS

AMERICAN CHEESE

INTRODUCTION

A Glimpse of Dairy Narnia

I USED TO BE A NORMAL PERSON. RELATIVELY SO, ANYWAY.

Whenever someone wearing an apron would ask, "Do you want cheese with that?" I'd say things like, "Sure" and "Obviously." You know—normal stuff.

When that question comes up now, though, well, I mostly still say those things, but only after performing some milky calculus.

Back when I was a civilian, I'd walk into a corner deli for a breakfast sandwich and slobber over sweaty slabs of Velveeta stacked into lactic ziggurats. My fridge was never without pepper jack, the most exotic cheese in my repertoire at the time, along with Trader Joe's burrata, its squishy center erupting in a sluicing gush like a McGriddles.

Cheese was my all-hours food, a welcome guest in any meal and something to mindlessly gnaw on during *Fleabag*. Whenever I saw a pristine party tray packed with toothpick-lanced Colby cubes, I greeted it as warmly as a friend. Possibly warmer.

Cheese was the deal breaker that made veganism a fridge too

far. Eggs, I could do without if need be; cheese, absolutely not. It could only be stripped from my life, much like the internet, in the event of some unspeakable global tragedy, possibly one involving zombies.

And somehow it never occurred to me back then that I had only glimpsed a tiny wedge of the greater sprawling cheesescape through a keyhole, possibly while squinting.

There were hints. Clues. Hansel and Gretel–esque blue cheese crumbles marking a path not yet taken. One night, I invited a few friends over for a wine and cheese party like grown adults. I went to the nearest overpriced gentrification hut in Crown Heights and picked up five vacuum-sealed wedges—Gouda, Brie, Jarlsberg, and both extra sharp and garlic cheddar—pairing them with Rosemary and Olive Oil Triscuits. (At that point, I was miles away from knowing that cheese people consider flavored crackers a class A food felony.) After I'd proudly enshrined this murderer's row of curds on Instagram, we began to devour it. Five minutes later, I noticed a withering comment a bartender friend had left beneath the photo: "Basic-ass cheese plate."

Basic? Did he not see there were *five* cheeses?

The heckle stung. Who was this guy to tell me—an enthusiastic and inexhaustible cheese lover—that I was doing something wrong? And which missing cheese did he think would elevate my board to the level of respectability? Was it Manchego? Rather than mull it over any further, I let the offending comment slip my mind and went back to living my basic-ass cheese life.

For a while, anyway.

The version of me who was enchanted by pepper jack is now dead. It's not that I no longer eat anything less than the world's finest cheese at all times; it's that I can't pretend not to be aware of it. That's the thing about cheese snobbery: Once you've opened Pandora's pantry, it remains open. You might as well try putting Cheez Whiz back in the can.

I will never again eat an omelet without knowing how amazing Gruyère d'Alpage would taste slowly sinking into it, like a fluffed bedsheet collapsing onto a pillowy pile of eggs. I have a hard time looking at green cylinder Parmesan, the scentless sawdust inside practically mocking Giorgio Cravero's Parmigiano-Reggiano—a cheese comprised entirely of guitar solos. I can't eat a grilled cheese sandwich without wishing molten Clothbound cheddar were in the middle, maybe with some Roquefort mixed in, too, for contrast and spice.

Once you know about knee-buckling cheese, you can't unknow it. You can try to ignore its salty siren song, but your taste buds won't let you forget it.

Why would anyone ever want to forget cheese, though?

HERE'S HOW I ceased to be a normal person.

It all started when I wanted to surprise my wife for Valentine's Day. Being a continuously surprising partner is hard work. If two people stick together for a certain number of years—let's call it five—they start telegraphing their every move like weary prizefighters. Each knows what to expect from the other, and comes to rely on it in a way, but they're always grateful for upended expectations. Otherwise it all starts to feel like choreography. By early 2018, I'd already surprised my wife, Gabi, with just about every blow-you-away vegetarian restaurant in New York, over various Valentine's Days and the mere virtue of living in one of the world's greatest food cities. Non-edible romantic gestures were part of the drill, too—a mechanical bull ride, maybe, or a haunted house that was open in February for some reason—but an event meal was central to the experience. And it was getting harder to find an herbivore-friendly one in uncharted territory.

Before I started strategizing that year's Hallmark holiday, I'd never heard of Murray's, the Bleecker Street bulwark of New York's indigenous cheese scene. Murray's is about as famous as a cheese shop can get. It began life as an egg and dairy wholesaler in 1940 and evolved into one of America's most prominent cheese brands, with kiosks in four hundred–plus Kroger supermarkets nationwide. But to whom exactly is a famous cheese shop famous? Certainly not me at the time.

I first heard of Murray's in an online ad touting the Most Decadent Valentine's Day Ever.

"We're pulling out all the stops for this one-of-a-kind, first-in-class, top-of-the-line tasting event," the ad promised. "Nothing—and we mean nothing—is too good for our guests."

The assurance of food that verged on being too good for my wife was quite a hook. It would be a guided tasting through the shop's top-shelf inventory, paired with equally impressive wine and a smattering of luxury goodies. The romantic gesture and the food itself were baked into one cheesy package. It was just what I was looking for—a bougie jackpot.

Perhaps I'd been in other cheese shops before—I *must* have been—but walking into Murray's for the first time felt like the first time ever. The center aisle was flanked by wicker baskets packed with stegosaurus backs of wedges. Enormous wheels of Grana Padano the size of kick drums stood on shelves behind the counter, beneath which lay a marathon glass case packed with rough-hewn hunks of edible gold. Each cheese inside the display case looked like a gallery piece, complete with a little placard noting title and artist. The air was thick with a robust, meaty aroma, one with depth to it—the kind of smell you'd imagine making a hungry dog levitate in a cartoon. It was coming from the sandwich press, but it interlocked with the almost oppressive amount of cheese in the glass case, the staff unwrapping and wrapping them up again like a never-ending wardrobe adjustment. I'd been vaguely aware of just how many different kinds of cheeses must exist, but I'd never given it much thought. How many cheeses could there possibly be? Like, a hundred? (There are thousands.)

In the back of the shop, a velvet rope blocked off a narrow staircase only for those attending tonight's special tasting. At the top of the steps stood a group of people who had clearly put Valentine's Day strength into their hair and clothes, everything spectacularly un-mussed, while Gabi and I had more of a relaxed, sixth Valentine's Day vibe, both of our outfits lightly basted in cat hair. As soon as we joined the queue, an instructor swept us into a room and sat us at a glossy wood-top table. A widescreen on the front wall flashed glamour shots of various cheeses, a televisual brochure for the inventory downstairs.

The cheeses in front of us were decidedly not basic. Sitting on charcoal slates the Flintstones might have used as dishes, the six pieces barely resembled one another in the slightest, each a luscious mystery. They were all punctuated with driblets of cherry confit and black truffle, a gleaming pool of caramel, and other accoutrements, all neatly arranged like a painter's palette.

The two instructors stood in front of the TV, which soon ceased its slideshow. Christine, the resident cheese expert, was taller, with a swoop of Nutella-brown hair hanging down the side of her face, while Emily, our wine master, wore an eggshell turtleneck beneath a cloud of dark curls. They had both worked at

Murray's for years, with Christine boasting the added gravitas of being a Certified Cheese Professional (CCP), a real credential which, at the time, sounded to me like something invented for a goofy dad's apron, like Official Baby Back Rib Commander.

"Who here knows nothing about cheese—you buy string cheese from 7–Eleven to snack on sometimes and that's it?" Christine asks. Several shy hands go up as Gabi and I look at each other and silently agree not to out ourselves. "Who here knows a little?" she continues, and significantly more hands raise, including Gabi's, which feels like a betrayal. Finally, Christine asks, "Who here could teach this class?" Only one brave soul owns up to this high level of either expertise or misplaced confidence.

Our hosts encourage us to nibble from baskets of baguette slices and jars of dried cherries and Marcona almonds at each table, but to hold off on any cheese until after they've introduced it—and even then, to eat each piece slowly and savor it. As someone with the impulse control of a Gremlin, this is what I'd call a counterintuitive approach. At the time, it seemed to me that if you were lucky enough to find some cheese, you ate the cheese until it was gone and then you double-checked that there wasn't any you'd missed. If pressed, I'd have said my favorite kind of cheese was More Cheese. But I was willing to pace myself that night, if only to avoid embarrassing Gabi.

First up appears to be a dimpled dollop of cheesecake that gets mushier the closer to what I called the "brie-skin"; a splat of raspberry jam arching alongside it.

"This is Kunik," Christine announces, "a bloomy rind triple-crème goat cheese from the Adirondacks."

I recognize some of the words in that sentence, but not many.

"A bloomy rind is that thick, rubbery coating a cheese has

when it ripens from the outside, and triple-crème is just a cheese with a high butterfat content, not three separate kinds of cream," Christine continues. "This one is super-rich, but its flavor profile is very subtle. It's creamy and a little goaty but mostly mild and mellow."

Creamy didn't begin to describe the taste. It was like biting into a butter cloud. The flavor is rich but subtle. Maybe too subtle. I look over at Gabi for confirmation that whatever made Kunik special was inscrutable, but she is busy swirling a forkful in raspberry jam. When she slides the fork in her mouth, her eyes light up. She nods at me and I try it too.

Whoa. The tart raspberry not only amplifies Kunik's milkiness but also introduces a new hybrid flavor: raspberry buttercream. I chase it with champagne, which washes over my tongue like scrubbing bubbles. Kunik had officially become . . . interesting. (I didn't yet have the capacity to describe it any other way.)

A couple of cheeses later, we're onto something called Greensward, a gleaming puddle the exact shade of Nilla Wafers.

"This cheese is something you can only get here," Christine explains. "It's a collaboration between Murray's and Jasper Hill up in Vermont. If you haven't heard of Jasper Hill, they're kind of the rock stars of the cheese world right now."

It had not occurred to me that the cheese world could have rock stars. What did that even *mean*?

"The idea was to make a cheese specifically for one of the fanciest restaurants in Manhattan: Eleven Madison Park," she continues. "They wanted a cheese for their limited-time Iconic New York menu, and yes, technically Greensward is made in Vermont and not New York, but Murray's brings it to the city right after it's born, and we age it in our caves in Long Island."

She does not elaborate on what she meant by "caves." Did I hear that right? I look around and everybody is either nodding along or horking down Marcona almonds. No one else seems lost in a cheese cave reverie, imagining some kind of Roquefort *Fraggle Rock*, where dozens of Doozers transport cheese in wheelbarrows all day. It was probably just me.

Greensward had a lot more going on than Kunik, flavor-wise. It tastes as though an evil wizard had magicked bacon into a salty squish of cheese. For a vegetarian, this is very exciting.

"This is a particularly intense batch," Emily says as she eats along with us, a delighted look on her face. "Cheese is a living food, and it's constantly changing. You could try your favorite cheese one year and find it tastes distinctly different than the flavor you remember."

New information is flying at me faster than I can grasp it. In addition to everything else, cheese could *shapeshift*? It was a superhero.

"What does everyone think of Greensward?" Emily asks.

"Outstanding," says a guy whose blazer fit him too snugly. "It's London broil on the nose, with a bit of a piney note, and roasted shiitake mushrooms at the finish."

Gabi squeezes my knee and when I look over at her, she offers her most devastating eye roll.

"Wow," Christine says, through a sphynx-like service industry smile. "That's quite an analysis!"

The final cheese we try is Rogue River Blue, yet another American offering. I'm surprised there are so many of them. The one thing I'd known about cheese all my life was that the best stuff came from Europe. Everybody knew that, right?

Rogue River Blue is a sturdy scoop of vanilla ice cream,

flecked with jade-green divots of mold. The thin, cocoa-colored rind is gift wrapped in grape leaves, like a present from the garden of earthly delights.

"Blue cheese tends to be the most divisive," Christine says, "but I would encourage everyone, even those who are a little skittish, to give this one a shot. Prepare to be surprised."

I have never been put off by blue cheese, so no coaxing is required. I take a bite.

Holy. Shit.

The first word that comes to mind is "dank"—not in the way of a dingy basement, but like a guttural current of whooshing weed-buzz. This cheese is *dank*. It packs a dizzy drug-punch that reverberates throughout my body. Rogue River Blue tastes like Fruity Pebbles cereal milk baked into savory fudge, with a brittle crunch in every other bite. It tastes impossible. No way could this stuff exist, and you could just go to the store and get some anytime you were in the mood.

Looking back now, eating Rogue River Blue for the first time felt a little like how falling in love feels; like being let in on the great cosmic secret of somebody's existence. I was instantly smitten. And on Valentine's Day, no less. I wanted to run outside doing full Kermit-arms and scream for everybody to try this cheese *right now*, which probably wouldn't be the weirdest thing anyone overheard on Bleecker Street that day.

It wasn't just the taste of one spectacular cheese, though. It was the dawning realization that cheese was a miracle food, an edible unicorn. So many things had needed to go just right in order for each piece we'd tried that night to reach us and taste the way it did. The animals needed to be exactly whichever kind they were, they needed to eat exactly what they'd eaten, be milked at a certain time of day, at a certain time of year; all before the cheesemakers could apply certain techniques to turn that milk into cheese, and then age it in a cave at a certain temperature for a certain length of time, until it was distributed out into the world and cared for in a certain way by an apparently famous cheese shop. If any of these steps had changed even slightly, those cheeses wouldn't have tasted the same—and because cheese is a living thing, they might not taste quite the same next time anyway. Hearing about everything involved in this complicated process made me understand, for the first time, that although cheese had just four basic ingredients—milk, rennet, starter culture, and salt—it had an infinite galaxy of potential outcomes. And we got to live in the multiverse where they were all happening simultaneously. How lucky are we?

Unlike my sweaty efforts at keeping Valentine's Day fresh, cheese was something that might never cease to be surprising.

Over the course of the year and a half that followed my cheese epiphany, I heard enough how-I-fell-in-love-with-cheese stories to fill an entire podcast network. All cheese people seemed to have them. Although the recipe changes from story to story, they're all comprised of the same basic ingredients: a location, a situation, and the one that did it.

"We were in Florence for our anniversary and had fresh buffalo mozzarella."

"I was in Vermont for a bris and tried some chèvre."

The details vary, but the conclusion is always the same. It's just a matter of how hard the person fell, and where they landed.

I was in a Manhattan cheese shop for Valentine's Day and I tried Rogue River Blue. That was what did it for me. How hard I'd fall and where I'd land remained to be seen. The experience had definitely awakened something within me, though—an inner cheesemonster, with a hankering for knowledge and experience and much more Rogue River Blue. I'd only seen a glimpse so far, but it felt like discovering an entire world hidden in plain sight.

After ninety minutes spent within a sensory tsunami, we left Murray's and I took out my phone. What had happened in the real world while we'd been smearing raspberry jam on a bloomy rind, and how many "likes" had my picture of it fetched? Once I started scrolling, I could have just ignored the impulse suddenly brewing inside me and gone right back to my basic-ass cheese life. If you gamed it out in simulations, nine times out of ten, that's probably what would have happened. But it's not what happened. Instead, I wrote myself a reminder to look into cheese some more the next day and took my first step inside Dairy Narnia.

CHAPTER ONE

The Big Cheese Bang

A FEW YEARS AGO, A GROUP OF TOURISTS WITH UNIDENTIFIABLE ACCENTS asked me to take their photo.

"Say cheese," I said, once they were frozen in pose-faces, because of course I did. But they did not take the suggestion. Instead, they looked at me like I'd just said the strangest goddamn thing they'd ever heard.

Their blank, softly distressed faces made me defensive. I wasn't weird for demanding they say cheese, they were weird for not knowing how this interaction works. To their credit, if you've never been told to say cheese before, it is kind of a weird ask. It makes sense as a trick for getting hummingbird-distractible children to lock in for one second, but you can say almost anything else to anyone who's ever filed their taxes before, like "Here we go" or "Bombs away" or some kind of countdown, and get the same reaction. Why do we still go with "Say cheese"? How did we land on it in the first place?

The reason is simple: cheese makes people smile. Well, technically, any word with a long ee-sound physically forces mouths into a smile shape, but it must mean something that out of all vernacular possibilities, *this* is the word that became industry standard. Whichever enterprising photographer first figured out the trick, and etymologists can't place him or her exactly, they probably chose this particular word because of an obvious truth: the very thought of cheese makes smiles appear.

Cheese is literally heaven. It's what happens after milk sheds this mortal coil and ascends to a higher plane of existence. The fact that its eventual destiny is to be consumed by me while standing in front of an open fridge door in pajamas doesn't really matter. It still got to live its best afterlife briefly upon meeting its maker, and perhaps heaven is just as fleeting as Earth. More importantly, though, cheese *tastes* like heaven. In one single piece, you can detect individual notes of disparate foods like hazelnut, pineapple, and pot roast, all seamlessly merging into a dulcet symphony of flavors. Tracking them all while also absorbing the robust aroma and sumptuous texture is a sensory roller coaster, a digestible sex act, a magic trick. It's the kind of thing that makes a person glad to be alive—so they can eat more cheese.

Long before we all knew that guac was extra, there was cheese: the evergreen cheat code for improving any meal. Salad, fries, nachos, pastries, pie, pretzels, every sandwich, every pasta, everything that goes inside a flour tortilla; cheese makes it all better. People love it, can't get enough, lose their minds over the stuff. It's the most shoplifted food in the world, providing succulent sustenance for so many Jean Valjeans. It's the heart and soul of pizza, the most-consumed dinner option in America. It's so widely, fantastically adored, it's become cultural shorthand for epic relatability in sitcoms, movies, and memes: anyone depicted spending their twilight hours couchbound, munching on block cheddar, is all of us.

Cheese is forever etched into how we interpret reality. The indoctrination starts when we're young, in children's books like *The Stinky Cheese Man* and every story that involves mice, and then it continues when we're old enough to receive a copy of *Who Moved My Cheese?* from a well-meaning but off-base boomer. For at least the past thousand years, people all over the world have even told their children the moon is made of green cheese, although the myth was debunked in 1968 when Apollo 8 crewmember Bill Anders returned from space and was immediately asked whether it was true. His answer: "It's made out of American cheese."

This level of cultural obsession hints at something much deeper than a snacking preference.

One night, not long after I decided to dive deep into the world of cheese, I was watching *Blade Runner 2049* when something shocking happened. Midway through the movie, Ryan Gosling, a cyborg space cop, discovers the man who might be his father, Harrison Ford, hiding on a distant ghost planet. Upon being found, Ford's first words are: "You mightn't happen to have a piece of cheese about you, now? Would you, boy? . . . Many is the night I dream of cheese."

Excuse me?

I was so busy choking on a taco after this inexplicable cheese solicitation that I nearly missed Gosling's character acknowledge it as a reference to *Treasure Island*. Since I wasn't exactly off-book on *Treasure Island*, having not read it since high school, when I didn't actually read it, I had some homework to do. As it happens, the *Blade Runner* lines allude to a scene where the book's hero, a young Jim Hawkins, stumbles on marooned seaman Ben Gunn, for whom cheese has become the very symbol of civilization itself. Gunn's profound longing seems meant to convey the character's dire straits more than the general awesomeness of cheese, but perhaps not. You could do far worse than cheese as far as symbols of civilization. It's the food of peasants and the food of kings. It unites the urban and the rural. It's nature. It's science. It's art.

But just like most of nature, science, and art, I had enjoyed cheese throughout my life in an incomplete way. I recognized that it was very good, without ever having much of an idea of what made it good, how it did so, how good it could get, or just how I was supposed to feel about it. Now I wanted to know everything.

To paraphrase disgraced former US Secretary of Defense Donald Rumsfeld: in life there are known knowns, known unknowns, and unknown unknowns.

When I woke up the day after my Valentine's Day tasting at Murray's, I had just about enough known knowns around artisan cheese to plug up a single hole in a slice of Swiss. In fact, I didn't even know that those holes are called *eyes*, and that what most Americans think of as "Swiss" is actually Emmental, a nutty wonder that makes for a far superior national representation of Switzerland than waxy Kraft singles do for America.

My known unknowns were legion, encompassing cheeses yet untasted, which ones paired well with what, why the most common visual depiction is usually a wedge filled with holes (I mean *eyes*!)—despite how few cheeses actually have them—and even just the slightest gist of how cheese is made. There was much to investigate. Over the next couple of months, I began reducing my known unknowns—a project I soon realized I could spend years of Talmudic study on without ever completing.

First up, was the question of how cheese is made. I thought the easiest way to learn would be by making it myself, like riding a bike for the first time but in a very small New York kitchen.

Making cheese at home seemed so simple, from the breezy way the Urban Cheesecraft kit described it. No matter which kind of cheese I chose, there were only four ingredients. First came the milk, along with the babbling brook-like gurgle of a whole gallon pouring into a pot. Then I added the starter cultures, good bacteria that convert the milk's sugar into lactic acid so it can separate into curds and whey. It was hard to reconcile the fact that bacteria come in both good and bad varietals. Bacteria is just one of those things that automatically scans as bad but actually resides along a spectrum, like fats or prestige drama drug dealers. Next up is the rennet, that crucial enzyme from the animal's fourth stomach chamber that acts like a lightning bolt from God. It converts a pot full of milk into a raft of clumped curds soaking in a lake of whey the color of lemon Gatorade. Finally, once the curds are removed, you add salt, both to help dry out the cheese and encourage flavor development. In the case of the ricotta I made in my kitchen, I had to first dry out the curds by squeezing them in the microscopically ventilated bridal veil of a cheesecloth.

When my ricotta was ready, I took a bite. Even though it was too salty, my heart was full with accomplishment. It was edible! I remembered later, though, that we actually had some Trader Joe's ricotta in the fridge, and when I tasted it back-to-back with what I'd made, the truth sunk in. The Trader Joe's version was light, fluffy, and mild, with a subtle undercurrent of sweetness, while mine tasted like a gummy salt lick soaked in Elmer's Glue.

My cheesemaking project continued, with minimal success. I made queso blanco, the soft white cheese often sprinkled on tacos, and it turned out better than the ricotta. When I tried mozzarella, though, the plane crashed into the mountain. After all the effort up to and including yelling at the almost-mozzarella, I had to throw it out. It was a crushing defeat, but at least now I had an appreciation for how hard it must be to make great cheese, let alone to make it consistently.

The other place I turned to learn more, besides my stovetop, was Steven Jenkins' *Cheese Primer*, long considered the bible of cheese. Originally published in 1996, for many years it was all anyone had. To this day, it remains a useful if slightly outdated reference for what to expect from hundreds of cheeses, despite being filled with dubious advice such as, "Put your left index finger on your eye and your right index finger on the cheese . . . if they sort of feel the same, the cheese is ready." Of course, by now you could fill a tiny library with cheese books, and the breadth of blogs on the subject probably requires several satellites to maintain all those archives. I bought some more books, devoured online resources like the encyclopedic Cheese Science Toolkit, and started listening to *Cutting the Curd*—a long-running podcast that hosts luminaries from the cheese world and beyond. (Kyle MacLachlan's episode falls squarely in the "beyond" category.)

One day, I was sitting in my apartment, reading about Montgomery's Cheddar, said to smell of freshly cut grass from the rural English countryside where cheddar was born, and wishing I could taste it. Then I realized: Duh, I could! In fact, I could use the entire literary cheese canon as one big Cheesecake Factory menu and order a quarter pound of anything that piqued my curiosity. (So, pretty much everything.) I proceeded to spend the spring of 2018 slowly eating my way through cheese books and cheese shops. Each bite was an experiment—hypothesis:

scrumptiousness—but it was more than that. I was building a vocabulary of flavors in my brain. Every time I tried something new, I would lock the taste away in my cheese memory palace, ticking off another known unknown. After a few months, though, it was the third category of cheese knowledge that continued haunting me the most: the unknown unknowns.

Most of what I didn't know about cheese would in all likelihood stay forever unknown if all I did was read a bunch of books, eat a lot of Halloumi, and make terrible apartment cheese. I had to go much deeper into the cheese world. As luck would have it, a lot was happening there at the moment. Unbeknownst to me, American artisan cheese had been riding a wave of popularity for the past two decades, and the wave was now cresting.

In the year before my fromage immersion, Americans consumed thirty-seven billion pounds of cheese, fully doubling the amount in our diets four decades earlier. We were more than lactose tolerant—we were *woke*. Not only were we eating more cheese in general but also more of the top-shelf stuff. Specialty cheese sales were soaring as the dominance of mealy, processed "cheese food" continued to crumble. At least eight states now have artisan cheese guilds, many of which throw annual festivals, bringing in crowds of thousands. An entire subculture appeared to have quietly risen up around American cheese, and the excitement was beginning to echo around the globe. After centuries of being a nonentity, American cheese had finally made a grand entrance on the world stage.

The only way to understand how we got here, though, is to go back to the very beginning. The beginning of it all.

NOBODY CAN AGREE on exactly how the Big Cheese Bang happened, only that it happened well before recorded history. If you want to

make a dairy historian laugh—and why wouldn't you?—tell him
or her the "definitive" era in which cheese was first discovered. A
new World's Oldest Wedge seems to emerge regularly, as inquir-
ing archaeologists cover more ground with better equipment. No
sooner had I started researching the topic when some Indiana
Jones of Parmigiano-Reggiano found 3,200-year-old cheese in an
Egyptian tomb, and then another found traces of 7,000-year-old
cheese shards on a piece of pottery in Croatia. By the time you
read this, someone else may have found an even older specimen
in some Mesopotamian mess hall.

Like many of history's most significant discoveries, the world's
first cheese was probably a fluke. Of all the theories to account for
how it happened, my favorite is the one about Egyptians leaving
out milk as tribute for the gods—an early precursor to leaving
cookies and milk for Santa—with the arid heat turning the hon-
orary offering into a divine gift for mankind. The most widely
agreed-upon theory, though, involves a happy accident in the
Gobi Desert. According to legend, the pioneering cheesemaker
was an anonymous Arabian merchant who brought along milk
for his camelback voyage. (You know how it's refreshing to drink
hot milk in the desert?) At the time, it was fairly common to use
a sheep's stomach as a traveling flagon, which is what makes this
theory more plausible than others. The merchant's intestinal thermos would have contained rennet, the enzyme from an animal's
stomach lining that helps coagulate cheese, and the confluence of
rennet, solar heat, and that camel's jostling gait could've conceivably separated the milk into curds (white, fluffy solids) and whey
(the protein-filled leftover fluid). Then that merchant just had to
be hungry and weird enough to take a bite.

Voilà: cheese.

No matter how it was first discovered, though, by the time the Roman Empire started pitting man against lion, cheese had become an industry unto itself. Since milk is such an unstable, quickly spoiling liquid, there was no good way to transport it in the pre-refrigeration days. But once civilization discovered how to not only preserve milk but also transform it into its most heavenly form, cheese became a widely sought-after commodity. Everybody wanted some. Over the centuries that followed, the Romans spread their cheesemaking techniques far and wide throughout Europe, like a schmear across a bagel. Cheese evolved into a dietary staple for many cultures, each producing its own signature style. Manchego was created in the La Mancha plains of Spain sometime before the dawn of Christianity, from the milk of Manchego sheep. Cheddar emerged out of its namesake village in Somerset, England, around the twelfth century, with the name eventually becoming a verb to describe its production technique. (To cheddar a cheese is to dice the curd for whey-draining purposes and then, Missy Elliott–style, flip it and reverse it.) Gruyère was developed in the mountains of La Gruyère in Switzerland, also during the twelfth century, although its place of origin was bitterly contested by the French, who lost that contest and legally had to start calling their version "Gruyère de Comté," or just Comté. Overall, the French may have gotten a little carried away with the sheer volume of signature cheeses they invented. In 1962, President Charles de Gaulle would famously say of France, "How can you govern a country that has 246 varieties of cheese?" Leave it to a politician to blame the complexities of postwar governance on cheese. (Since that time, by the way, the number of French cheeses has ballooned to at least 1,600.)

And then, far down on the roster of cheese-producing nations, is America. Sad, barren America.

Had the Native Americans created a cheese of their own, surely Columbus would have stolen the shit out of it, and we'd all be eating Columbo Cheese to this day. Since they did not, however, the United States remained without a cheese of its own until the 1700s, when Franciscan friars in Monterey, California, created Monterey Jack, perhaps the earliest American original. A century later, another of the more dominant deli-tray cheeses was born—in a place called Colby, Wisconsin. Monterey Jack and Colby may have each tasted like cheddar's nearly identical, annoyingly well-behaved cousins, but both became seminal American cheeses all the same.

The most significant kind of cheese America invented, though, was "mass-produced" cheese. Dairyman Jesse Williams pioneered this process in his New York factory in 1851, producing one hundred thousand pounds of cheese in the first season—more than five times that of a typical maker at the time. America then continued pumping out tons of cheese throughout the twentieth century, but as far as the rest of the world was concerned, well, they weren't. The New World didn't have a seat at the grown-ups' table. And after James L. Kraft began marketing his shiny slices as "American Cheese" in 1911, that was a wrap on our reputation. The country's fate was as sealed as a moist, yellow yarmulke in its hermetic envelope. The words "American cheese" were officially synonymous with processed cheese food. The Kraft slice became America's lasting lactic legacy; our hit single, if you will.

Or at least it used to be that way.

There's been a lot more going on with American cheese than American Cheese for a long time. People finally started to hear about it, however, in the 1980s, thanks to a loose collective known as "the goat ladies." They were spread out all across the country—Laura Chenel and Mary Keehn in California, Laini Fondiller and Allison Hooper in Vermont, and Judy Schad in Indiana, among others. They all had different reasons for getting started, and different reasons for how they came to possess goats, but they were connected by a desire for a self-sufficient, rural lifestyle. Mary Keehn was a single mother and prizewinning goat breeder who started making cheese in her kitchen before a friend, who worked at a restaurant, encouraged her to expand. Allison Hooper was a twenty-four-year-old with wanderlust who returned from France appalled that nobody in America knew what she meant when she mentioned chèvre—the soft, fluffy goat's milk cheese to which she'd become addicted. Her solution? Move to Vermont and make chèvre herself. Despite the many unforeseen challenges of turning goats into a business, Chenel, Keehn, Fondiller, Hooper, and Schad managed to whet America's appetite for fresh chèvre and more, with companies that are all still thriving today: Laura Chenel, Cypress Grove, Lazy Lady Farm, Vermont Creamery, and Capriole, respectively. It was only a matter of time before restaurants, distributors, and cheese shops wanted other home-grown takes on European cheeses.

Many had been right under their noses all along.

The United States has been welcoming European cheese-makers and absorbing their techniques for centuries—the British resettling in New England (naturally); Swiss, Dutch, and Germans moving to Wisconsin; and Italian and Spanish immigrants conquering the West Coast. Back in Europe, those cheesemakers were shackled to long-standing cheesemaking traditions. Their work was closely guarded by certification such as the *appella-*

tion d'origine contrôlée (AOC), a protected designation of origin (PDO) that dates back to the year 1411, when Charles VI signed a charter giving the villagers of Roquefort-sur-Soulzon sole right to make Roquefort, one of the most popular blue cheeses in the world. Since then, several other forms of PDO have sprung up in various countries, with exacting standards for producers selling famous styles of cheese by their official names. (The Consortium that protects Parmigiano-Reggiano, for instance, is especially litigious. Mess with them at your own peril.) Although this admirable commitment to preserving tradition has helped sustain ancient recipes in modern times, it's also limited cheesemakers' creativity. Once free from the binding of protective initialisms, European cheesemakers who moved to America began to go off-roading, with new variations on centuries-old cheeses.

While America never moved to officially protect its cheeses beyond the FDA's lax standards of identity, instead keeping everybody on the honor system, we eventually got something like a governing body. In 1983, Dr. Frank Kosikowski of Cornell University founded the American Cheese Society (ACS), a national trade organization bringing together cheesemakers from across the country to advance their mutual cause: cheese appreciation. A couple of years into its existence, the group added a competitive element to its annual conference. It was an opportunity for cheesemakers to be judged and critiqued by a panel of experts, while meeting fellow travelers from places they'd never been. It was also a chance for the ACS to create a steady supply of "award-winning" American cheeses to promote, since, at the time, the idea that these makers could ever place at an international competition was practically unfathomable. Nearly four decades later, the annual ACS conference and competition arguably remains the pinnacle of the year in American cheese.

Around the same time ACS was born, another organization formed in Italy that would change the way people ate in America. Slow Food began in 1986, when Italian writer Carlo Petrini lost his mind over a McDonald's opening near the Spanish Steps in Rome. The automated, globalized monstrosity was antithetical to everything he believed food should be: traditional, local, made by small businesses, and devoid of clown-based mascots. Petrini presented Slow Food as an alternative to fast-food restaurants, a campaign to promote sustainability along with regional cuisine. The movement and its motto—Good, Clean, and Fair—gradually spread to 150 countries, including America, sowing the seeds that would eventually culminate in the United States' ongoing farm-to-table mentality. Slow Food made American artisan cheesemakers with European-style products seem more appealing to shoppers set on thinking globally and acting locally. Imported cheeses remained popular, but lots of shoppers suddenly became more inclined to seek out hometown alternatives as well.

It was only in 2003, though, that America truly hit the turbo boosters on artisan cheese. The Atkins-inspired low-carb craze was peaking, giving calorie-conscious eaters license to go buck wild on cheese; nascent rock stars Andy and Mateo Kehler of Jasper Hill Farm opened for business, and an American cheese surprised the entire world by bringing home a gold medal in its category at the 2003 World Cheese Awards for the first time ever.

Nobody saw it coming, nor was anyone prepared for the demand that would follow. The paperwork for exporting an American artisan cheese hadn't even been invented yet. It took years of untold emails between Whole Foods, customs, and Neal's Yard Dairy in London, one of the world's most famous cheese operations, to find a way to export the first American cheese to gain recognition on the world stage. On the day that cheese finally arrived at Neal's Yard, a visiting American cheesemaker stood on top of a full pallet and sang the national anthem in honor of the American cheese sending shockwaves around the world: Rogue River Blue.

It turned out the cheese I'd fallen for on Valentine's Day had been the very same one that made many people around the world fall for American artisan cheese. Or at least notice it. Rogue River's win for Best Blue at the World Cheese Awards was admittedly a smaller scale victory than the Judgment of Paris, the 1976 blind tasting where wines from Napa Valley triumphed over the heavily favored French wines. *(Sacré bleu!)* That moment, whose lack of video documentation cruelly denies us a view of the judges' faces as they realized which wine they'd chosen, forever changed the wine industry. The myth that stateside winemakers couldn't breathe the same rarefied air as their French counterparts—as smugly ludicrous as the idea that New York has America's only good pizza—was permanently punctured. Well, almost permanently: After French winemakers insisted California wines wouldn't age well, another blind tasting was held in 2006 with the original vintages. California won again.

The gains in America's worldwide cheese reputation after 2003 were not exactly the same as those the California wine industry enjoyed following the Judgment of Paris. They were enough, however, to instill cheese lovers at home with a sense of pride and purpose, and ensure that anyone paying attention abroad knew something was happening with cheese in America.

The more I paid attention, the more I wanted to know. At a time when America's reputation seemed to be getting worse by the day, it was gratifying to discover something we were doing that made people happy and actually earned some well-deserved respect. I could now see the bigger picture: Cheese wasn't just something you did, it was something you did with your life. There were so many people, way more than I'd ever considered, whose whole existence revolved around it in one way or another. Farmers, makers, cavemasters, importers, distributors, and buyers all driven by the same force that propelled the goat ladies to kick off the movement decades earlier. Some of them were bitten early by the cheese bug—not to be confused with mites, the actual cheese bugs—and worked toward a career in the dairy arts their whole lives. But most people ended up there after taking a sharp left turn somewhere.

The cheese world is made up of misfits, rebels, rogues, and romantics; venturing forth from all corners of the country, leaving their old lives behind, to work with something tactile and tasty that they truly love. In the months that followed my cheese awakening, I would meet former accountants, psychologists, literary agents, and many others whose professions had once involved open offices, Slack channels, and stand-up meetings first thing in the morning. They too were possessed by the kind of adventurousness and curiosity that led that mythic Arabian merchant to eat the curds in his sheep's stomach pouch. And the only way to tune into their frequency, to find out what fueled all this devotion, was to fully immerse myself in their world.

My mission began to cohere: I would spend at least the following year exploring the subculture around artisan cheese, from its trenches to its command centers. I would visit farms, creameries, high-end restaurants, and the laboratories that elevate cheese to its optimum level. I would eat, sleep, and breathe cheese, learning how to enjoy with all my senses this ancient art form that is today created in part by high-tech robots. The journey would take me around the world, from a basement cheese cave in Paris to the mountains of Gruyère, leaving no curd unturned, until I cultivated a full appreciation for what America brought to the table. I would go from cheese bozo to expert, documenting everything that happened along the way, and preserving it the way cheese preserves a season's milk; so that when people find it later, they know how that year tasted. Basically, I would find out why the world seems to smile when you see it through the lens of cheese. Here we go. Bombs away. Three . . . Two . . . One . . .

CHAPTER TWO

A Man Called Mr. Moo

WHEN YOU TELL YOUR FRIENDS THAT YOU'RE WRITING A BOOK ABOUT cheese, more often than not, they respond with a bathroom joke. Something along the lines of, "Well, good luck to your bathroom!" but probably grosser than that.

It's unclear whether the joke is supposed to be that, LOL, a heavy cheese regimen gives you nuclear-grade IBS or, conversely, that it puts your intestinal tract on lockdown. I don't think even they know which joke they mean exactly. Either way, there seems to be some connection in the popular imagination between eating lots of cheese and having to poop, or not being able to.

Since I'm as susceptible to popular imagination as the next person, I wanted to know whether I was actually in danger of any stomach-related side effects from all the cheese I was about to ingest. I consulted a gastroenterologist about it, and he answered in the starkest terms possible.

Consider this a trigger warning: we're gonna go there.

"Most often, the effect cheese has on the bowels is loose

stools," Dr. Nitin Ahuja of the University of Pennsylvania tells me over the phone one day. "Constipation is much rarer."

Well, that settles it! Now I could correct anyone who landed on the wrong version of the two available jokes about eating too much cheese. Neither outcome was very likely, though, barring lactose intolerance, a condition that is apparently quite misunderstood.

The much-vilified lactose is just a sugar contained in milk, which is metabolized in our bodies by an enzyme called lactase. But that doesn't always happen. While lactase is necessary for nursing newborns, lots of people lose it during childhood, hence the dreaded intolerance. According to Dr. Ahuja, those among us who can endure limitless dairy products have a genetic mutation that keeps our lactase intact into adulthood. In other words, cheese lovers are technically X-Men. But even people who don't have The Gift are still able to eat more cheese than they might think. Lactose is most prominent in softer, fresher, and processed cheeses, which are more likely to agitate lactose-sensitive colons, but the owners of those colons should be able to eat harder, aged cheeses without incident.

And that is the last time the word *colon* appears in this book.

Dr. Ahuja assured me that as long as I am tolerant of lactose, as the five pounds I'd gained since February suggested, there was no real physical danger in eating too much cheese—at least not beyond the danger that comes with eating too much of anything.

He said nothing, however, about the psychological danger.

There is probably no good way to prepare oneself for being around a truly unlimited avalanche of amazing cheese for the first time. By any metric, though, I had failed miserably. The Cheese-monger Invitational (CMI) had only begun about an hour ago and I was already fuller than I'd ever been in my entire life, aching with the exquisite pain of gustatory blitzkrieg. I'd indiscriminately inhaled untold cubes, sticks, wedges, and slivers, chomping on autopilot like I was favored to win Coney Island's hot dog eating contest. Rather than a trophy, though, I was in contention for becoming the world's first case of lethal cheese poisoning.

I'd made a classic rookie mistake. Over five hours remained in CMI, during which I would continue to be surrounded by an infinite buffet of mouthwatering morsels. Yet I already felt as though if I ate even a single niblet more, the contents of my stomach would become abstract expressionist art all over the floor.

It was like that *Twilight Zone* episode where the book-loving nerd who never has time for reading stumbles across a library, postapocalypse . . . and immediately breaks his glasses.

"That's not fair!" he says of his symmetrically ironic fate. "There was time now!"

I was the nerd, my stomach was the glasses, and the books were every kind of cheese I could ever want to taste. It wasn't fair. There was cheese now!

IN THE MONTHS between my awakening at Murray's and my arrival at the Cheesemonger Invitational, I had prostrated myself before the alter of cheese shops many times. I had gone to Di Palo's in Little Italy, one of the oldest specialty shops in New York, where you take a number and wait your turn among a vulgar display of dangling salamis; and I'd been just down the street to the French Cheese Board in SoHo, with its prepackaged, pudgy bundles of St. Nectaire (pronounced like "sonic tear") lying in grab-and-go rows along the wall. The great thing about walking around New York City, even when you're not going from cheese shop to cheese shop, is the way your surroundings abruptly shift depending on where you suddenly find yourself; the knockoff bag vendors, aggressively aromatic fish markets, and bustling tea rooms of Chinatown dissolving into the cannoli-filled confines of Little Italy, with its red and green streamers hanging above the streets as cigar-chomping locals intersect with pizza-seeking tourists; the gonzo fashion, polyglot accents, and mournful sax buskers of SoHo suddenly replaced by the upgraded grime of Greenwich Village with its ancient jazz clubs, baby-faced gender-fluid NYU students, and so many vape shops and sex toy emporiums that they start to seem like the same thing. As I ventured to more and more cheese shops, I realized that canvasing their counters reminded me of what I liked about walking around the city; how abruptly the cheeses suddenly ceased to resemble each other, the cakey blues giving way to bloomy rinds and then marbly cheddars. You could easily get lost in it all, hence the mongers. They're professional cheese Sherpas.

Talking with mongers didn't come naturally to me at first. It was more like getting a haircut, that uncomfortable feeling of barely having any idea what I want or how to describe it. Maybe it was just a trim (cheddar), or a little off the top but bring in the sides (aged Gouda). Maybe it was something really specific, like Two-Days Unshowered Rami Malek (Cabrales). The problem was that I kind of only knew what I wanted after I'd already had it, and I didn't prefer technically being the one in charge of getting it. The whole process would be so much easier if the person cutting my hair, or my cheese, were psychic. Seldom is that the case, though. Instead, both professionals just tend to learn how to read the minds of sphynx-like customers and deliver the goods. But while a barber can look at a shaggy salon patron's face shape for clues, few mongers can look into someone's eyes and intuit which buttery euphoria will nourish their very soul.

Fortunately, mongers can simply stuff cheese in a customer's mouth to figure out if it's what they want. A barber can't just start hacking away to demonstrate how a bob will look, only to switch gears midway through and preview a bouffant. At least not until deepfake technology improves dramatically. Mongers, though, can guide their customers through an evolving matrix of options on a choose-your-own-adventure food safari, with sample cheeses every step of the way. *Do you like sweet or salty? Hard or soft? Sheep, cow, or goat?* It's a deeply human algorithmic ability. And in addition to guiding rookies like me, mongers also have to be knowledgeable enough to go toe-to-toe with full-fledged aficionados. One of them told me about his experiences mongering then-neighbor Padma Lakshmi, and the pride he felt each time he helped the woman with "the most exacting palate I've ever witnessed" find just the right cheese.

About a decade ago, veteran monger Gordon Edgar of the famous San Francisco co-op Rainbow, wrote a book called *Cheesemonger: A Life on the Wedge* to shine a light on what people like him actually do all day. Part memoir, part manifesto, it's a down and dirty look at day-to-day life in a cheese shop: deciding on the inventory, calling bullshit on sales reps trying to unload subpar product, dealing with defective wheels, playing caretaker to nondefective ones, and knowing which customers need to be enticed with a story and which ones do not. Reading about Gordon's early struggles with figuring out how each wedge is supposed to taste made me feel less alone in my quest to learn the language of cheese—and gave me a greater appreciation for what mongers do.

"When I wrote that book, honestly, I used the word *cheese-*

monger kind of ironically because nobody was saying it at the time," Gordon told me when I eventually visited him at Rainbow. "Back then, me and my friends would call each other cheesemongers, but mostly people used it as a goofy way to describe anyone who liked cheese a lot. Now it's the official term."

Mongering has taken on more dimensions in America in the decade since Gordon's book came out. Anyone who humps a counter at Whole Foods can rightly call themselves a cheesemonger, but more people now approach the job like a higher calling. They're mavens who are professionally excited about cheese and want you to be just as excited. They aspire to be as knowledgeable as sommeliers, minus the reputation for pretentiousness. And they even have a cheese analog to the legendarily difficult Certified Sommelier Exam.

In 2010, the American Cheese Society introduced its Certified Cheese Professional (CCP) program, which hinges on a grueling three-hour, 150-question exam. The test requires an encyclopedic body of knowledge spanning broadly, if not too deeply, across every aspect of working in cheese, including regulations, retail best practices, production, and cave-aging. It's a credential that makes mongers more attractive hires, not just at cheese shops but almost anywhere in the industry, and lets customers know they're in good hands. (Although, CCPs tend not to display framed copies of their certificates on the wall like psychologists.) The ACS rolled out a second certification at its annual conference in July 2018. The Technical, Aesthetic, Sensory, Tasting Evaluation (or T.A.S.T.E. Test, naturally) would be a hands-on exam in which CCPs diagnose defects in cheese, with a forensic intensity that is frankly disconcerting.

There's another way ambitious mongers can distinguish

themselves in a crowded field, however: competing in the Cheese-monger Invitational.

The flyers promised nothing short of Wrestlemania for curd nerds, with inverted knives like a bull's horns adorning a *Simpsons*-yellow cheese wheel. I pictured an unsanctioned cage match, cheese boards nimbly blocking rind shards tossed at eye level. The event probably wouldn't rise to that deranged level of mayhem (or *would it?*), but I had to find out.

THE INDUSTRIAL RUBBLE of Long Island City in Queens looks a little bleak, even in the daytime. Empty roads. Water towers. The specter of Manhattan and all its possibilities looming in the distance. As I walk along the gravelly edge of a street with no sidewalk, I text Adam Moskowitz that I'm almost at Larkin Cold Storage, the warehouse where we're scheduled to meet. He responds with just the word "Gouda," and somewhere, presumably, a rim shot rings out.

Adam has a scruffy, dad-bodded Beastie Boys vibe, with closely shorn hair the same length as his beard, and eyes that are permanently mid-snicker. He's wearing a black T-shirt and dark rinse jeans, along with the checkered black-and-white Vans beloved by both ska hornsmen and TikTok kids the world over. Beneath his shirt sleeve is a tattoo that revolves around his bicep, a gothic depiction of the entire cheese-making process, like the cover of an H. P. Lovecraft book set in farm country. It's the first of many cheese tattoos I will encounter in the months ahead.

"So, you're becoming a turophile," Adam announces, broadly. "Welcome to the club, bro. I don't really fuck with people who don't like cheese."

"Why waste time on people who can't experience joy?" I say.

Adam smiles, but we have only just met, and he is obviously still making up his mind about me. I had let him know over email about my mission to explore the cheese world—that's why he's invited me here—but still, I'm an unknown unknown.

Pretty soon, we leave Adam's office and he leads me through a tour of the facility. Larkin Cold Storage is notable for its breadth (it feels practically mall-sized) and for its cleanliness (no way all these damp floors are sparkling just for my benefit). We pass a woodworking nook, where Adam's employees can upcycle pallets into makeshift art or furniture when feeling inspired on a break, and he starts telling me the story of the Cheesemonger Invitational, which is also the story of himself.

Adam is the third-generation scion of a specialty foods dynasty, a family that's made its living importing cheese and other high-end foods since the 1940s. He started out, however, as a cheese skeptic. Despite driving forklifts of Stilton in his adolescence, he grew up uninterested in following in his father's footsteps.

"It seemed like failure," Adam says as we walk through the freshly scrubbed surfaces of his warehouse, dodging stacks of pallets. "I thought going into the family business was a sign that you didn't make it in the world. I tried it for nine months after college and it wasn't for me."

After that brief initial stint working at Larkin in the late nineties, Adam became a salesperson at Yahoo! Unfortunately, he did so just before the dot-com boom entered its "final third of *Goodfellas*" phase and the small fortune he'd just amassed evaporated. Along with all that internet money, Adam lost his enthusiasm for selling digital widgets. He spent the next few years juggling jobs at short-lived startups while trying to make it alternately as a rapper and an actor. Eventually, while Adam was plotting a move to Los Angeles, his grandfather passed away. Since Adam's father, Joe, who'd been surprisingly supportive of his rap career, needed help forging the way forward with his importing empire, Adam decided to stick around and help out. He accompanied Joe on a business trip to Spain soon after, and something clicked. Seeing how it all worked up close flipped his whole idea of the cheese world on its head.

"That's when I realized the people in this business are some of the most passionate, thoughtful, incredible people I've ever met in my life," Adam says. "I was used to the internet world where everyone was motivated only by stock options. Cheese was totally different."

Adam wanted in. But he wanted to understand the business from a street-level perspective before jumping in any higher. He took a job as a monger at Formaggio Kitchen, a tiny nook in the terminally hip Lower East Side's anomalous mini-mall, Essex Marketplace. As he began hawking his store's rind-wrapped inventory, Adam fell in love with cheese—the product itself, sure, but also the deeply human interaction at the point of sale, the moment every other element in the supply chain is inevitably charging toward. Adam only worked in an actual cheese shop for a year, but the experience guided his thinking when he eventually took over the business in 2007. Without that experience, he probably never would have had the idea to create the Cheesemonger Invitational a few years later.

The last stop on the tour is Adam's private office, a surprisingly long, narrow shrine to the cheese business. The walls are crowded with still-life paintings of various wedges, along with certificates from fancy-sounding organizations like the *Guilde In-*

ternationale des Fromagers. On the floor, propped against the wall, is an enlarged promo of Adam leaning dangerously far back in his desk chair, sporting a cow costume with a bulging pink udder, feet dangling in the air like a baby. The plastic sheath around the giant photo is ripped, which suggests it's been moved around a lot.

"Nice cow costume," I say.

"Thanks," he says, smirking. "It's what I wear at CMI. I'm Mr. Moo."

It's unclear whether he means Mr. Moo is his alter ego while hosting the Cheesemonger Invitational, or if the cow costume is representative of who he is all the time.

The idea for the Cheesemonger Invitational was born a decade ago at Burning Man. Adam was blissed out in the desert night air, feeling one with the wayward tech CEOs and purveyors of moon-charged energy crystals around him, when inspiration struck.

"I wanted to throw a cheese rave," he says, settling into his desk chair. "An industry party bigger and crazier than anything anyone had ever thrown before."

He had no idea what such an event would look like, or if anyone would even be into it. Long after he returned from the desert and rehydrated, though, he continued to brainstorm, eventually settling on a concept that split the difference between a "Coacheesa" Festival and *American Gladiators.* Mongers would face off in feats of cheese mastery, while friends and colleagues watched, schmoozed, and feasted on sponsor-donated wheels. It would be an artisanal battle royale for the ages, combining the elite competition of the Olympics with the hedonistic abandon of an Olympic village after-party. It was a hit.

CMI grew each year, spawning a second annual edition

in San Francisco each January, to the point where the summer 2018 event, just a couple of weeks away, would be moving out of Adam's warehouse for the first time and into the massive Brooklyn Expo Center.

One of Adam's assistants knocks at the door just then before hauling in a thick wooden cheese board and placing it on Adam's desk. I can't tell whether Adam asked for the board in advance or if it was a matter of routine that someone brought one in every afternoon promptly at 2:00 P.M. Either way, once the cheese is here, Adam's tone changes. He becomes a motivational cheese speaker.

"We're all programmed from the day we're born to love cheese," he says, as his assistant walks away. "What's the first thing any of us has to eat?"

Before I can even nod, Adam answers what I'd assumed was a rhetorical question.

"Milk from your mama's tit!"

"Right."

"Everyone loves cheese," Adam continues, "but they don't know what they love about it. They don't seem to think too much about what it tastes like. Whenever I eat cheese with people, I always ask how it tastes and they always say the same thing."

"What's that?"

"Creamy," he says, giving me a look like I just asked for ketchup to put on my cheese. "*Oh, it's so creamy!* Yeah? It's cheese! Of course, it's creamy! What does it actually taste like?"

I roll my eyes in the style of a person who would definitely never describe cheese as creamy. But I'm more nervous now than I've ever been about eating cheese, and that includes the time I tried some back-of-the-fridge cheddar of unknown origin that felt as hard as a LEGO.

Thin triangles of pale, firm cheese lay fanned out across the board in twin apertures. First up is the light-mocha one on the left: Gruyère 1655. I pop a wedge in my mouth and relish its luxurious denseness. The only tasting notes I have right away are: "very good" and "tastes like cheese." I concentrate hard on finding a more profound observation.

"I'm getting a hint of potato?" I offer.

Adam nods patiently.

"Okay, that's something," he says. "Some people might say there's a nuttiness to it. They might say there's kind of a fruity flavor. And others might say it's like a lightning bolt hit 'em in the head. There are no wrong answers."

It sure felt like there were some wrong answers—like "creamy," for instance.

Searching your mental flavor index for the Dewey Decimal number that corresponds with any one cheese is stressful when your library is limited. I wondered how many flavors the people competing at CMI could recognize from any random bite.

I eat another piece, slowly grinding the Gruyère into a mushy paste in my mouth. What I clocked as potato before could have been a nuttiness—those are both mild, starchy flavors. As I chew some more, the taste further reveals itself, even though it defies easy description. Did I detect fruit? Maybe. Fruit might be what's blooming in my mouth, or Adam might have just tricked my brain into thinking that's what it tastes.

The other cheese we try is OG Kristal, an eggnog-hued aged Belgian Gouda that Adam has recently begun importing, and whose name sounds very much like a strain of weed. It tastes way different than the previous cheese, like toffee filled with flavor crystals. Each of my molars seems to be getting blasted by a caramel-dispensing car wash.

"Oh wow," I say through a mouthful of heaven. "This one reminds me of butterscotch or crème brûlée, but it's still savory. It's like making out with a sexy Keebler elf."

Adam grins and points at me.

"Sounds like you just got hit in the head with a lightning bolt, bro."

The phone rings, and Adam picks up. While he's on the call, I gingerly help myself to several more pieces of OG Kristal. It continues to taste criminally rich.

Had I just been mongered? I mull it over for a moment and decide that Adam hasn't mongered me so much as given me a taste of what he does: he mongers the mongers.

ON A SERPENTINE line outside the Brooklyn Expo Center, where it's hot enough to make cheese in a sheep's stomach pouch, me and the other 1,400 CMI ticketholders stand waiting for the chance to eat Asiago in air conditioning while watching hot monger action. Just as I hit the sweaty T-shirt crisis point, it's go time.

Much of the competition would unfold during closed-door qualifying rounds over the next few hours, with the top six of the forty-eight competitors eventually facing off on stage. For now, though, the event belonged to the spectators, the cheese freaks. Throngs of munching millennials spill out in every direction, ready to consume unlimited cheese and beer to a thumping house music soundtrack. The space is enormous and flooded with sunlight. All of the walls except the brick one in the back are comprised of unobstructed windows. No vampire could possibly survive. Aside from the forbidden area where the mongers are competing—and a hot food section to the left, with chafing dishes full of gooey mac and cheese and even gooier fondue—the perimeter is lined with tables. Cheesemakers are stationed throughout the space, smiling as the masses devour samples, which stretch across connected tables in a magnificent trough.

The Cheesemonger Invitational has literal tons of cheese. Some of it is lumpy and formless, as though flung haphazardly onto a plate; much of it is cut into perfect cubes, rectangles, and other rudimentary shapes. Every table is another lactic tableau, a visually pleasing configuration of supple paste and rugged rind, with gentle beams of Vermeer sunlight washing over it all. It's almost too much to take in, but I give it my best shot. Even more so than usual, I'm eating like a prisoner on the run finding windowsill-pie. The nuances of each individual piece barely register before I'm on to the next one. Had I meditated deeply on every pungent chunk, though, I did not yet possess the language to describe what I tasted. Sure, I could say that Försterkäse, which looks like banana pie filling with a coral crust, tastes like a large, violently deceased mammal to me, but that just exposes my inexperience with stinky cheeses, whose presence I can scarcely distinguish from occasional whiffs of high-octane body odor.

The other spectators don't seem to share my hang-ups. One group stands clustered around a tray of Taleggio, discussing its characteristics with goatee-stroking focus, like museumgoers evaluating a painting. Who even are these people? Many in the crowd are rocking heat-beating jorts and Allbirds, along with multiple tote bags—the one they got at the door plus the one they came in with, promoting NPR, perhaps, or Ruth Bader Ginsburg. One couple I chat with is celebrating their "cheesiversary," since they began dating after attending their first CMI together as pals six years ago. They now come every year to further their dairy edification and have made a lot of friends along the way. After a while, I start to get it. This is more than a competition or a chance to eat a disgusting amount of cheese: it's a place where stray cheeseheads come to find each other.

In the back corner of the building, the competing mongers' entries in the Perfect Bites, Perfect Pairing, and Perfect Plates competitions are spread across rows of tables cordoned off by stanchions. Each monger has had months to plan out how they would prepare an assigned cheese, and now their work is on display with high school science fair flamboyance. One monger has designed her signage to look like movie posters—the one for her Perfect Bite reads, "For Love, Cheese, and the Sea," in the style of a beach-set Harlequin romance novel, with the bites themselves— cheddar and cider gelée with spicy relish—served in giant, presumably well-scrubbed seashells. Just beyond these display tables, behind dark curtains, is the off-limits area where dozens of mongers are hunched over mixing bowls in perpetual motion. They've been working for hours already, and now they're making hundreds of Perfect Bites for the crowd. Their reward for impressing the judges and winning a spot in the top six is that they will get to repeat the most audience-friendly qualifying rounds—cutting and wrapping, for instance—on stage. The grand prize for coming in first, though, raises the stakes considerably. The winner will walk away with $1,000 cash, a trip to the Vermont Cheesemakers Festival, and an additional trip to Neal's Yard Dairy in London. There were other less tangible benefits to winning as well, but I had no way of knowing what those were just yet.

One monger I recognize from Bedford Cheese Shop in Williamsburg is exhausted from the written portion and from making so many cheese Pac-Men surrounded by jelly ghosts.

"I sincerely hope I do not make it onto that stage," she says.

Eris Schack of Eataly, on the other hand, is in it to win it.

It's Eris' third time competing at CMI, and she is pumped. Eris is sharply dressed in a salmon button-up and a *Saturday Night Fever* vest. The words "milk" and "salt" are scrawled in Sharpie across her knuckles like crude prison tattoos. She placed second at the San Francisco CMI last winter, and has been preparing for today's competition ever since, making a spreadsheet of factoids such as every European cheese with a protected designation of origin (PDO). Her Perfect Bite sounds like it was created in a laboratory: Kirkham's Lancashire, a beloved British farmhouse cheddar, on a Lancashire-gougère base, balanced with Lancashire-infused crema, soy candied shiitake mushrooms, jalapeño pickled carrots, and cucumber skin. Eris has been practicing with dry runs of this dish for the past month and by now she might be able to crank them out blindfolded. It helped matters not at all, though, that the Brooklyn Expo Center's excessive windows have given the sunlight direct access to the cheese. Anything that was meant to be cold refuses to stay cold and anything meant to remain at room temp is hanging on for dear life.

By the time the Perfect Bites are available to the masses, some of them are getting runny. This does not seem to be an issue for most of the attendees. Ravenous crowds instantly fan around the mongers wheeling out their Bites on speed racks, like zombies finally breaking down the fence at the surviving townspeople's stronghold. It is at this point that I truly feel the trauma of having maxed out my stomach real estate on random cheeses I encountered that first hour. It's painful to see all these rare creations go around without trying any, but I'm done. I am drowning in cheese and the colorful wheels on each table are life preservers made of even more cheese. The only thing to do is go outside, where the food trucks and Juuling cheese lovers are stationed, and lay on the ground like a beached whale.

Finally, it's time for the actual competition. Adam emerges in his bovine onesie, a farm-bound Cruella De Vil, on a stage that's backlit in ominous red like the inside of a toaster oven. The crowd, previously spread out around food-filled tables throughout the expo center, is suddenly concentrated in front of the stage.

"Can I get a Moo Baa Maa?" Adam yells, raising the roof.

"Moo Baa Maa!" the obliging crowd thunders.

Adam's rallying cry represents the noises a cow, sheep, and goat make, respectively. I'm not sure goats actually say "maa," but my knowledge of goat noises is entirely based on memes.

"These cheesemongers are the caretaker-shamans, the connoisseur-makers, and the food-fear therapists," Adam stabs the air with his cow arm as he says each phrase he's coined. "They're the ones who find the flavors that'll make you say, 'Oh yeah!'"

The crowd erupts again, hundreds of buzzed Brooklynites cheering for the very concept of cheesemongers, or perhaps their favorites. Scattered throughout are a dozen people in sky-blue T-shirts that read KIRI THE GREAT, which feature the happy, embarrassed face of a blonde monger named Kiri from the Cheese Shop of Salem. Some of the shirt-sporting friends have traveled from as far as Phoenix to watch Kiri compete, and they won't be disappointed: Kiri Endicott is the first name Adam calls to the stage. The crowd goes nuts, and the enthusiasm remains roughly the same as Adam calls up the other five finalists. Last up is Eris Schack, who flips a humid tendril of curls off one side of her eyeglasses and runs on stage.

"Alright," Adam yells, turning from the crowd to face the contestants huddled on the stage. "For the first round, I'm gonna ask you the one question cheesemongers hate being asked the most."

An outsize section of the crowd shouts the question, as if they'd been waiting for it all day: "What's your favorite cheese?"

Of course, mongers hate that question, I realize. People must ask them all the time—at the shop counter, at parties, during Passover Seders—and the answer probably changes just as often, as they try more cheeses and more versions of them over the years. The sheer gall of asking a monger which cheese is their favorite! You might as well ask an astronomer which star they like best.

During the next part of the competition, the mongers have to cut some cheese. One of the first things that happens when immersing yourself in this world is that the expression "cut the cheese" ceases to be funny ever again. Not that it was so hilarious to begin with, but for many adults, it carries the residual whiff of juvenile naughtiness that goes along with anything fart-related. After spending even a little time with cheese people, however, the phrase becomes boringly, immutably literal.

Each competitor has a minute and a half to cut the cheese, hacking as many perfect quarter-pound slices as possible from a wheel of cheddar. Eris Schack places her wheel on a white plastic wire cutter and pulls the thin cord across to cut it into a more manageable half. Then she expertly severs slices until the wheel is no more. When Adam places the first piece on his scale, its weight flickers between .25 pounds and .26 pounds and the crowd alternately cheers or hisses. This goes on for an insane amount of time, until Adam finally declares it a good slice and the crowd explodes. When a wedge isn't the proper weight, which is what happens most often, the DJ hits a sad trombone note, and the crowd falls briefly silent.

Each of these contests is the NFL version of the tasks that make up a cheesemonger's day: talking about, handling, and improvising with cheese. The competitors are just cinematically performing a regular work shift, with hundreds of people watching, rather than one or two.

After the trivia round ends, Adam solicits yet another *moo baa maa* from the crowd and invites anyone who has ever competed in CMI to join him on stage. The space soon transforms into a swaying scrum of linked arms and nearly tangled beards, the group as jittery as a graduating senior class in which everyone is the valedictorian. Each member of this motley crew of cheese pirates has a story about how they came aboard the ship, rather than landing anywhere else in the world. Nobody appears to have worked themselves into a frothy cut-throat fervor to come out on top. Just like the friends finding each other in the crowd, this is as much a congregation for them as it is a competition.

Somebody has to win, though, and we're about to find out who. Once the stage empties except for the finalists, Adam announces the runners-up one by one until he gets to the winner. It's Eris Schack.

Eris' entire body is gyrating as she jitterbugs up to the front of the stage, where a trophy crowned with a blasphemous golden calf awaits. "We Are the Champions" pipes in over the speakers as Adam sprays the champion with champagne. Eris appears too overcome to say anything at first, but then she finds her footing.

"This industry, it saves lives. It makes people incredible," she says into the mic, fighting off tears with sniffles. "I've had some of the most amazing mentors. I've had some of the most amazing friends. A lot of them are here right now. Some of them are no longer with us."

Eris starts flat-out sobbing as she trails off. At the moment she seems finished with her speech, though, she adds one more thing, something that might as well be CMI's slogan:

"I just fucking love cheese!"

CHAPTER THREE

Consider the Platypus

THE AMERICAN MUSEUM OF NATURAL HISTORY IS A MUSEUM THAT, IT-self, could live inside a museum. Newer additions like the immersive insectarium, with its supersize beehive straight out of a 1950s monster movie, exist alongside creaky wildlife panoramas—time capsules from a technologically primitive point in the history of history museums. The 150-year-old New York institution is home to world-class wonders like its famous fiberglass blue whale, so big it takes three days to scrub the skin when it turns from midnight blue to dusty gray, suspended from the ceiling at a disturbingly sharp angle like it's coming right for you. Of all the marvels, ancient and modern, that the museum holds, however, I have come here today for cheese.

On the museum's fifth floor, which is strictly forbidden to the public, tucked away in a labyrinthine corner of the paleontology department, a group of researchers and fossil preparators meets once a month to participate in the ancient ritual of feasting on fromage.

Cheese Day is only a three-year-old tradition and so not exactly historical enough to merit an exhibit, but it has already become an institution among those who partake. For months, I'd been searching for some kind of cheese-tasting club, but I'd come up short. There was one at New York University, currently on summer hiatus while the students were off backpacking through Prague or whatever, and there were the WiChes, a monthly gathering that Elena Santogade—host of *Cutting the Curd* podcast and an all-around cheese celebrity—had started for her fellow women in cheese. I never even tried to fish for a WiChes invite, seeing as I was neither a woman nor "in cheese," so to speak, and because Elena described it to me as not so much an opportunity to learn about cheese and more of a chance for people already intimately familiar with it to talk about other stuff. ("My life is a cheese club," she said with a shrug.) And that was about it, as far as New York tasting clubs were concerned.

Thankfully, one monger mentioned that she'd once curated a platter for the Natural History Museum's secret cheese society. Many emails later, here I was walking down a charmingly musty, panzer-wide hallway, lined by gunmetal gray cabinets with wide, wooden drawers on top, stacked to the ceiling. A low-key formaldehyde funk hung in the air, transporting me back, kicking and screaming, to a long-ago biology class. It was the smell of preservation. This is where the museum kept certain species alive, if in memory only.

"These are the collections," says Kendra from Communications, a swift walker in a crisp white sweater with perforated stripes all over it like pastry dough. "The museum has more than 34 million specimens and only 2 percent are actually on display at any given time. Everything else is here, in locked cabinets."

She points at one with a label that reads LEPIDOPTERA in tiny caps, a block of unpronounceable words beneath specifying just what type of dead butterflies lay within.

The Natural History Museum was officially goth.

After a while, we make it out of the rat maze of stairways, and into a more traditional office setting. At the end of a short hall, we head into a conference room crowded with people partaking in a different kind of paleo diet. A makeshift midday banquet lay upon a slate gray table, the entire surface thick with food debris: flaxen hunks of cheese in various states of unwrap, kitchen knives caked in cheddar residue, shiny grape tomatoes, shriveled tusks of sausage, and crusty baguettes poking out of a paper bag. It was a feast fit for a king of some ancient civilization the people in this room could probably help carbon date.

Kendra introduces me as a writer and fledgling cheese enthusiast, and everyone says *hi*.

"You've got to see this," declares a goateed man with mischievous eyes dancing behind rectangular glasses. As I take my seat, he flings a plastic packet my way, vacuum-sealed cuttlefish kebabs with a Japanese logo on the front. I look from the fish jerky packet, to the beaming gentleman who'd tossed it my way—Carl Mehling, Cheese Day cofounder—and back again. Carl urges me to read the ingredients, and I start reciting them aloud. After *white granulated sugar* comes the words *a small head*, prompting the entire group to break out in cheers as though I'd said the Magic Word on *Pee-wee's Playhouse*.

This is my introduction to paleontology humor.

About three years ago, Carl and two other officemates had bonded over a shared love of cheese, and a willingness to eat absolutely anything during various fossil-related travels around the world. Since their curiosity about the barely edible often led them astray, they'd decided to aim that curiosity at cheese, a food that rarely ever did. They've been meeting once a month ever since, always throwing in some questionable accoutrements on the side to zhuzh up the spread, hence today's tiny sea rodents on skewers.

Although the tradition started with just a trio, it gradually ballooned to nine people, with at least as many cheeses. One member of the group departed the museum for greener pastures—literally, she'd become a park ranger—but she still returns just about every month for Cheese Day, and today is no exception.

"We used to keep a spreadsheet of which cheeses we tried before and whose turn it was to bring the next round," says Lindsey, the park ranger. "I still have it somewhere."

Of course, she does. You can take the girl out of Collections but you can't take Collections out of the girl.

"Dutch Knuckle," Kendra reads off the label of a champagne-colored wedge like Hamlet hoisting Yorick's skull. "That's a great name."

The name reminds me of *moose knuckle*, a term for the unflattering bunch-up when men wear too-tight pants, but I can't argue with the cheese. It has the kind of chewy texture and nutty flavor I was starting to associate with alpines. I traded Dutch Knuckle to Verne, a fossil preparator sitting on my right, for an Australian grocery store cheddar called Old Croc. Anybody at the table who wasn't actively eating a cheese was passing one around so they all eventually orbited the room.

Knowing that Cheese Day was coming up each month had inspired everyone to venture out to New York's lesser known specialty shops looking for something different, something impressive. It had also gamified traveling into an opportunity for scouring new cheeses far beyond the five boroughs. One of the specimens on the table was a Carl find called Um Grama, which he'd brought back from a recent trip to Portugal. It was a goat and sheep mixed milk cheese, floating in a fist-sized jar of olive oil and rose pepper. The viscous amber-tinted liquid lent the container a laboratory look, as though it might hold some kind of serum. I dipped a knife in and pierced a compact ivory cube. It was salty and spicy, the olive oil obscuring whatever the milk was trying to express. Still, it was something new.

A conference in Australia was coming up soon, and then the museum's annual field expedition in Mongolia. Surely, these trips would produce some fresh gems as well.

"Maybe we'll bring back some of that camel cheese," Alena says, alluding to the deeply rich, feta-like delicacy she'd had on a previous Mongolian adventure.

"Since you're gonna be in Australia, you should know that one of my goal cheeses is platypus," Lindsey says, steepling her fingers almost in prayer. "You could use its eggs, too. A whole breakfast: platypus eggs, platypus cheese, and platypus bacon."

Everyone laughs, considering the duck-billed, beaver-tailed breakfast beast.

"Platypuses don't have nipples, do they?" asks a graduate student named Anna. "They just secrete milk, I think."

Muted murmurs of agreement spill out around the table.

"What's the hardest mammal to get cheese out of?" Carl asks.

"Whale, what about whale?"

"That's supposed to be insanely rich," Carl says. "Mostly fat."

"Would that be the fattiest cheese ever?"

"Penguin cheese!" offers Alena.

"You don't want to know how penguins make milk," Carl says.

The table leaves it at that, but I google later, and apparently penguin milk comes from a pouch in the penguin's throat which she pukes up into her baby's mouth. I quietly cross Penguin off my ever-expanding list of goal cheeses.

Although cow, goat, and sheep are far and away the most common producers of cheese milk in the animal kingdom, they're not the only ones. Yak cheese is popular in Nepal. Moose cheese is a Canadian delicacy. The Serbian donkey cheese, Pule, is actually the most expensive cheese in the world. And then there's human cheese.

In 2010, New York chef Daniel Angerer started using his wife's breast milk to make cheese, quickly becoming the subject of national media attention. It all started as a storage issue. The chef's then-wife and business partner Lori had been running out of freezer space for her breast milk. Little pouches full of it, with dates scribbled on them, were starting to flood their kitchen. Meanwhile, a devastating earthquake had recently struck Haiti, and Lori wanted to ship over her breast milk, so it wouldn't go to waste. Quite understandably, however, donating breast milk for disaster relief required a whole sheaf of forms to fill out, and then the milk had to be tested in a lab. It was all too overwhelming, so that idea was out. Since her husband was in the process of opening a restaurant called The Little Cheese Pub in Manhattan at the time, Lori asked, half-jokingly, whether the chef knew how to make cheese.

Angerer, who had grown up in the Austrian alps and in fact did know how to make cheese, did not take it as a joke at all.

At first, the chef had trouble with the project. His curds wouldn't properly thicken, because the protein makeup of human milk is very different from other cheesemaking mammals. The cheese came out edible, but it wasn't quite right. Angerer kept tinkering around with the recipe, though, and landed on what he called Mother's Milk Cheese. When he wrote about it on his blog, cheekily adding, "Whoever wants to try it is welcome to, as long as supplies last," he had no idea the shitstorm he'd just provoked. Clickbait-starved media outlets incorrectly reported the story, making it sound as though the chef was serving human cheese in his restaurant. Soon, gourmands from as far away as Australia and Japan called asking if they could fly over for a taste, and concerned citizens sent hate mail to the cheese sicko they'd read about online.

"I don't actually know where those people were finding my address, but they would show up out of the blue," Angerer told me over the phone one afternoon.

Worst of all, the added attention failed to drive any business. In the coming years, both of his restaurants closed, he and Lori separated, and he became a vegan. (Angerer attributes none of these outcomes to the Mother's Milk Cheese experiment.)

It seems fitting, though, that human cheese would end up producing trouble. According to Carl Mehling, cheese may be the single food on earth that's entirely invented for humans. Making human cheese meant messing with the primal forces of nature.

The paleontology crew's adventurousness never quite led them to human milk, but it did take them to some dark places. Carl had once brought with him some processed cheese slices he'd excavated from his fridge after a year or so, the entire surface a patchwork of discolored crusty cracks. The atrocity Carl shows me on his phone is barely recognizable as cheese.

"I gave it a test drive the day before Cheese Day," he says, "and I told everyone, 'If I make it into work tomorrow, you guys have to try it.'"

When Carl did show up the next day, alive, not everyone in the group actually tried the cheese. But those who did had no regrets. Now they knew what it tasted like: sour, bitter, the texture of uncooked spaghetti, yet possibly better than its original form.

The mystery of this particular flavor was solved. Now they could catalog and stow it away in their internal archive of cheese collections and await the next exploration.

PALEONTOLOGY ILLUMINATES HOW certain organisms interact with their environment.

So does cheese.

The flavor of the milk that cows, sheep, and goats create through biological alchemy is an expression of whatever they've eaten and wherever they ate it. When you taste cheese, it's not as though you're getting down on all fours and chewing crabgrass alongside the cows, but it's closer than you might imagine. Or at least it is, if the cheese is made with raw milk.

As I had very quickly learned, there is a lot of controversy around raw milk in the cheese world. Americans may have the freedom from PDOs to experiment with creating and selling any wacky hybrid cheeses that tickle their fancy, but Europeans have a staggering amount of more freedom with raw milk. Cheese lovers in France can legally gorge themselves on a wide range of fresh young cheeses, while the FDA has long had draconian laws in place around raw milk production, forbidding Americans from selling it any younger than sixty days. This limitation forces stateside cheesemakers to search their souls and decide whether they really want to jump through all the hoops it takes to make raw milk cheese, or just pasteurize instead.

Like many schoolchildren who learn about Louis Pasteur, the genius dairy science man of history, I grew up believing that heating up milk to kill bacteria was unambiguously a good thing. Before I knew much about cheese, I might have thought raw milk lovers were as reckless as anti-vaxxers. It's not at all true, though. Our ancestors were using raw milk all over the world for centuries. The act of pasteurization assumes all bacteria is harmful, when it's actually part of what gives milk its flavor, with the bad bacteria dying off as the cheese ages. The world's most ardent fromage lovers swear by raw milk cheese. Some of them don't even consider any pasteurized cheeses to be real, even if they come from reputable artisans like Cowgirl Creamery. To them, a pasteurized product will always lack the vibrancy and complexity of the raw. ("You can really taste the dirt in raw milk cheese," one monger told me, and she meant it as a compliment.)

The sixty-day rule was implemented in America about eighty years ago, after forty-seven people died from cheese-related listeria infections over the course of a decade. That death toll may sound high, and it is, but safety technology was pretty lousy across the board back then. Seatbelts wouldn't even be required in cars for another thirty years. While the sixty-day rule may have saved some lives, it's almost certainly out of date at this point. Despite the fact that every phone now has a computer with powers once only attributed to sorcerers, and we have robots capable of performing heart surgery, we're still relying on a cheese decision made during the FDR administration. Complicating matters further, that decision was based on studies of cheddar, and might not apply to all other cheeses. The sixty-day rule has come under review many times, but the FDA has held firm again and again.

As I learned more about raw milk cheese, I had a hard time figuring out whether raw milk counted as its own category of cheese or if it was just a description.

This was an issue I was bumping up against all the time.

Cheese had proven an unwieldy beast to bring to heel. There were just so many kinds and the differences between each were profound. Whenever I tried to wrap my head around the myriad permutations, to impose some semblance of order over the endless variety of types and styles, I understood even less than before. One monger I met liked to convey the vast spectrum to customers by explaining, "There are thousands of cheeses and only six hundred species of shark."

It was a premise I found oddly comforting. Sharks are losing a Darwinian evolutionary battle with cheese. Not so tough now, are you, you razor-toothed, fin-flapping jackasses?

Scientists tend to identify sharks and other members of the animal kingdom by breaking down their evolutionary traits into seven subcategories: kingdom, phylum, class, order, family, genus, and species. The cheese world mercifully had no such system of classification. You'll never hear David Attenborough soothingly narrate, *Tarentaise by Spring Brook Farm hails from the cow phylum, raw milk class, natural rind order, traditional rennet family, hard cheese genus, and alpine-style species, and thrives best in a panini-style environment.* Most of those things are true, but nobody would ever describe Tarentaise that way. Cheese, unlike sharks, can be handily lumped into one of several broader categories.

Unfortunately, nobody can agree on just what those are.

Some experts like Liz Thorpe, the cheese consultant and author, claim there are six major groups—fresh, bloomy rind, washed rind, pressed, cooked, and blue—while others put it at more like eight or nine. Some break it down across rind lines, others go by production style, geography, or some other radical rubric. The more I asked around, the more I realized there is no one true taxonomy of cheeses, no skeleton key for easy identification. Instead, chaos reigned. As soon as I understood that washed rinds—the cheeses regularly bathed in brine or alcohol as they age—were pudgy, pudding-pasted stinkers, I found out that hard, aromatic alpine cheeses like Gruyère and Comté were also considered washed rinds. *What the hell?*

I didn't know my semisofts from my natural rinds, and I probably never would. But the almost terrifying breadth of the cheese world only truly dawned on me about a month after CMI, when the American Cheese Society announced the results of its annual competition, which happened every summer during a week-long conference: the prom-slash-Oscars of the American artisan cheese world.

How naïve I'd been to expect a tight field of straightforward categories like Best Supporting Asiago and Most Improved Mozzarella! Instead, what I found was more than two thousand entries in 120 specific subcategories. (The American Kennel Club, in contrast, had narrowed down the 192 recognized dog breeds to a svelte seven categories for its National Dog Show.)

I perused the ACS winners list with the studious scrutiny of a seasoned zoologist.

There were categories like "Farmstead Aged 60 Days or More—Less than 39 Percent Moisture—Made from Cow's Milk" and "Rubbed-Rind Cheese with Added Flavor Ingredients Rubbed or

Applied on the Exterior Surface of the Cheese Only—All Milks."
Those couldn't be types of cheeses; they sounded like weather reports or directions for putting together an edible IKEA dresser. I
couldn't imagine how the judges had chosen the 2018 Best of Show
winner, Jasper Hill's Harbison, as superior to the 119 other category winners. What could these judges possibly taste in any one
cheese that revealed its inherent superiority? I had wanted to witness the judging firsthand, but I knew that going to ACS—where
all 120 winners were available at the conference-closing Festival of
Cheese—would be wasted on me at this point. Next year, I'd be
ready. In the meantime, I needed to learn how to be less like a paleontologist poring over history and more like an animal wrangler
dealing with something very much alive.

Luckily, it was only a few weeks after missing the ACS conference that I got an email from Adam Moskowitz inviting me to
the Barnyard Collective.

THE FIRST THING I saw when I arrived was the cheese car. Not a car
made from cheese, obviously. That would be silly. But it seemed
only marginally sillier than what I did see parked in front of the
Larkin warehouse in Long Island: a bumblebee-yellow Kia Soul,
boxy as block cheddar, with vanity plates that read CHZLIFE. At
least now I knew I was in the right place.

Of course, I had been here months before, but Larkin looked
different under a blanket of night. Every building along the road
had the dull patina of a toothpaste factory beneath the sparse
streetlights. Adam's warehouse looked that way too—except for
the Barnyard space. From outside, you could see a triptych of
windows facing the street, portals to an incongruous wooden oasis that could either be a rustic ski chalet or the hull of an ark. Pal-

lets hung from the ceiling at canted angles, with pendant lights dangling from either side like scales of justice. The clean lines of hardwood planks ran across the walls, and a red light glinting off a disco ball bathed them in rows of pursed cherry lips, slowly spinning like they were trying to kiss the contents of the room, or perhaps eat them.

I eventually found out who belonged to the cheese car, but it could have been anyone inside. They were all cheese people, or the people who loved them, and the latter group tended to be de facto cheese people as well. There were about fifteen souls milling about inside, talking animatedly above the Motown tunes blasting from wall-mounted speakers. Almost everyone was in their mid-twenties and looked like they'd just stumbled out of a kombucha dispensary. Some had round tortoiseshell glasses and rounder unmanicured beards. One woman had seafoam green hair like a mermaid. Another woman whose face was steeped in concentration wheeled around a beer trolley, and a guy with a chestnut Caesar cut doled out cheese fragments on plates with a black leather glove.

When Adam came out of his office, he appeared to be down maybe twenty pounds from his Cheesemonger Invitational weight, the result of a gluten-free diet implemented by his wife. He hadn't been chubby before, but now he looked notably slim. A forest green hoodie hung from his frame, and a matching wool cap hovered just above his hairline, connecting with his cinnamon beard like a knight's mask. As soon as he saw me, Adam said my name in an overly formal way as though announcing me at a debutante ball.

"Did you have a good time the other night?" he asks.

The only time I'd seen Adam since CMI was a few days before, when he'd agreed to meet me at Bedford Cheese Shop so I could pick his brain. The moment he started choosing wedges for our board that night, I realized he was not the easiest customer to monger. It turned out that one of the country's leading specialty food importers—the very person responsible for putting several cheeses in that case—just might have some opinions on which of them went on his board. Our monger dutifully offered options, and Adam either approved or shook his head dismissively, saying, "Not my cheese." I couldn't tell whether he was consciously mimicking J. K. Simmons' mercurial music teacher from *Whiplash*, but I chose not to address it.

"I had an awesome time," I say.

"What was awesome about it?" he asks.

I wasn't blowing smoke up his ass by saying I'd had fun. I had! But I didn't know how to tell him that watching the cheese-tango between him and that monger—her offering recommendations and him either accepting or shutting them down—was as entertaining as the cheese had been tasty. Not without it sounding like a sideways insult, anyway.

I kept my response super simple: "Good cheese, good company."

"I agree," he says, smirking again. "So how would you describe it?"

Adam often seemed somewhere between expressing pure happiness or an ironic funhouse-mirror version of it, depending on which way each sentence went—conversational freestyling. Talking with him could sometimes feel like trying to pass a pop quiz full of trick questions.

"It was a cheesy delight?" I venture.

The smirk became a smile.

"I like that," he says, lightly knocking me on the shoulder as he walks away.

After I grab a beer from a pallet in Adam's beer trolley and sit down, a loud clang rings out, as jarring as non-holiday fireworks.

"I bet that scared the shit out of some of you," Adam says, releasing the crank of an enormous bell near the entrance. The meeting was officially called to order.

"Welcome to the Barnyard," he says, striding toward the center of the room. "I created a space to get really nerdy about cheese because I'm a grown man who likes to wear a cow costume in public. The email list is mostly mongers and other cheese professionals. It spills over a little into cheese enthusiasts, too, but I try to delete those people whenever I get a chance."

A knowing laugh ripples through the room.

"I'm serious," Adam says.

It was an exclusive club. Everyone here had been recruited into Xavier's School for Gifted Curd Nerds, where they would refine their powers away from all the cheese tourists like me who had packed CMI this year. They had come, for the budget-friendly price of five dollars, to mingle, gossip, eat, and learn, like one of Gertrude Stein's Saturday night salons but for cheese. It was a much different warehouse party than the kind of molly-fueled loft-apocalypse that took place not far away in Bushwick, but everyone seemed almost equally enthralled. I had stepped into the Cheese Underground.

Tonight, Adam was hosting a cheesemaker he'd met in Spain, whose wares he'd begun importing.

"I happen to know this cheese goes good with sherry, so we have a few different sherries for you," Adam says. "If you find a good pairing, shout it out. I'm sure we'd all like to know. For now, though, let me introduce, all the way from Madrid, Clara Díez of Quesería Cultivo."

As everyone starts applauding, a woman with big, amused eyes and striking brows stands up and looks around slowly, as though trying to figure out where she is. Clara is in town for a quick East Coast tour of the shops that would soon be carrying her product. She and her partners had begun working together four years earlier to build Cultivo, a retail hub that brought together cheeses from three different family farms in Madrid. The group had modeled their store after Neal's Yard Dairy in London, one of the most influential cheese operations anywhere.

Before Clara can say too much about her cheese, Adam launches into the story of how they'd met. It apparently happened the previous autumn at Cheese in Bra, the festival Slow Food held in Italy every two years, bringing together top cheese producers from all over. It was generally considered the biggest cheese event in the world. While Adam was there, he'd asked his right-hand man, Jonathan Richardson, to find some Spanish wedges worthy of bringing back home. Jonathan poked around in the area called Affineurs Alley, where more and more people he knew and trusted seemed shocked that he and Clara didn't know each other. Jonathan made appointments with two outfits in Madrid for the following month, including one with Clara, and when he and Adam finally tasted Cultivo's cheese, they knew the hunt was over.

"What I'm describing to you is the best part of my job," Adam says.

As he went on, I realized that in a way, being an importer was sort of the opposite of being a paleontologist. Instead of traveling around the world to examine fossils, the permanent record of a species that once lived, Adam was trotting the globe looking for cheese, the temporary expression of animals who were very much alive. They both help people understand or experience something they otherwise would not, although on only one side could you experience it on a sandwich. I pictured Adam wearing a pith helmet and khaki jacket, on the hunt for cheese you couldn't find on the internet, so that he could capture it and bring it back for stateside explorers to taste for themselves.

And that's what all these people were: cheese explorers. When it's time to taste, they pinch and stretch with anthropological interest. They break the pale-yellow pieces in half and take little bunny sniffs at the center, eyes clenched. They chew with intention and feeling, some looking far off as though trying to remember a word in another language just out of reach. Adam and Clara both mush theirs up with their fingers, a move I later learned helps get cheese to room temperature and aerates it like wine.

"The two cheeses on the left are both Malacara," Clara says, "which means 'Grumpy Face' in Spanish. It's based on a traditional Manchego recipe."

She holds up the piece furthest to the left and continues.

"This one is the four-month and the one in the middle is the seven-month. It's interesting to see people tasting them both. The reaction has been that they taste like two different cheeses."

I look at the craggy, canary-colored wedge in the center of my plate, half-expecting it to morph into another cheese like a Transformer. This is what's called a vertical tasting, when you try the same cheese at different ages, back to back, like meeting multiple generations of your significant other's family all at once over Christmas. It's the easiest way to understand the wild flavor journey a cheese travels as it ages and to choose a favorite leg of that journey, *Goldilocks and the Three Bears*–style. Producers will often hold vertical tastings to make sure everyone on their team knows that, say, Jasper Hill's Bayley Hazen Blue tastes a little bitter at its youngest level but gains caramelly notes as it ages. Some producers even offer wheels at different ages to retailers, depending on which flavor profile the shop prefers.

The two Cultivo cheeses taste markedly different. The younger one has a fresher and almost custardy flavor, while the seven-month is nuttier and more herbaceous. I try a sherry with each, the sweet amber liquor cutting the rich, salty taste in a pleasing way.

"I prefer the younger one," Clara says, after a while. "Manchego is usually much drier and spicy at the end, and makes your tongue feel a little weird. This one is light and fresh and a bit sweet and doesn't have a lot of acidity. It's balanced. What do you think?"

"Delicious!"

"I taste roasted peanuts on the seven-month."

"The sherry brings out some sweetness."

"It's like a bizarro-world Manchego. An Un-chego."

Mongers rarely hold back at the Barnyard. Untethered to the politeness that goes along with describing cheese to customers, they speak their mind and say whether, as a monger at Barnyard once put it, a cheese tastes like it has "rolled through a horrible animal's sopping wet sickbed, collecting shit along the way like a snowball down a mountain" if that's how they feel. It's doubtful anyone feels that way about the Malacara, though.

As the tasting continues, everyone plays travel agent for Clara, throwing out options on where else she might visit during her American excursion. At the precise moment it seems as though the conversation might sag for the first time that night, Adam asks, "Does anybody like fondue?"

The response is roundly affirmative.

The final phase of any Barnyard gathering is an all-out cheese party. Adam stations himself in front of his pro-grade DJ equipment, next to a kibbutz of record crates that reminds me of the collections back at the Museum of Natural History, and starts mixing. Doug Jacknick, a recent hire of Adam's whom I'd observed setting out cheese earlier with a sleek leather glove, begins cooking down cheese in a pot on a hot plate. As soon as it begins its witch cauldron metamorphosis into fondue, the air fills with the smell of oily, buttery oblivion and induces something like survival hunger.

A bearded monger in chunky glasses boasts to Doug about his own estimable fondue prowess, and Doug invites him to use the twin burner nearby. Suddenly, there are dueling fondues sloshing around twin pots, both chefs pouring in little spritzes of wine at odd intervals. The following month, Adam would host a formal eight-way challenge called Fonduel that pit mongers from around the city and as far away as Connecticut and Pittsburgh against each other, with Doug coming out on top. (His wife, who also worked in cheese, had won a previous iteration, making theirs probably the only double Fonduel-winning household in the country.)

Adam switches the music from Motown to electro, and the beat knocks. I want to compliment him on his selection, but I fear he might ask me to describe what I like about it—lots of funk and a long finish?—so I flash him a thumbs-up instead. He is in his element here, a bona fide tastemaker. I imagine him rooting through record bins, panning for gold in a different way than he had at the Slow Food Festival. A Spanish cheese. A white-label record. Trawling for what people wanted, and what he wanted to make people want. Rare flavors. Special blends.

I join the group gathered around each finished fondue like a campfire, spear a baguette slice with a wooden pick, and dunk it in Doug's pot. I have to swirl the smothered bread that emerges, like a rotisserie, so none of the ropy cheese threads are lost. When it seems as though the cheese will never cleanly separate, I clip it off with my fingers—the thick, gooey glops enveloping the bread like an inverted grilled cheese sandwich. It's salty, savory perfection, a pop of tang from the wine sending it into hyperdrive. In this moment, it seems like nothing could ever taste better. What else would anyone want to eat but more of this, forever?

I ask Doug, the victorious fondue maker, the question I'd been asking everybody lately, whether he happened to know of any cheese tasting clubs. He did not.

"Why don't you just start one?" he says.

It was such a simple solution that I was embarrassed I hadn't thought of it.

The next day, I sent an email to forty-five friends and acquaintances I'd never ordinarily invite to any one thing together. I wanted people from different backgrounds with different appetites who processed flavors differently to eat and talk cheese together on a regular basis. It would be just like the movie *Boyhood*, except instead of a coming-of-age story filmed over twelve years, they would get to watch me slowly gain weight. The response was overwhelming. I had created a herd of my own.

CHAPTER FOUR

The Cheese Internet

PUMPKIN SPICE LATTES, THE LIQUID EQUIVALENT OF A TAYLOR SWIFT SINGLE, are as reliable a harbinger of fall as red and gold leaves dancing on a windswept sidewalk. As the treacly autumnal beverage leaves a trail of coffee rings and quenched apple pickers in its wake, it's a reminder of time's inexorable march forward. Winter is on its way, the year is winding down, and if a Halloween costume hasn't organically occurred to you yet, it probably never will.

But there is no Pumpkin Spice Latte of the cheese world. There are several.

While seasonal cheeses pop up regularly year-round, just before winter comes an avalanche of America's most rabidly anticipated fromage. There's Rogue River Blue from Rogue Creamery, Rush Creek Reserve from Uplands, and Jasper Hill's Winnimere, all of which could fit on a Mount Rushmore of artisan excellence.

Elsewhere in the cheese world, though, the slide into winter is celebrated in a much deeper way.

Every September, high up in the Swiss Alps, hundreds of herdsmen finish a months-long mountaintop sojourn. It's part of an age-old process called transhumance. While only somewhat as metal as it sounds, transhumance is the production method behind incredible alpine cheeses like Gruyère and Appenzeller. Early in the summer, village cheesemakers collectively squire their cattle up to higher elevated areas filled with lush wildflowers only found in certain microclimates, and spend the next three months grazing. (The cows, I mean.)

Transhumance ensures that those cows are eating the best of what the land has to offer: vibrant floral flavors from the season's most eligible pastures. The cheesemaker rotates the areas where the cows graze all summer so they keep coming upon untapped meadows, flush with fresh grass and herbs, ensuring that their milk produces the year's most exquisitely complex cheeses.

When the weather finally turns in late September, the cows come home, which is also where that expression comes from. They then spend the winter keeping warm in barns, eating hay instead of pasture grass, and producing different, fattier milk as a result—milk whose makeup lends itself to a creamier, spoonable cheese called Vacherin Mont d'Or. In towns like Fribourg near Gruyère, the villagers commemorate the shift into winter with a Désalpe festival, leading a parade of cows covered in flower garlands down mountain roads like conquering heroes. It's a much more profound, if equally undeniable autumn omen than drinking syrupy coffee while jumping into a pile of leaves on a hayride.

Although there isn't a stateside Désalpe festival, some American cheesemakers have imported the Swiss concept of a seasonal switchover. In Vermont and Wisconsin, which both have similarly unforgiving winters, Jasper Hill and Uplands send their pasture-fed cows to the barn, where they feed on only hay during the frigid months. So long, summer milk; welcome back, winter.

As the season's first batches of America's answer to Vacherin Mont d'Or—Rush Creek from Uplands and Winnimere from Jasper Hill—begin to arrive in stores this year, I've just begun my own winter cheese transition: volunteering at Murray's.

ONLY THROUGH SHEER dumb luck did I find out about the Murray's volunteer program, one of the best worst-kept secrets of Manhattan. It was one of those coincidences that might fetch a sentimental "only in New York" from saps, but one I chalked up instead to the relative smallness of the cheese world.

One night, Gabi and I ate at Raclette, the Alphabet City enclave devoted to a Swiss style of cheese cuisine. The servers scrape sharp knives across heated half-wheels, drizzling alabaster waterfalls of molten Morbier, along with rivulets of rind, over roasted potatoes and vegetables. It's a cinematic way to serve a meal. If anyone ever dared rob the joint, they'd be captured in a panopticon of concurrent Insta Stories. During a shared Lyft ride home, our fellow passenger knew where we'd eaten because she could smell the cheese on us. Raclette is, after all, impossible to enter without getting roundhouse kicked in the face by the murdered-gym-sock aroma inside. Our car companion knew all about the place, and once she clocked it from the smell, she started rattling off her own personal cheese story.

Natalie was a marketing exec and a nascent cheese hound. After she took a few classes at Murray's, a monger friend of hers who worked there suggested she start volunteering instead. It was typical of the whispery way New Yorkers passed on knowledge of the volunteer program, which isn't advertised on the company website or anywhere else. You have to know someone, or at least meet someone in a Lyft who knows someone.

It works like this: In exchange for helping instructors set up each tasting event, refill wineglasses during it, and wash dishes afterward, you could essentially audit classes at Cheese University and walk out with whatever cheese is left—and sometimes just any loose wedges that happened to be lying around.

"It's a little work, a little wine, and then you're done cheese shopping for the week," Natalie said, her curly hair flapping in the breeze after lowering the window a crack. "I'm actually supposed to do a Cheese 101 this weekend that I can't make anymore, if you're interested . . ."

That's all it took. Suddenly, I was plugged into the Murray's matrix.

Every month, the volunteer coordinator sent out a link to a Google Doc spreadsheet listing all available classes. Each one required two volunteers. First come, first served; you snooze, you lose. Once I received the first spreadsheet and wrote my name in the row for Cheese 101 instead of Natalie's, I giddily scrolled through rows of other options, ready to jam my name in as many open classes as I could without arousing suspicions that I was a highly dedicated undercover health inspector.

Nothing was available for the entire next month. The spreadsheet was a rich mosaic of edible academia, all of it off-limits. Beer and Cheese, Burrata Making, Viva Italia!, and many others, all already spoken for by able-bodied turophiles. I would have to play the waiting game.

The first time I got an email blast with a spreadsheet of fresh classes, it vividly brought back traumatic college memories of registration day. By the time I started perusing, all the best options were full and a couple of open fields in the Google doc were rimmed in different colors as other volunteers typed in their names in real time. Next month, I would have to be quicker.

In the meantime, there were mostly just Cheese 101s. Setting up for these involved the kind of impossible-to-screw-up tasks I prefer in my manual labor, like arranging tables in whichever *Tetris*-configuration made most sense for the class size, setting out the right number of chairs, and distributing silverware. We would carefully unload some of the cheeses onto rustic gray slates in triangles or foot-shaped strips, saving others until just before class began so they wouldn't get too runny. The other volunteer was always either an amateur cheese enthusiast like Natalie, coming straight from her office job, or a monger trying to learn more about cheese on the side. I always preferred it when it was a monger because invariably there would be cheese gossip between her (almost always a her) and the instructor (almost always a her, too).

"The head monger at my shop finally got fired," says Lisa, a volunteer with microbladed eyebrows who works at a cheese shop in Brooklyn. She's attempting to balance a basket on the knee of her jeggings with one hand, while loading baguette slices into it with the other.

"Which one was he?" asks Michelle, an instructor with ice-sculpture cheekbones framed by sleek sheets of chestnut hair, dangling perilously close—but not too close—to the cheese she's cutting.

"He was that snotty guy who would never tell us anything about the new cheeses he brought in," Lisa says, walking the basket over to a table. "The guy who'd always say things like, 'Lake's Edge is like Humboldt Fog, if Humboldt Fog didn't taste like it was sold at Walmart.'"

Shots fired!

Humboldt Fog is a canonic cheese made by Cypress Grove, the creamery founded by original goat lady Mary Keehn. Even though it was still early days, I already knew enough to know that dismissing Humboldt Fog so savagely was like proudly shit-talking the Beatles: it said more about your arbitrary aversion to popular things than it did about your impeccable taste.

"Eww," Michelle says, making a face without looking up from the cheese.

When Michelle runs a class, she commands the room like someone with a performance background—because she has one. Like so many others in the cheese world, the singer-slash-actor-slash-et cetera took a dramatic left turn to get here. She came to Murray's originally as a volunteer, but after two years she had a breakthrough. One day she had the option of shooting a scene in a movie with a famous actor or being on volunteer duty at the shop. Obviously, she chose the movie, but in the middle of shooting her scene, she realized where she'd truly rather be. Her priorities suddenly clarified. Afterward, she ended up volunteering so much at the shop, and so well, Murray's pretty much had no choice but to hire her.

"The other night, my cat knocked my boyfriend's wallet into my purse," Michelle genially announces, placing long slices of Stockinghall Cheddar on a row of slates. "I found it right away, but I'm surprised he didn't find it first since he's always looking for cheese in my purse."

I'm about to offer my own story about cats and wallets when it occurs to me I'd almost let the weirdest part of her anecdote go by unchecked.

"Wait, you just carry random cheese in your purse?"

"Yeah, and I'm like 'Don't you know not to go through a woman's purse?'" she says, tossing her hands up like the shrug emoji. "It doesn't matter if there's cheese in there."

I knew not to go through Gabi's purse, but my position might change if she regularly used it as a cheese humidor.

Once everything is prepared and the tasting is underway, my lone job is to closely monitor everyone's wine level. I watch the wealthy Upper East Side couples who want their money's worth of tipsiness, along with the decidedly non-debauched bachelorette parties pacing themselves for a long night. It's not un-fun. Pouring endless drinks while I too am buzzed makes me feel like a magnanimous party benefactor—Jay Gatsby with somewhat less baggage. Most people glance over and quietly thank me as I refill their glasses. Every now and then, someone politely waves me off, because they've had enough. Other people look a little embarrassed at already needing a refill, not realizing this is a mostly judgment-free space and we only make fun of the truly depraved wine-goblins afterward.

Each month, when a new spreadsheet arrives, volunteer slots fill up fastest according to one metric: quality and quantity of take-home bounty. Burrata Making was by far the least popular class among volunteers, because you only got to bring home the burrata you made and you probably made it incorrectly because you were too busy refilling wineglasses to pay close attention. (Poorly made burrata tastes like mushy, salty Silly Putty that is crying milky tears.) Whiskey and Cheese, though, might get you a bulging grab bag of cheddar and alpine cheeses and a quarter bottle of whiskey or two, with the caveat that there will be way more dishes to wash because classes with beverage pairings require several extra fishbowl-sized glasses. Pairing Perfection was a consensus favorite because in addition to learning unconventional creations like the Snickers Bar, which is Gruyère paired with caramel and almonds, you got to take home the Gruyère, the caramel, and the almonds, all while learning about cheese and drinking a bunch of wine along the way.

Whether dead sober or pushing it a little with the wine, the educational part of a tasting can go in one ear and out the other, easily overshadowed by the tasting part. It's hard to internalize all those science terms while simultaneously having a flavorgasm. When you start volunteering for cheese classes a few times a month, though, more and more details tend to stick. Suddenly, I knew a lot about fungi, and a lot of other things too.

I knew that *Geotrichum candidum* is the mold that gives bloomy rinds their wrinkly, brain-like texture and sourdough aroma, while *Penicillium roqueforti* is the one that gives blues their minerally mold, originally found, as it were, in a moldy loaf of bread accidentally left in the caves of Roquefort. (Another case of how curious cheese people can change history with their willingness to try ill-advised food mutations.)

I knew that you could always tell a goat's milk cheese by its blinding whiteness, since goats convert the golden-hued beta-carotene from plants into color-free vitamin A.

I knew that the little starbursts I called flavor crunchies were actually an amino acid known as tyrosine that formed in aged cheeses like cheddar and Gouda. I also knew that I would definitely continue calling them flavor crunchies.

Some of these factoids resurfaced in every class, and some of them I overheard afterward, when guests would linger to pick the instructor's *Geotrichum candidum*–textured brains. The other volunteer and I would start clearing the tables while those folks were still asking questions, an unmistakable passive-aggressive message for them to wrap it up. Finally, after washing the dishes, I would arrive home with several cheeses, which were destined to join the New York skyline of wedges already populating my fridge, and perform a half-assed version of the class for Gabi. (". . . And goat cheeses are always white, because of beta-carotene or some shit.")

It was through spending time at Murray's, though, that I ended up discovering the world of cheese influencers, who practiced what instructors like Michelle did but on a mass scale. However many guests showed up to one of these classes, there would always be a tiny fraction of people who eagerly ate up every Instagram dispatch from Madame Fromage.

A CHEESE BUYER I'd met through Murray's over the summer had recently relocated to Philly by the time autumn rolled in. Lauren Cunningham, who had jump-started her cheese career after realizing she was unhappy working in finance, was just getting to know the lay of the land when I emailed to ask about her newly adopted city's cheese scene. In response, she forwarded me an invitation to the Cheese Ball, an upcoming party hosted by an influencer who went by the name Madame Fromage. Lauren knew of Madame Fromage as a friend of the artist, Mike Geno, who specialized in cheese portraiture, and from whom Lauren's husband once purchased a couple of paintings to celebrate her promotion to the Murray's buying team. Immediately after emailing with Lauren, I looked up Madame Fromage's blog, which promised the upcoming ball would be "Philadelphia's largest cheese party." Attendees need only bring a wedge or a condiment and "don your cheesiest suit, overalls, or ball gown." As I debated which of my suits was the cheesiest, I scrolled through a gallery of photos from previous balls on Madame Fromage's website. A woman in a cheetah-print blouse and Cheeto-flecked necklace flashed by, followed by a lady dressed like one of those red Babybel cheese-briquettes that only exist at continental breakfasts. The message was clear: it was a cheese costume party.

Gabi's eyes lit up when I told her the news, and I knew why. We had recently returned from a trip to visit her cousin in Germany, where we'd acquired authentic lederhosen (for me) and a dirndl (for her). Now that we owned this ceremonial garb, we were desperate for any excuse to get more mileage out of it. Following Oktoberfest and then Halloween, we'd sadly accepted that another chance might not present itself for some time. It was only early November, though, and now a golden opportunity had fallen right in our laps. There wasn't necessarily a clear connection between cheese and traditional German folk wear, but there was enough overlap that we figured the logic would track.

Since we knew what to wear, the only question remaining was what kind of cheese does one bring to a cheese ball?

On the day of the ball, I go by the cheese shop nearest my apartment, which I'd somehow never visited before. The cherry-red font spelling BKLYN LARDER on the storefront promised "Cheese & Provisions," as though the shop's Brooklyn-ness wasn't sufficiently telegraphed by the name alone. Past the checkout section's impulse-buy Matzo Chips (just in time for Rosh Hashanah!), next to a barrel-sized dummy wheel of Gruyère is a refrigerated case packed with soft cheeses, and a counter topped with free-standing, plastic-wrapped wedges. Lately, cheese shops had taken on the allure of record stores for me. I wanted to stop in every one I passed, just to see what they had—a reflection of the staff's taste and personality. I'm in the middle of imagining the choices that went into

BKLYN Larder's selection—imports versus domestics, perennial bestsellers versus up-and-comers—when a woman in a gray T-shirt and tilted orange beanie appears in front of me.

"What are you thinking?" she asks, as though we'd already been chatting for several minutes.

"Well, I'm going to a cheese ball . . ."

"Whoa," she says, slamming her hands on the counter. "You're going to Philly?"

"Yeah, how did you know?"

"It's a big party. I mean, I've never been but a lot of cool people are going."

My knowledge of the Cheese Ball seemed to have the same effect as the password at a speakeasy. The woman behind the counter introduces herself as Kristina, the general manager, and we formally shake hands.

"I want to bring something that's interesting, unexpected, and tasty as hell," I announce, as if ordering off the secret menu. "I know that's a tall order."

"Well, I love a tall order," she says.

"Let me put it this way: If you were going, what would you bring?"

"Oh my goodness," Kristina says, drumming her fingers on the counter. "Okay, a couple different ideas. Black Betty and Symphonie Comté are both holiday release cheeses. They only come out this time of year. One is a year-old Dutch Gouda, the other is a thirty-month Comté. You'd get a lot of cheese cred for bringing one of those in."

I'm ready to stop her right there, at the promise of cheese cred, but she keeps naming other rare offerings that might impress, including Rush Creek, the seasonal cheese from Uplands.

"Oh, I would bring that—it's great—but somebody else will definitely bring it, too," I say, as though I hadn't just heard about and tasted this cheese for the first time ever the previous week.

"Yeah, you're probably right," Kristina says.

I have never felt prouder.

All four cheeses she samples out are fantastic, and they're all different from one another. It's like listening to The Supremes, Joy Division, Tame Impala, and Ariana Grande back-to-back. Ultimately, though, I'm most struck by Black Betty, a goat Gouda that is ivory white but pink near the rind, like an inverted Himalayan salt lamp. It packs a butterscotch punch, and sticks to my teeth. I pick up a half-pound, and now Cinderella is ready for his first ball.

THE RUBA CLUB is a century-old venue in a bohemian area of Philly known as Northern Liberties, or NoLibs, which is probably also the name of a message board for young conservatives. It's part of a formerly working-class Polish neighborhood that went through a hipster gentrification in the early aughts, and it's the site of tonight's cheese party.

One thing is clear immediately upon walking through the ruby red front doors: This is *not* a costume party. Nobody is wearing anything they wouldn't wear to an opening at the Philadelphia Museum of Art; not the ticket taker, not the young woman in flame-colored eyeshadow offering felt-tip pins for labeling my cheese, not the partygoers just beyond the threshold. Just us. There's been a mistake.

I clutch Gabi's upper arm by the lacy white sleeve of her dirndl and shout-whisper in her ear: "It's not a costume party! What do we do!"

Gabi takes a quick survey of the main room and looks me up and down, the Bavarian brown lederhosen exposing my shaky knees.

"I think we'll be just fine," she announces, patting my suspender-strapped shoulder.

Easy for her to say. With her outfit, she looks like a brunette St. Pauli Girl fantasy, while I look like a background extra from *Shrek*. She was right, though. The only other option was to go back to our Airbnb and change into the clothes we'd worn on the bus ride over. I sigh deeply as we start to make our way through the throng of partygoers.

In the back parlor, on the opposite side of the room from the bar, draped across a pool table covered in brown butcher paper, is the mother lode. It's a Last Supper layout of cheese, bathed in shadowy mood lighting. The centerpiece is a tall tower of accoutrement: a bundle of baguettes stood upright in a wooden basket, surrounded by a swirl of plump grapes and apricots, perhaps as much for visual texture as to counteract the gathering smell of cheese anarchy. I write BLACK BETTY on the brown paper in Sharpie, realizing nobody will know that it's mine and the whole "cheese cred" idea is moot, and check out the spread. There's a Rush Creek after all, validating my decision not to pick one up; a five-year Dutch Gouda I break a plastic knife on trying to cut into; a prototype bloomy rind labeled INTERGALACTIC that a local cheesemaker brought to test on the crowd; and a bowl full of garlic pepper bombs, little dried-up bits of cheese the size of croutons that explode in your mouth, rendering your breath uninhabitable.

In just a couple of minutes, I taste a cheese with the luscious sunk-tooth texture of a Hershey bar, one that has the Plasticine chewiness of Twizzlers, and another that has the grainy crunch of, well, a Crunch bar. It feels like trick-or-treating.

"This is an overwhelming amount of cheese," Gabi says, her eyes wide and mouth half-full. "I've seen so much cheese in my life."

I would have surely felt the same way if I hadn't gone to the Cheesemonger Invitational over the summer. But even though I've already been surrounded by more cheese than I could possibly eat, this is the most I've seen concentrated in one area.

Out of nowhere, an older man with sporadic tufts of white hair appears at my side, inexplicably decked out in my exact outfit.

"These are my formal lederhosen," he says, wheezing with laughter at his own joke. Then he claps me on the back and disappears, as quickly as he arrived.

"I love your outfits," says a woman dressed in head-to-toe black, her ashen face framed by Creamsicle swirls of hair, blonde at the roots.

"We were a little worried we'd look out of place," I say.

Our new friend dips her knife in a tan mound of cheese with a creamy center and brings it to her lips. "You just look like serious beer and cheese advocates," she says.

Erika Kubick is herself a serious beer and cheese advocate, but mainly the latter. Since 2015, she's been blogging under the name Cheese Sex Death, on a quest to make her favorite food seem as achingly alluring as sex and as morbidly fascinating as death. Her specialty is fleshing out click-worthy concepts like Your Perfect Cheese According to Your Zodiac Sign with provocative photos of herself holding cheese in her multi-ringed, methodically manicured fingers.

"I've always had a very sexual approach to food," she says

when I ask about the name. "And I've always connected to the very dark elements of cheese. Fermentation itself is a death born from life or a life born from death, whichever way you want to look at it."

Whenever I'd thought of cheese as heaven, milk's final form, I hadn't really dwelled on the part of the analogy where milk has to die in order to get there. Was cheese haunted?

There's a phrase for videos like the ones Erika films, showing a Raclette landslide smother some potatoes: food porn. She knows that this is mostly what fans want from her, which is why she calls her 35,000 Instagram followers "Cheese Sluts."

When I mention I'm from New York, she recites a laundry list of Empire State dwellers from her Facebook friend group, the Cheese Influencers. I have never heard of any of them, but that's not surprising. An entire ecosystem of cheese people were thriving online unbeknownst to me. There was Lilith Spencer, the former CMI champion monger who sparked a cheese plate revolution. Her inventive arrangements of cheese, fruit, nuts, and charcuterie were so busy and colorful, so bursting with unexpected shapes and hidden patterns, they looked like undulating motion paintings. Although Lilith stopped posting photos of her creations by the time she started working at Jasper Hill earlier this year, Marissa Mullen, who started gaining a following around the same time as Lilith, carried the torch even further. The music industry hustler's website, That Cheese Plate, caught fire over the past few years, spinning off merch, a book deal, daytime talk show appearances, and classes teaching the paint-by-numbers system she'd developed for foolproof cheese plates. Elsewhere, there was Gavin Webber, the Australian YouTuber who filmed himself making cheeses he'd never even tasted before, with hundreds of thousands watching. There was the *New York Times* of cheese bloggers, Janet Fletcher of *Planet Cheese*, and Florence Fabricant of the actual *New York Times*, whose positive blurbs could launch new wheels straight into the stratosphere. There was an endless appetite for cheese knowledge and a battalion of enterprising experts eager to feed it.

In line at the table, which looks like an edible model train set, we're buffeted on all sides by an insistent whir of cheese-chatter. Newcomers continue adding to the decadent offerings, until the table is practically heaving with cheese. A woman in distressed denim and an open-front blazer holds up an LED fill light while taking a photo of the otherworldly table display.

"When did you go strictly video?" she asks a friend with an amber, asymmetrical bob.

"Over the summer," the friend says, moving her phone in a slow, clockwise, Ferris wheel rotation over the table. "My photos weren't doing so well, so . . ."

Everyone around us either works in cheese or appears to be auditioning to be a cheese documentarian. I start asking whoever is closest on the disjointed line at any given moment about whichever wedge I'm looking at. The responses always come packed with details. It's like being inside the cheese internet, or like the cheese internet had spilled over into the physical realm.

"That's Zimbro," Erika Kubick says of the fist-sized mound with a spoon in its creamy center—the same one she was eating from before. "It's a Portuguese thistle cheese, kind of a lemon bomb."

"This one's a French Crottin," my neighbor on the right says of a compact hockey puck dusted in flour. "A really hard goat cheese you usually grate over, like, pasta or something."

"That's Gjetost," someone else pipes in, pointing at a brick of what looks like un-jarred peanut butter magically maintaining its shape. "It's a Norwegian cheese that tastes like caramel. People put it in their snowsuits before skiing and take bites when they get hungry."

The mélange of aromas takes a turn from irresistible to a crime against humanity as we hit a corner of the table with pudgy pink discuses, their brainy tops peeled back like sardine cans. These would be the washed rinds, cheeses doused in alcohol or brine during the aging process to influence bacterial growth, flavor, and ultimately odor. Their title is somewhat ironic because these are the cheeses most likely to smell like a profoundly unwashed person on a long camping expedition through a landfill. Gabi and I smell the cheese at the same time, a concentrated blast of Raclette-level intensity, and she starts waving at the area in front of her nose.

So far, washed rinds have been my Achilles' cheese. Some people love pungent Époisses, but I can merely tolerate it. I just don't understand how smelling precisely like the animal a cheese is born from, or like effervescent sweat stains, could be a desirable quality in food. Milder washed rinds like Taleggio, I'd enjoyed from the get-go. But something like Époisses, which the French purportedly forbid from bringing on the Paris Métro because of its odor, were like impenetrable poetry to me. One of the cheeses on the table, Jasper Hill's Willoughby, was said to be especially pungent. Michelle at Murray's once told me a story about bringing home a couple ripe wheels one night, which incited a pair of dogs to chase her down the street.

"The smell is usually stronger than the taste," says Lauren, the buyer from Murray's, who has just joined us at the table.

This seems like my cue to taste it, so I prepare a Willoughby-smothered baguette slice.

In this case, the smell is exactly as strong as the taste, and they're both vaudevillian bodybuilders.

"Oh wow, that is . . . uh, something," I say, suppressing a gulp. "It's got a lot of character, but I don't know if I'm ready for that character."

"Should I try it?" Gabi asks, her nose twitching. "It seems like a hard nope for me."

"You should!" Lauren says, so reassuringly I can't contradict her.

Gabi nods with a grave look on her face and takes a bite. Right away, her eyebrows and mouth contract into the exact face she makes when a dog in a movie is in danger.

"If you pair it with something that has some acidity," Lauren says, "that kind of cuts that barnyard flavor and mellows it out."

Gabi's hands fly toward a nearby jar of cornichons so fast, she nearly knocks them over, before stuffing a trio of tiny pickles in her mouth.

"I'm sorry!" she says, as though Lauren personally made the cheese. "I'm sure it's great."

Our plates fully loaded, we retreat to the bar for a brief alcohol breather before hitting the upstairs area where, rumor has it, there's more cheese. A sign on the bar touts the official cocktail pairing: an Old Fashioned and a German cheese named Alex. The cheese has a dark chocolate rind, tastes lightly fruity, and goes along with an Old Fashioned in no discernible way beyond the fact that they both taste great separately. I ask Lauren where I can find Madame Fromage, a sentence that sounds like it comes from a *VeggieTales*-style children's book.

"She's out there," Lauren says, pointing toward a hallway we passed on the way in. "Trust me, you can't miss her."

Once we're there, I see what she means. The host of the party, whose real name is Tenaya Darlington, is wearing a foam Velveeta top hat, curly streamers of strawberry-streaked blonde hair spilling out, and fashionable granny glasses. I introduce myself as a born-again cheese-seeker, and it's the first of many times I hear her generous, uninhibited laughter.

"You are in very good company," she says. "There are no greater lovers than cheese lovers."

Hearing this from someone rocking the headwear of Mayor McCheese makes it sound incredibly convincing. If anyone would know, though, it's Tenaya. Cheese is practically in her blood. The future Madame Fromage grew up in Wisconsin, eating alpine cheeses like Gruyère, Comté, and Appenzeller, courtesy of her Swiss-born mother. She went to college in Madison and got a job editing the food section of a local alt weekly—just around the time that Uplands introduced Pleasant Ridge Reserve, a fantastic alpine-style cheese widely regarded as one of America's best artisan offerings. A chef friend invited Tenaya to taste an early sample, and she was in heaven. Pleasant Ridge had all the complex, meaty-sweet flavors she'd loved growing up, but was uniquely its own thing—and it was made right there in her backyard. Little did she know that much later, having tried Pleasant Ridge in its test phase would be the cheese world's version of catching an early Nirvana show in Kurt Cobain's mom's garage.

When Tenaya moved to Philadelphia in 2005 for a teaching job, she only knew one thing about the city: a Wisconsin neighbor had told her that if she ever got homesick, she should visit Di Bruno Bros., an old-world cheese shop in the Italian markets of

South Philly. One day, she went in and asked for Pleasant Ridge, which was then still relatively new. The mongers at the time were blown away. "How do you know about Pleasant Ridge?" they demanded. When she told them, they insisted she sample about twenty other cheeses too. Tenaya soon started hanging out at Di Bruno a lot. She texted cheese observations with the mongers, and they pinged her when new product arrived. It was her own version of *Cheers*, and she was drunk on flavor. Her superhero origin moment arrived when she got the idea to try all 350 of the shop's cheeses, and blog about each of them. Overnight, she became Madame Fromage—a cheese courtesan who helped readers find cheeses to fall in love with. Readers usually ended up falling in love with her too, and after a while, some of the cheesemakers she wrote about followed suit. Tenaya would write a post about hunting down a certain rare wheel, only to have its maker offer to send samples in exchange for her feedback—like a record label sending demos to Pitchfork.

By the time I met Tenaya, she'd become much more than a cheese blogger. She was the author of multiple books, one of which she cowrote with her friends at Di Bruno Bros., and she was a tour guide with Cheese Journeys, leading hard-core turophiles in a behind-the-scenes visit through the exclusive kitchens and caves of renowned European cheesemakers. Tenaya was so happy with the life she'd carved out in Philadelphia's cheese scene that a few years into it she decided to celebrate with all her new friends at once. She rented out Ruba Club for the first time in 2010, and threw up the cheese bat signal. In the years since, her ball has become a biennial tradition, growing so popular that it extended beyond her friends and into what she calls "the khaki crowd" of random cheese lovers. One year, the party coincided with Halloween, which is how some costumed photos ended up on her website, and why Gabi and I were now wearing anomalous German folk outfits.

By her third Cheese Ball, Tenaya had decided the party had room for some kind of charitable element. If so many people were excited about celebrating the Philly cheese scene, maybe they could also get excited about keeping it thriving. She dubbed the 2014 edition of the Cheese Ball a cave-raising party, and held a raffle to benefit Birchrun Hills, a local farmstead cheesemaker family she loved. The event successfully hit its target, helping the family complete construction on their caves.

Madame Fromage and her fellow cheese influencers were the midpoint between the cheesemakers and the public, and sometimes their influence flowed both ways.

More guests come by to greet Tenaya, so Gabi and I excuse ourselves and head upstairs where a twangy, countrified band called Chuck Darwin and the Knuckle-Draggers stokes the dance floor into a frenzy, and an un-tattooed Post Malone look-alike is making Raclette. We stick around the Cheese Ball until the entire table downstairs, which we hit up again later, looks like a crime scene of cheese rubble; full of wrinkly wrappers, hollowed-out rinds, overturned Camembert boxes, and oily residue seeping into the brown paper. It was a glorious, unruly mess.

While Madame Fromage only throws this party once every two years, I realized on the way out that what she and the other influencers do is make cheese feel like a party that was going on all the time. They take the gravitational pull of social media and apply it to cheese. *Here's a new bloomy rind you need to know! Here's a new way to prepare it that will change your life! Here's a method of making cheese in the Swiss Alps that's so cool you'll want to fly there to eat it fresh!* No matter where you are, or what you're up to tonight, cheese is happening out there, and it could be happening to you. And unlike the deep, burning FOMO so many other kinds of influencers carefully cultivate, cheese is a party everyone's always invited to, no RSVP required.

Come hungry.

CHAPTER FIVE

Between the Farm and the Table

I DON'T REMEMBER WHERE I FIRST HEARD OF THE CALIFORNIA CHEESE Trail, but I remember laughing about it.

Before I knew that was just the name given to a loose cluster of cheese operations throughout Marin and Sonoma county, I pictured the least perilous hiking expedition of all time. Wine-thermos. A backpack full of baguettes. Boots with grater-bottoms. Texting my wife that I'd injured my leg in a freak fondue incident: *please send help and more baguettes.*

Although the reality wasn't quite the cheddar wonderland I imagined, it was a way to hit up as many dairy farms and cheese-makers as I could handle in one trip. Since I was heading to San Francisco in January for the next Cheesemonger Invitational, it was an ideal time to tackle the Pacific Crest Trail of cheese. This would be my Cheryl Strayed's *Wild.*

Over the last several months of hanging out at Adam's Barn-yard, I'd heard a lot about the stories behind various cheeses. The history of the farms that produced the milk. The method of the make. How the recipe was passed down through generations, guarded as closely as the secret formula for Coca-Cola. A good story couldn't make mediocre cheese taste good, but it did seem to make good cheese taste better. The story need not have heroes, villains, or third-act twists. Nobody had to save a cat. All the story needed to do was leave its listener with a reason why the cheese in question was special. Virtually any reason at all.

"This cheese is called Eleven Brothers because the family that makes it actually *has* eleven brothers," I told Gabi one afternoon, breathlessly, upon returning home from BKLYN Larder.

"That's, uh, a lot of brothers," she replied.

"Right? I bought two pounds."

As much as I was a sucker for almost any cheese story, my reading comprehension, so to speak, was probably at about a second-grade level. I had never visited a creamery or a dairy farm in my life. My familiarity with the elements that make up most of these stories existed only in the abstract. It was like when I was younger and would describe movies and TV shows as "dense like a Russian novel," before I'd ever in fact read a Russian novel. When a monger told me about a "farmstead" cheese, I knew the cheese was made by the same people who raised the animals that produce the milk, but I had no concept of why that mattered or why anyone would do it. Would seeing the source of the food I was now eating more than any other food enhance my enjoyment of it? The answer was waiting somewhere in the eighty-three creameries and farms along the sprawling California Cheese Trail.

In order to make sense of the unwieldy trail map, I sought out the person who created it.

Vivien Straus comes from a family of California farm royalty. Her mother Ellen cofounded the Marin Agricultural Land Trust, which has permanently protected more than fifty-four thousand acres from developers, and her brother Albert established Straus Family Creamery, the first organic dairy west of the Mississippi. And then there's Vivien herself. In addition to being a journey-person in the California dairy community, she's also a writer and performer. A cursory google brings up a digital flyer for her one-woman show, *E-i-E-i-Oy: In Bed with the Farmer's Daughter*. The poster features an adult Ashkenazi Annie in overalls holding a menorah-pitchfork in one hand and tighty-whities in the other, an aloof cow lingering in a nearby pasture. It looks like a hoot.

Vivien was working part-time with her friends at Cowgirl Creamery almost a decade ago when one of the owners, Sue Conley, floated the idea of making a cheese map.

"Essentially, nobody knew there were cheesemakers out here," Vivien explains over the phone.

"I think in the last five to ten years suddenly everybody is talking about cheese and *now* it's very hip, but when I started doing the map, people didn't even know you could visit these farms."

I can see how that would be the case. Until recently, I had no idea California even made cheese, much less that it was one of the three top cheese-producing states in America—along with Vermont and Wisconsin—and that its rich, cheesy history goes far beyond the goat ladies of the 1980s, way back to even before the invention of Monterey Jack in the 1700s.

Soon after Vivien released her trail map in 2010, based on the model of Napa Valley wine-tasting maps, one of the larger cheese producers in Sonoma revealed that her retail sales had exploded in the first two months alone. More and more makers on the trail suddenly scrambled to find ways to quell the apparently insatiable market demand for agritourism.

Since Vivien knew the map better than anybody, she helped me narrow down a short list of options for my California visit. It felt like planning a hike after all, except instead of trekking poles and a breathable fleece, all I needed were shoes that could withstand a little mud, which I ended up forgetting to pack anyway.

IF THERE WAS any chance I was going to miss the turn for Bohemian Creamery, the quiver of orange arrow-signs that read GOT CHEESE? ensures I don't.

I've been driving for an hour and a half, directly from the airport in San Francisco, and the further north I get the less it resembles anything like what I know California to look like. I've spent time in sunny Los Angeles and foggy San Francisco before, both bustling and intensely metropolitan cities. Sonoma County couldn't be more different. (Well, except for the fog. That's still here.) I drive past rain-drenched pastures of grazing Holsteins, which are the black-and-white milk tanks most people picture when they picture cows. An honest-to-God purplish hue hangs over the mountain majesties in the distance, and the iridescent green grass practically vibrates like a video game set in farm country.

Bohemian Creamery operates out of a house that rests upon a hilltop dotted with skeletal winter trees, overlooking the marshy Laguna de Santa Rosa wetlands. Beneath the rusty, sheep-shaped weather vane on the roof, a sun-faded tangerine awning sports the creamery's funky logo: a silhouette of three SoCal surfer goats driving a Beetle with boards strapped to the roof. I can't say for sure whether I'd rather hang out with the person who designed it, or the goats themselves.

Inside is the Bohemian shop, which has the ramshackle feel

of a summer camp concession stand. A handmade sign on the paint-chipped fridge promises WHEY SODA, and a bushel basket on top overflows with twine-wrapped bars of goat's milk soap, an attached sign demanding: SMELL ME. (I do. It smells like goat.)

Almost as soon as I arrive, a door near the fridge opens and a woman in a shiny, yellow, hazmat-thick apron emerges. Lisa Gottreich is wearing a gray hoodie and a Rosie the Riveter–style bandanna, a flap of dirty blonde hair flooding out the back.

"Come on in," she says. "But don't bring your germs."

I dunk my shoes in the trough of disinfectant she points at on the floor and follow her over the threshold into the creamery.

For the past ten years, Lisa has been making cheese practically by herself in this spartan room. Loose curds dot the crimson floor like spiral notebook detritus, in a trail leading to the rectangular steel vat where Lisa has just finished making today's cheese. On a steel table nearby, the freshly made cheese sits in crooked rows of white plastic molds; gleaming, dough-like wheels draining out their stubborn remaining whey.

"This is cow's milk, from a neighbor down the street," she says. "I keep goats here, but I make cheese with all kinds of milk: goat, cow, sheep, and water buffalo when I can get it."

To the right are three open storage units, full of ventilated shelves, each one holding a different kind of white plastic mold: some shaped like cakes, others like pyramids, and others still like those big Folgers Coffee cans. Lisa uses all the different molds and milks at her disposal to make an ambitious, almost absurd variety of cheeses for such a small operation.

"How did you end up with goats?" I ask.

"Because I like them better than people," she says, grabbing a push broom from its nook on the wall and going after the loose curds on the floor. "I got quite a number of them while I was raising my kids. They're an entertaining animal, and I figured I needed an excuse to justify having them, so I started making cheese."

Like many before her, Lisa entered the cheese world via a surprising left turn. Although she was raised in Sonoma County, she made her living as a policy advisor in Washington, D.C., for many years before returning back home to start a family. She had no grand plans to become a cheesemaker. She simply had the goats already, and the idea for Bohemian Creamery sort of unfolded from there.

In the beginning, she was putting in fourteen-hour days as a one-woman cheese operation. It took years before her products began to pop up in enough restaurants around the Bay Area that she could breathe easier and hire an assistant. As I watch her push floor-cheese into a dustbin, I think of all the well-heeled diners at the Ritz-Carlton daintily auditing the menu and ordering cheese made from this humble creamery.

We head into one of her ripening rooms, where stacks of brown dish racks stand alongside the room's metal walls holding marshmallowish bloomy rind cheeses the size of vending machine chip bags. The bleachy sting of ammonia scorches my nostrils for the first of what will be many times during the new year. As I would later come to learn, when the proteins in fresh cheese break down, ammonia is released into the air. The fact that my face feels like it's going to peel off right now just means that the cheese in here is aging properly.

"These cheeses move through time," Lisa says, running her hand along the side of one of the plastic racks. "They shed some qualities, and gain some others. Just like we do."

The process of aging a cheese—either in a no-frills room like this one or a fancy, humidity-controlled cave—is called affinage. It's a complicated, scientific part of cheesemaking that involves a lot of turning, salting, washing cheeses in brine, and intuition.

"So, this one's not ready to eat," she says tapping an ash-covered, pyramid cheese. "And this one is," she says, thrusting an enormous butter-yellow hunk in my palm. "You can have it if you want."

The imminent snack in my hand is ShredHead, one of sixteen cheeses Lisa makes. It has a constellation of tiny holes in the paste, which is held together by a pizza crust–colored rind. I take a whiff and pick up a yeasty sourdough aroma beneath the ammonia in the air.

"I probably have more kinds of cheese than I oughtta have," Lisa says. "I'm like the little old lady that lived in the shoe. I wish there were contraception for cheesemakers, because I kind of don't want any more, but I get inspired sometimes and I just can't help myself—I've gotta do it."

ShredHead is Lisa's latest inspiration, an effort to shut up the cheese buyers at restaurants who hound her about making a cheddar. She didn't understand why they kept asking. Plenty of cheesemakers do cheddar, but very few make Italian-style cheese infused with bee pollen (FlowerPower) or goat's milk cheese rolled in nori seaweed (Surf and Turf). If people weren't interested in those, then why were they even ordering from Bohemian? In an effort to meet her buyers halfway, Lisa played around with the idea of what kind of cheddar an Italian maker might produce. The piece of ShredHead in my hands is the result: grudge-cheese.

Although Lisa takes after one of the original goat ladies, Mary Keehn of Cypress Grove, in falling into cheesemaking while raising goats and children, her experimental side puts her more in line with one of the others: Laini Fondiller of Vermont's Lazy Lady Farm, who is always testing out new ingredients like smoked paprika and Russian stout beer, and who keeps upward of eighteen different cheeses in rotation. This is the freedom American cheesemakers have, unbound by European PDOs.

Europe has definitely noticed what America has done with this freedom, too.

"They're jealous that we have so much play with our recipes," Cowgirl Creamery cofounder Sue Conley says with a measured half smile when I visit later in the week. "And the truth is that the European companies are investing in American cheese companies, including ours."

In 2016, the multibillion-dollar Swiss conglomerate Emmi acquired Cowgirl Creamery. Soon afterward, they began purchasing other California cheesemakers including Cypress Grove and Redwood Hill, both of which were founded in the 1980s and 1990s by goat ladies. If nothing else, it's proof that European companies see the wallet-incinerating passion for artisan cheese in America, along with how much easier it is to simply snap up an already-trusted brand rather than build one here from scratch.

The buyouts have proven a controversial development in the cheese world. Some independent producers see them as an existential threat, the pathway to artisanal homogeny. Others see it as more of a well-earned golden parachute for old-school pioneers. Here's what's undeniable: After the Cowgirl Creamery sale, its founders were suddenly able to afford a new creamery in Petaluma, allowing them to make more cheese, both in terms of volume and new products. They have since brought back their previously discontinued Clabbered Cottage Cheese—think kernel-sized curds in luscious cream—and created Hop Along, a cider-washed soft cheese I first tried when someone brought an early wheel to the Philly Cheese Ball in November. In other words, Cowgirl is using its surplus money to be as nimble as Bohemian Creamery.

Eventually, I thank Lisa for her time and her cheese and head out to my rental car. It seems like there's no good place to put the ShredHead, until my eyes alight on the center cupholder, which is conspicuously cheese-sized. With a shrug, I set my silent, edible passenger in the holder and take occasional nibbles as I drive down the highway; it probably looks as though I'm either incredibly hungry, running late, or possibly both. The cheese is buttery, sharp. It only tastes kind of like cheddar, a bit tangier than usual, but I smile thinking about Lisa inventing it as a middle finger to the chefs asking her to make something she didn't want to make.

THERE IS ZERO cell reception on this particular winding stretch of Highway 1, so I'm unable to either look up how to get un-lost or let my host know I'll be late. All I can do is continue driving along the foggy bay that keeps area restaurants up to their elbows in oysters, trying to remember roughly where I'm supposed to go. Just as I'm about ready to give up, I find a sloping gravel path riven through a grassy hill that leads to Point Reyes Farmstead Creamery.

As my car crawls through a light drizzle, alongside a herd of Holsteins and past two chrome-colored feed silos, I see a giant black blob rising from the ground, hemmed in by a short chain-link fence. From its bulbous outward appearance, I'd never have guessed it was a methane digester filled with electricity-generating poop fumes. I hang a right by a stable filled with more cows, pass a small fleet of ATVs, and park near the head office, which looks like the kind of resort that might have a lobby DJ spinning inside. Across from the reception desk is the entrance to Fork, the folksy-fancy culinary and educational center where Point Reyes hosts agribusiness event meals and corporate retreats. (A group from Whole Foods is currently in there, talking quarterly reports over crumbly blue cheese.) It looks like the type of space a couple might get married in, depending on how much they love cheese and are indifferent to jokes about it.

Although the Giacomini family, who owns and runs the business, appears to be doing very well, that wasn't the case twenty years ago. Like many other smaller dairy farms around the country, they had been finding it difficult to stay competitive selling only fluid milk. America simply had too much, and it sold for way too cheap. By the late 1990s, when the prospects of keeping the farm began to look bleak, Bob Giacomini considered selling. The only alternative, it seemed, was to diversify. Switching to commodity cheese, which is what a majority of dairy farmers make and a majority of Americans eat, would leave him subject to the fickle whims of the Chicago Mercantile Exchange, which determines its fluctuating price. If he made artisan cheese instead, though, Bob could charge whatever people were willing to pay.

He and his wife, Dean, decided to go for it.

Since they didn't think they alone could do all the work of converting to artisan cheesemaking, they asked their four adult daughters to come along on this uncertain cheese adventure. Three said yes, and together they produced California's first artisanal blue cheese. Nearly two decades later, Point Reyes Farmstead's Original Blue has become a nationwide cheese shop staple, affording the Giacominis this impressive, state-of-the-art facility.

Many other dairy farmers tried turning to artisan cheese as a means to save their farms before the Giacominis, and many more would try afterward. Not very many are able to make it work.

"You caught us on one of our rainy weeks," says a Point Reyes employee named Stacey in a navy parka. Stacey has a freckled face and a frizzy ponytail, and even though she looks young enough to belong to a sorority, she has the composure and infectious pleasantness of a local morning news anchor. She hands over an umbrella as she greets me in the lobby, and I follow her through the doors back out into the mid-morning mist.

The first place we visit is the milking room, located in a bunker just across from the creamery. Each machine is an octopusian jumble of tubes, all of them ending in apparatuses topped with suction cups. It seems like a room where cows might gear up before a scuba diving mission.

For some reason, it's disappointing to find out that cows are milked by machines and not by hand, like they are in every movie or TV show to ever feature a cow. It's like the first time I went to a casino and saw everybody just pushing buttons instead of pulling the slot machine handles. Little did I know at the time just how advanced milking technology has become. A couple of months later, I would visit Rogue Creamery's farm in Oregon, where the cows milk themselves. Whenever they're ready, they simply clomp over to a waiting vestibule, where milking robot arms first spray their udders with iodine and then latch on and start sucking, the machine pinging the farmer's phone if there's ever a problem. (Old McDonald has an app, E-I-E-I-O.)

"We pride ourselves on our sustainable practices," Stacey proudly announces, pointing out the solar panels on top of the milking room.

Sustainability is a buzzword lightly tossed around in restaurants and coffee shops and Peloton classes, and my grasp on it is tenuous at best. I know, at least, that it is a good thing and I am in favor of it. The concept fully sinks in for me, though, when Stacey explains, in a relentlessly upbeat tone, how Point Reyes uses by-products from the farm and from other local industries in every way they can. They use cottonseed from cotton farmers. They use brewer's grain from the nearby Lagunitas brewery. They use solar energy from the sun. Not only are these by-products super affordable or free, they also represent the concept of using the whole buffalo, and not letting resources go to waste.

"The biggest by-product on our farm is methane from the cow's poop," Stacey says as we stroll past a chill-out area where cows lay in repose on dirt beds, their legs folded up underneath them and their butts jutting out. "It, uh, comes without fail, so we have to put it to good use somehow."

Converting cow poop into useful energy is the ultimate example of turning lemons into lemonade, and a stronger candidate for that expression's mantle in my opinion. When life hands you poop, make power.

All the waste the cows leave behind on the pasture stays there, because it's too hard to capture from the porous earth, and goes on to fertilize new grass for those same cows to eventually eat. Yada, yada, the circle of life, and so forth. The poop in the barn, on the other hand, slides down a gravity slope system, which the dairymen flush out with recycled water a couple times a day. That waterborne poop floats from the barn to the Giacominis' methane digester, which extracts enough gas from it to power 60 percent of the farm on average, including the creamery.

"Another by-product is whey," Stacey says as we head toward

the barn, "which is high in protein, so we feed it right back to the girls."

Once I realize that Stacey means the cows and not the Giacomini sisters, whom she also refers to as "the girls," a shiver travels up my spine. The idea of cows ingesting whey from their own milk sounds an awful lot like cannibalism. It's at least cannibalism-adjacent. But it seems from Point Reyes' success that they know exactly what they're doing and only feed these cows substances that enhance their lives. "Happy cows make happy milk" is a dairy industry slogan that sounds like it was written by cows but it's actually true. Scientific studies show that stressed-out animals secrete cortisol and other non-delicious hormones in their milk. You can probably taste the psychic trauma trapped in the milk of poorly treated cattle, and I bet it tastes like shit.

I survey the cows and try to discern their level of happiness. The eight-ball-like pupils in their wide-set eyes reveal nothing. They look healthy, though, each with a beefy ripple of ribs. At least part of the reason why, as it turns out, is because they come from good stock.

"We source our semen from around the world," Stacey says as the cows meander past. "From professional breeders who advertise traits like longevity, high production, and strong legs."

I look at the cows a little differently, now that I know they're genetically superior specimens.

Months later, I'll actually get a glimpse at a semen catalog where professional breeders advertise bulls with names like Taurus Commander X Force alongside pictures of his progeny, with stats on their milk production. It sounds an awful lot like eugenics for cows. It's at least eugenics-adjacent.

"Our herd manager and master cheesemaker are in constant communication with our nutritionist about how to best feed our girls and how it will affect the milk," Stacey continues.

"Wait, the cows have a nutritionist?"

"Uh-huh," she says. "Dr. Kennedy looks at all the data we get from the milking barn and he decides whether they need more sugars or more omega-3s, and we fluctuate as needed."

Incredible. I picture a team of doctors in lab coats taking notes as an electrode-covered cow runs on a treadmill, like a bovine Ivan Drago. These cows are being optimized in every way and getting more help with their fitness than I can afford to get with mine. They're leading an aspirational lifestyle.

Soon, we come upon an isolated section of the stable with a lumpy dirt floor, which Stacey refers to as the maternity ward. A Holstein with haunted eyes is helping a wobbly baby calf, the size of a Golden Retriever, remain standing beneath her. She was apparently born just a half hour ago.

"There's the placenta," Stacey says, pointing to a slurry of red, membranal goop that resembles a beached jellyfish in shape, consistency, and my desire to avoid it. I've barely recovered from the sight when Stacey mentions that the mama cow will soon be eating it.

"Wow," I say, and then bite the inside of my cheek to keep from barfing.

It is in this weak condition that I hear what's coming next, the information that turns my whole cheese world upside down.

"The girl calves go on to join our herd," Stacey says, in the exact key of chipper she's said everything else, "and the boys become beef cows."

Whatever she says after that gets a little fuzzy. Because I'm spiraling.

For the last ten years, I've been a vegetarian. It's part of my identity. The words "beef cow," however, pierce the veil of my deeply internalized denial. Suddenly, I see my own complicity in all the hamburgers I've forsaken for seitan. It had somehow never occurred to me that having a steady supply of milk is contingent on cows being pregnant all the time, and while girl cows keep producing milk for many years, boy cows are single-use only. Their purpose in dairy starts and ends with sperm donation. And for all the cost associated with raising a calf to adulthood, you might as well just artificially inseminate. The longer the boy cows stay on the farm, the more they soak up resources, take up space, and exude methane. Ideally, these unmilkable boy cows would be able to roam free on a utopian cattle sanctuary, but this isn't an ideal world. Meanwhile, the boundless demand for beef continues. So, boy calves become beef cows: pre-veal. That's why we associate cows with the name "Bessie." All the Benjys are dead.

I had eaten cheese, guilt-free, my whole life—a decade of which I spent patting myself on the back for being kind to animals as a vegetarian. Now I understood that artisan cheese simply could not exist without people eating meat, the dairy industry and the beef industry working in symbiotic harmony. Even if dairy farmers didn't sell their boy cows to be butchered, there was still the matter of rennet, the cheese-making enzyme that comes from a calf's fourth stomach. I suddenly realized that it can't possibly be extracted from those calves with a syringe like I'd quietly told myself when I first heard about rennet. Deep down, I probably always knew how farmers got it.

Even in the best conditions, at a top-of-the-line farmstead creamery where the animals are mostly treated like guests at a day spa—happy cows making happy milk—this process was still pure subjugation. I had shielded myself from some hard truths about it in order to remain a blissful, cheese-loving vegetarian. But I couldn't do that anymore. Santa isn't real, love doesn't always last, and baby boy cows are slaughtered for rennet and veal.

MY EXISTENTIAL CHEESE crisis continues when I visit the next stop on my tour of the California Cheese Trail: Achadinha Cheese Company in Petaluma.

As soon as I get out of my rental car, the air is filled with a horrible chamber chorus of moos. It sounds like a forest full of werewolves just discovering their curse, one after the other, in a circle-dirge of sadness. *(Ah-oo. Ah-OO.)*

I'm parked in a sludgy mud patch, across from a massive barn with a long, raised roof, and a corral of cows in front, bellowing with what sounds like deep, all-consuming grief. A woman in a forest-green bubble vest soon appears heading toward me, waving her hands.

"I'm sorry for all the noise," she shouts over the cacophony. "We sold their babies this morning, so they're upset."

Donna Pacheco gestures toward two rows of white maternal yurts running perpendicular to the barn, to demonstrate where the baby cows are no longer staying.

I try not to let my face betray the sheer horror coursing through me. Instead, I suppress it and listen to Donna's story.

Achadinha Farm is a family operation, but in a very different way from Point Reyes. While the Giacomini sisters and their father are hands-on in every decision, they're a layer removed from any of the actual farmwork at this point. Not so with the Pacheco family. They are intimately involved in every aspect of making and selling the cheese, the couple and their four children waking up at 4:30 A.M. every morning to start the day's chores.

Achadinha sells most of its cheese at farmers markets, which I mostly know of as the tent-filled shantytowns I pop in to pick up hot apple cider on a chilly fall New York day. Farmers markets are also, of course, outlets where small-production cheesemakers could cut out the middleman and sell directly to consumers and chefs, get exposure, build a grassroots fan base, and possibly get scouted by a Whole Foods professional forager. The Pachecos hit about thirty-five of these markets each week during the winter, and seventy-five in the summer. On a Saturday in July, they might reach thirteen in one afternoon; loading up four trucks with umbrellas and coolers, each headed to a different spot, a cheddar armada.

The Pachecos are nothing if not scrappy. They started out selling cow's milk in the 1980s, moved on to raising beef cows, then switched from all cow to all goat, and now they have both. Somewhere along the way, they also bought a vineyard and experimented with making wine for a time, before settling on cheese. Once they got started, they took Best of Show at ACS back in 2002, with a goat's milk cheese called Capricious that lives on now as the mixed-milk Cowpricious. Donna chalks up their big win to having far less competition back then, though.

Once we head off to the barn, the queasy feeling from earlier returns to my stomach. It's half to do with hearing the bereft cows outside inundating us with their feelings, and half to do with the smell. I'd heard the word *barnyardy* used to describe fecal-smelling cheese many times by now, and it's proving only too accurate. We walk through the center of the long barn, a trio of ducks in tow behind us. Brown Jersey cows are fenced in on one side, while Holsteins run along the other, both groups sticking their heads through the open slats in the fence to munch on some hay in the barn's center. They all have yellow numbered tags on their ears that look somewhere between fashion-forward earrings and price tags. Bales of stiff hay lay in the far back of the barn, stacked in an M. C. Escher staircase almost to the ceiling.

"Are you being nice?" Donna says to a cow, who has sucked Donna's entire fist into her mouth. Then, turning to me, she adds: "They like to pacify."

The cow that is pacifying on Donna's fist has a piece of tape tied around her tail, a designation to show that she's pregnant.

Raising kids on a farm provides ample opportunity to teach them about the birds and the bees. (Or the semen-syringe and the cow-uterus.) It also offers plenty of chances to explain a rather unpleasant fact of life: what happens to old cows and goats when they're ready to retire.

The lie that some parents tell their children about the beloved family pet going away to live on a farm doesn't work when you already live on a farm. There's no way to sugarcoat it. These animals are going off to be butchered.

"I believe we, as a small farm, have a strong connection to our animals," Donna says, letting her hand rest on the pregnant cow she's stroking. "The person that feeds the animal is generally the one who takes it to the butcher yard. If you're just unloading them, they get freaked out. But if that person is there for it, even if it's just a whistle they hear, they know that whistle and they calm down."

I want to cry. Instead, I try to think about anything else except a sad-eyed cow taking a last moment's comfort from a familiar noise just before meeting its fate. I try so hard not to cry that I go too far the other way and crack a half smile, which feels wrong.

"It is a business, even with the dairy cows," Donna says, patting the pacifying cow on the head as we turn to leave the barn. "They may have names and we may know their personalities, but at the end of the day we need to make the ranch payment so we have to be realistic."

Being realistic is something I have to do, too, as a vegetarian. People are always going to eat cheeseburgers and drink milk, and so the subjugation of cows will continue. But my trip along the California Cheese Trail has convinced me what a difference it makes in who is doing the subjugating. Factory farms milk their cows so aggressively they stop producing after five years, while smaller farms can keep theirs going for eight to ten years. And even if the reason those smaller farms do it that way is because "happy cows make happy milk," rather than pure animal altruism, at least those eight to ten years will probably more closely resemble the fictional Cowtopia I had let myself innocently imagine before.

On the way back to my car, I walk past the cows in the corral, who have just lost their babies and continue their moaning. I would surely think of them again the next time I ate cheese, which for the first time in as far as I could remember, I don't particularly feel like doing.

I START TO recover as I head toward the last company I planned to visit on my whirlwind tour of the Trail, which also happens to be the newest.

Folly Cheese, which sold its first-ever wheel roughly half a year ago, is a company that operates independently within a larger company, like a Russian cheese doll. All week, I'd seen different operations that were thriving at different levels. Now I'd see one that was just getting off the ground.

Christian and Ashley Coffey are a married couple in their mid-twenties who had been working at Tomales Farmstead Creamery for years before deciding to go into business for themselves. Unlike most aspiring cheese entrepreneurs, they had access to all the equipment they would need to get started, and the kind of relationship with their employers to ensure they'd be able to use it. Incredibly, though, the moment they chose to launch coincided with Ashley's pregnancy.

"They rolled out a new cheese and a new baby in the same year," says Tomales cofounder Tamara Hicks, sitting at the marble counter of her well-appointed kitchen. "We're very impressed."

Beyond overseeing her cheese business, Tamara works as a psychologist, while her husband and partner in cheese, David, heads up the thoracic surgery unit at the University of California, San Franciso. Tamara hovers over her laptop, with a jaunty scarf around her neck, slowly picking at a quinoa salad. Christian is seated on the other end of the table, absently itching his mossy brown beard. Ashley is nowhere to be seen at the moment because, as Tomales Farmstead's head cheesemaker, she's currently working the vat.

Christian and Ashley have worked at one dairy farm or another—sometimes together, sometimes not—since their first mutual job while they were still in college in North Carolina. Five years ago, the pair moved to California, with Ashley taking a job at Tomales and Christian splitting his time between buying cheese for Amy's Kitchen brand and helping out here on the farm.

For the past two and a half years, they'd been playing with the idea of launching a cheese of their own, until finally they just up and had the conversation with Tamara and David. They asked for access to the Tomales Creamery one day a month to make cheese for themselves, and to borrow against their retirement funds for material costs. It was a $10,000 investment, they reasoned. If it didn't work out, they wouldn't be completely wiped, and at least they would have tried. Most cheesemakers who don't have a creamery at their disposal need $500,000 or more to get started. Christian and Ashley just needed to secure their employers' blessing.

There are many reasons why a cheesemaker decides which kind of cheese to make. Some stick with chèvre, for instance, because generally you only get paid for cheese once you sell it, and fresh goat's milk cheeses have a much quicker turnaround time than aged ones. The reason Christian and Ashley modeled their cheese after the alpine Beaufort, though, is because that cheese is fucking awesome.

"Sometimes when you work for another company you don't get to make the cheese you'd like to make," Christian says, after we leave the kitchen to go pick up his baby from where she's napping down the hall. "We decided to make this cheese because it's the cheese we always want to eat."

Although Christian and Ashley enjoyed the soft-ripened goat cheeses Tomales was known for, they wanted the sautéed onion and hazelnut complexity of a hard Beaufort in their kitchen all the time. Lillian, the sole offering from Folly Cheese Company, ultimately didn't come out that way exactly, but the pair is happy with what they created.

Christian returns from the bedroom with an angelic red-headed baby in a light blue onesie strapped to his chest. She is cooing nonstop, clearly loving the ride.

Aside from having access to the creamery, which is where we're headed now, Christian and Ashley have a leg up on other cheese start-ups in that they are already deeply immersed in the California cheese community. They're both members of the California Artisan Cheese Guild, a trade organization that includes other makers, shop owners, distributors, and some enthusiasts. They had an entire community to reach out to for advice and feedback, and shops that were eager to carry their cheese.

"The first batch we made was not up to par but starting out with very little money, you kind of have to sell that first batch," Christian says. It's hard to concentrate on what he's saying because there's a baby on his chest looking at me with a goofy grin as he talks. "We made about a half dozen wheels, and sold half of it, and that enabled us to keep going."

That fall, Christian took five of the thirty wheels he and Ashley had made in Folly's first year to the San Francisco Cheese Festival and sold them all. The response was so enthusiastic that they invested their profits in a Dutch press, with the goal of shooting for sixty wheels in this, their second year in business.

When we get to the creamery, which I can only see through a window for sanitary reasons, Ashley has a hairnet on and is working with a bunch of square molds of cheese. Before coming outside to greet her baby, she goes into a ripening room and retrieves a big yellow wheel from Folly's second season for me to examine through the creamery window. This is as close as I will get to tasting it now, since it won't be officially ready for another few months. The wait feels pre-emptively excruciating.

After hearing the story behind this cheese, I'm dying to know how it tastes. But when I think of how this story would sound over a counter in a cheese shop, I draw a blank. Theirs is a story that doesn't neatly boil down to a counter-pitch, not that any of them really do.

"This bee pollen cheese is from a restless experimenter who makes it all by herself."

"This sustainably made cheese is the first blue ever produced in California."

"This alpine-inspired cheese comes from a couple who worked for another cheesemaker and—well, why don't you just taste it?"

When I finally try Lillian months later, it's so rich and nutty, I can't tell whether the story made their cheese taste better or if their cheese makes their story sound better.

I just know I want more.

CHAPTER SIX

What I'm Talking About
When I'm Talking about Cheese

piece of slang for the first time.

It's the moment of truth. Will your friends just accept you calling a hot song "a slap," or will they suspect instead that you've been body-snatched?

Hopefully, more often than not, any efforts at zhuzhing up your word bank will go unremarked upon. (Unlike the first time I took "zhuzh" out for a spin.) But what's even more fraught than conspicuously trying out a new word is learning you've been using an old one wrong all along.

The more time I spent with cheese people, the more my vocabulary evolved to keep up with theirs. Nobody blanched at any of the new-to-me words now regularly dotting my descriptions, like "squidgy," even as I labored over whether I was using them correctly. But there was one word that made cheeseheads react so strongly I had to remove it from my repertoire.

That word was *sharp*.

Despite its grocery store cheddar ubiquity, "sharp" doesn't actually mean anything in terms of flavor. It's merely the word some Wisconsin cheese people concocted to describe a cheddar whose acidity is so high it drowns out any other attributes. Cheese sharpness is a shared hallucination that means whatever anyone needs it to mean. Heat. Tang. General strength. They're all tucked away inside the same vernacular Swiss Army Knife, which is ironic because knives actually are sharp, and cheese in Switzerland never is. That Goldilocksian lineup of mild, sharp, and extra sharp on store shelves? It's designed to make people who always choose the most extreme food option (me, for instance) feel like they're slaloming the culinary expert slope, instead of eating chemically unbalanced cheddar.

Suffice it to say that mongers don't often describe cheese that way to each other. Not that *sharp* doesn't have a place in their lexicon. It's a euphemism, and euphemisms help ease civilians into cheese. Since it's hard to make *high acidity* sound all that sexy to customers, *sharp* is a handy word for when batches turn out that way.

There's plenty more where that came from too.

Cheese noobs might be scared away by the fumes of something that's *pungent* or *stanky*, but who wouldn't want to try something *funky*? That sounds like a party!

Just as a boring movie might be described as *deliberately paced*, a bland cheese could either be *elegant*, *understated*, or *restrained*. Where's the lie?

But my favorite cheese euphemism is another one for powerfully smelly fromage: *assertive*. It's the perfect way to describe a cheese that simply insists you take a Chernobyl shower after coming in contact with it in any way.

However, when mongers talk about cheese, evasively vague or piercingly precise, it's always intentional. Cheese people dig deep to find exactly the right words for descriptions, not because their careers depend on it, but because they love the challenge almost as much as they love the taste. It's an infectious quality to be around. And I would have ample opportunity to absorb it as I headed to San Francisco for the next Cheesemonger Invitational.

AFTER A WEEK of scenic winding roads overlooking the Pacific coastline, driving in San Francisco is a nightmare. It feels like constantly going up the first hill of a roller coaster, if every other roller coaster kept swerving into your tracks or double-parking on them and you had to constantly stop at almost-vertical stretches of hill that test the tensile strength of your roller coaster's brakes. The driving is already uniquely stressful even before it's time to park, at which point: good luck. The only spots are coin purse size voids between attached driveways, and whoops, they're all taken.

As much trouble as it is to get around the city, it's all worth it once I arrive at The Midway, the venue for this winter's San Francisco Cheesemonger Invitational. It's a performance space on the east side of the city, in an artsy, post-industrial area called Dogpatch, named after either the fictional setting of the comic strip Li'l Abner or the gangs of feral dogs that rumor has it, once roamed the streets freely.

It's 8:00 A.M. and The Midway is already a shaken beehive of activity. Out on the breezy deck, a monger with light chocolate hair in Pippi pigtails not-so-gently strums her acoustic guitar, improvising a happy tune about birds for an audience that includes a fellow wearing the bowler hat and vest of a person who's definitely addressed someone as "milady" in recent days. Inside, a man in a black hoodie stalks the long central corridor with a bullhorn, herding up the thirty-five or so competing mongers. Eventually, he gets them all into a snazzy reception hall with the words GODS AND MONSTERS imprinted over the entranceway. The room is lined with diamond-tufted plush leather couches you can practically hear just by looking at them, but most of the space is occupied by rows of foldable tables filled with chatty mongers. There's a stage up front, empty except for a stuffed buffalo head with winsome eyes mounted just above it. Adam Moskowitz's cow costume hangs from an amplifier on the right side, representing him in spirit since he is home with the flu, missing CMI for the first time ever.

When I went to last summer's CMI in Brooklyn, I didn't know Adam yet, and had only gotten to see the outer layer of the event—its rind, more or less. That public-facing portion was actually just the climax of an entire weekend in which makers and mongers came together in the lead-up to the qualifying rounds and an eventual face-off between finalists. Some people call it Cheese Camp, even though that's also what they call the week-long ACS conference at the end of each summer, and it's the name of a biannual training program for mongers at Jasper Hill as well. For the San Francisco edition, Adam agreed to let me come for the entire weekend and see everything, all the delicious paste behind the rind.

Soon enough, Adam's colleague Jonathan Richardson takes the stage, his small black hood flopping as he thrusts both fists to the sky. Once he gets through the unexpected news about Adam's absence, he switches to motivational mode.

"So, what are we doing here today?" he asks, conjuring up Adam-like enthusiasm. A couple of hands shoot up before their owners realize it's a rhetorical question. "Today is not a day to worry about the competition. Today's the day that we feed you. We feed you passion. We feed you education. We let you sit down with some of the people you've read about in books, whose cheeses you lust after in shops and on Instagram. We put you at a table together so you can find out about them and they can find out about you."

Several of the puffer jacket–clad mongers in the room hoot and holler, as though they've been waiting to ask questions of Neal's Yard Dairy partner Jason Hinds for many untold years.

"If you want to know anything about how to win, we have some people right here who have intimate knowledge of how it's done," Jonathan says, gesturing to a triad on one of the nearby couches. I recognize Jordan Edwards from last summer's CMI right away, because how could I not? He has a nearly shaved head, a dagger on his right temple competing with all his other tattoos for prominence, and he dresses like a longshoreman crust punk. The other two previous winners are Rory Stamp and Lilith Spencer, who look more like coffee shop philosophers, but probably mostly because they are sitting next to Jordan. All three wore prescription glasses, and as I found out later, each had the word *cheese* somewhere in their email addresses.

"Most of you will not win anything," Jonathan says after rattling off all the prizes on hand for the winner and runners-up. "But what you'll all walk away with is a way to explain to your family and friends what you do. This is cheese. It's not just a job, this is a lifestyle for us."

A stadium wave of spirited nods flows through the room. The competitors are all keenly aware that most people know nothing about what mongering entails. Whether or not they actually learn how to describe their occupation any better over the next forty-eight hours, it would still be cathartic to spend that time hanging out with other people whose expertise is equally underestimated.

Soon, it's time for the mongers to break out into four groups and settle in at different round tables in the long main corridor. Over the next few hours, cheesemaking luminaries like Andy Hatch of Uplands and Mateo Kehler of Jasper Hill would take turns stopping by each. It was kind of like speed dating, but if everyone was horny for cheese.

On the way over to my table, I pass former CMI champs and two of this year's judges, Rory Stamp and Lilith Spencer, and stop by to introduce myself. I knew Lilith by reputation as a former monger and cheese plate influencer, who had since moved on to work for Jasper Hill in production. It turned out Rory had also left mongering behind, eventually opening a cheese consulting firm after a variety of other jobs within the industry. Both judges are examples of the uncertain trajectory of a career in cheese—and proof that what you learn as a monger can apply to many jobs.

Before I can ask about any of those things, however, a monger with a wily smirk and a flat-brimmed hat perched on a nest of wavy hair interrupts to say hi to Lilith. She matches his exact smile intensity and the two proceed to do a complicated handshake, which ends with either person pulling on the other's upside-down thumbs. It takes me a moment to realize they're milking each other's digits like cow udders.

At the other end of the room just then, Jonathan blows a whistle. The speed dating is about to begin. Alex and I leave the two judges and join the nearest table.

Although sitting down with marquee cheesemakers was

supposed to be the highlight of the day, I was ready for some variety by the time Rachel Juhl, a sparkplug in an extremely cozy-looking sweater, joins our table. Well, she doesn't join the table so much as attack it, plunking down well over a dozen vials of odd substances; tiny, aromatic pipe bombs. One is loaded with peels of butter, another contains bits of brioche, and there's a black smudgy one labeled EARTH, the entire contents of our planetary existence reduced to wet dirt.

"Let's talk cheese," Rachel says, slamming down a tube of lactic yeast, her fingernails the color of red cabbage. She then launches into a rapid-fire, uninterruptible spiel, with breath control any high-speed rapper would envy.

"What we do at Essex St. Cheese is we're importers. That's the boring side of the job; logistics, making sure we're kosher with the FDA, all that stuff. Boring. The cool part of what we do is selection: trying to represent these classic cheeses that are really well known in the world but are misrepresented or underrepresented in the United States."

It seemed strange to me at first that Adam would invite another importer to CMI, since he owned and operated an importing company himself. What I didn't realize is that the two companies weren't in competition with each other; they were both in competition with the American consumer's indifference toward artisan cheese. Like everyone else here, they were on the same side.

"I'm chief educator," Rachel says, placing the last of her specimens on the table. "So, my job is to visit all of our producers, try to get as much information as possible about the cheese and the story behind it, and distill it down to something we can share with people."

Some of the cheeses Essex St. brings in are already iconic, like Marcel Petite Comté from the Jura mountains, L'amuse Gouda from the Netherlands, and Giorgio Cravero's Parmigiano-Reggiano, which many consider the world's finest. Other producers, though, the Essex St. team has sought out, starting with a type of cheese in mind and then scouring the globe for years to find, say, the Hellenic ideal of feta. Once they zero in on a producer, they focus on grading and selection, the process of meticulously tasting a creamery's cheeses to develop and adhere to a concrete flavor profile. It's the closest they can get to consistency.

No raw milk cheese ever tastes exactly the same every time. Discovering the little differences from season to season is part of what makes artisan cheese so richly rewarding. But grading and selection helps producers define and maintain a range of tastes and textures the cheese should always fall within. A lot of American artisan producers have their own sensory programs to do the same thing in-house. Rogue Creamery, for instance, uses twenty-seven levels of tasting to teach employees their cheeses' flavor profiles. Only the batches that hit a six or above out of a ten score are released into the wild. Jasper Hill regularly grades each of its batches, too, based on texture, flavor, salt, and appearance—along with a score for DF (Deliciousness Factor)—before deeming them salable. Essex St.'s program holds the company's producers to similar standards. Essentially, they help determine what language will be written on the little cards planted in retail shop cheese like moon-flags and ensure that it always tastes that way. Or as close to it as possible.

Now Rachel wants these mongers to taste her cheeses as though they are doing the same.

She and an assistant pass out paper plates with three cheeses on them: a briny block of feta, a crumbly slab of Manchego, and a supple slice of Comté. Between these plates, the tubes, scattered packets of papers, and the odd CamelBak thermos, the table is now in total disarray.

"We're going to learn to calibrate your palate so you can describe these cheeses as accurately as possible," Rachel says once everyone has a plate in front of them. "Sometimes we get real nerdy, like, 'This cheese tastes like a specific kind of moss in the Sonoma county forest.' And that's great! But it doesn't really add much value."

One monger looks personally offended at this suggestion. Probably because she knows that getting super-specific about a batch of cheese—describing the shadow flavor of the native herbs and berries the cow would have eaten to produce it—gives certain customers the warm fuzzies, as though the cheese had been cultivated solely for them. But not everybody wants that. A lot of people just want to know whether a cheese tastes nutty or not. And Rachel was imploring the mongers to go deeper in that direction and confidently say just what kind of nut the nutty cheese tastes like. Is it the almondy essence of Emmental, or the roasted peanut umami of Cowgirl's Red Hawk? Ideally, a monger's brain is an optimized cheese processing unit, able to churn out dictionary-precise descriptions in an instant. In the interest of getting everyone on that level, Rachel instructs us to take a bite of her cheeses, write down what we taste, smell the elemental flavors in each tube, and then taste again with our newly attuned palates.

Let the calibration commence!

The flavors of feta, Manchego, and Comté are all familiar by now, but for some reason, words fail me. The cursor in my brain blinks emptily. I'm so nervous about saying the wrong thing, I can barely think of anything at all. I jot down a few notes and start smelling. There's vanilla in one bottle, strong and concentrated like bourbon custard. The one with butter smells like movie theater popcorn. Then there's the tube labeled EARTH, filled with wet, black silt. I'd described many cheeses as "earthy" before, because I'd heard other cheese people describe them that way until a Pavlovian association stuck. But I now realized I'd been using "earthy" as a euphemism. I'd thought of it in terms of wild mushrooms plucked fresh from the forest; natural, granola-cruncher, Birkenstocky realness. But did everyone else think of it that way? One person's "earthy" might be another person's "actual mud." If I ever tasted mud-cheese, I decided on the spot, I would definitely describe it that way to avoid any confusion.

Eventually, after the last tube has circulated and everyone has taken a second bite, Rachel calls time. Bite number two had been clarifying in that the smell of olive oil matched the flavor of feta in a way I hadn't picked up on before. I'm curious to see what others had picked up on, though.

The first few descriptions of the feta that Rachel and her team had literally searched the ends of the earth to bring to America are in line with what I'd tasted: sourdough bread, lemon, sheep. Then it's Alex's turn.

"I just shotgunned a lot of them, so there's a bunch," he says. "Olive, sour cream, cooked milk, vanilla, coriander, salted egg yolk, anchovy, oregano, lemon rind, and rosemary."

All of these flavors make sense in retrospect—hindbite is indeed twenty-twenty—but they are beyond what I would have ever pulled out from just tasting the feta. It was like seeing a stumper of a math problem solved on a chalkboard, all the work rigorously illustrated.

"I really wish I don't have to follow that," I say. Everyone chuckles, probably because they didn't realize just how simple this was about to get.

"Olive oil and sourness," I announce. "The end."

"That's fine!" Rachel says, with the cheerful tone of someone complimenting my poise after I roll a gutter ball. "Your customers may not know what an anchovy tastes like, but they know sour. Most people are totally fine with that."

If I had any customers, I'm pretty sure they'd be more fine hearing that a cheese tasted like salted egg yolk and rosemary, but I accept my participation trophy and we move on.

For Manchego, nearly everybody comes up with wool, and either nuttiness or a type of nut in particular. Alex distinguishes himself once again by noting traces of boiled potato, cultured butter, roasted broccoli, hazelnut, brioche, and bok choy.

I kind of want to call bullshit on Alex. How could anyone offhandedly know the smell of cultured butter as distinct from not-cultured butter? Impossible. However, his descriptions were so "you-are-there" vivid they make me want to taste the cheeses again and tune in further; to close my eyes and concentrate on whether I could detect the bok choy hiding in this cheese like a secret assassin. That's talent, and my desire to challenge it is just jealousy. It occurs to me I'd definitely want Alex around if I ever came across a pack of Bertie Bott's Every Flavour Beans.

When it's time to describe the Comté, everybody pops off. It's such a complex cheese with so much happening that it tickles the imagination. Beef drippings, overripe melons, molasses, sweet corn, peanut butter; all of them get a shout-out. One of the mongers even says, "horse blanket," and everyone nods sagely. *Of course,* horse blanket!

Rachel dutifully jots down each of the monger's descriptions. Eventually, she reveals how many of them overlapped with the language she'd helped develop to describe these cheeses herself. That's when I understand that she isn't just teaching the mongers to better flex their descriptive muscles; she's using them as a focus group to double-check her own work.

It was a smart move. If part of your job was describing cheese and you had a table full of some of America's most skilled cheese-describers at your disposal, why let the opportunity go to waste?

CHEESE IS LITERALLY flying through the air. Dollops of butterfat, launched from a wire cutter, arc inelegantly onto my shoe.

It's Sunday afternoon, back in the GODS AND MONSTERS room, and every table is now a traffic jam of open jelly jars, unwrapped wedges, measuring cups, and goblets. The mongers are locked in an anarchic arms race to finish their perfect bites, perfect pairings, and perfect plates—so much perfection!—carving up cheese with reckless abandon. The room is abuzz with the sounds of culinary clatter; the pop of Tupperware forcefully unfastened, the crunch of ice bags pummeled with ceramic spoons, the squeak of sneakers seizing up as a floppy-haired monger calls an audible and lunges for an ingredient in the opposite direction. ("Behind!" one yells, with the unbothered air of a restaurant vet, the monger in front letting her breeze past.) The speakers on either side of the stage are blasting the stretch from "Bohemian Rhapsody" that sounds like the internal tug-of-war raging within an unstable Satan worshipper, as the mongers chip away at their cheese projects. Only a handful are able to resist singing along.

> *Bismillah! No, we will not let you go.*
> *Let him go!*

Graters, shakers, peelers. Crumbling, stirring, fizzing. Streaming, sprinkling, splashing. It's total chaos, in service of pristine presentation. And there are hours left to go.

The first half of the day featured a series of written tests, followed by the tech round, a nerve-flaying crucible of *American Ninja Monger*–style cheese obstacles. Most of them I'd seen performed onstage at last summer's CMI—cutting perfect quarter-pound wedges by eye before wrapping them in wax paper and their remaining wheels in plastic. The salesmanship round, on the other hand, was completely new to me and probably the most bizarre part of an already bizarre competition. It's the round where, in addition to displaying depth of knowledge, bedside manner, and expedience, the mongers also get to trot out their acting chops. They have to pretend that, say, Andy Hatch of Uplands, one of the most respected and recognizable cheesemakers in America, and someone they have quite possibly had a beer with in the last twenty-four hours, is a random, mildly befuddled civilian in dire need of cheese assistance. They also have to pretend that Andy, or whoever else the supposed customer may be, isn't also holding a clipboard and taking notes after everything they say, like the most ineptly constructed episode of *Undercover Boss* ever recorded, and that someone else, also in possession of a clipboard, isn't pacing the hall and calling out how much time is left throughout this farcical transaction.

In the long, white hallway, four mongers and four judges meet across the scrimmage line of a table posing as a cheese counter. Each judge is armed with a hypothetical situation and a surprise condiment, ready to test out how well these mongers know people, cheese, and how people interact with cheese.

"So, I'm throwing a birthday party for my aunt, who is pregnant," says a "customer" who is actually a cheese shop owner, trying not to look down at his clipboard, perhaps realizing it's rather unlikely a man who appears to be in his late thirties would have a pregnant aunt. "And I've heard that some cheeses aren't good for you when you're in that condition."

"Yeah, your aunt might want to avoid raw milk in that case," says the monger, whose shirt is unbuttoned down to his naval. He leans over to look through the pasteurized options on his silver tray full of cheese, which rests atop a table barely wider than an ironing board.

"She also loves this ginger jam," the faux customer adds, producing a small jar with a fancy, copper-colored label. "And she's traveled the world, so she wants something with a lot of flavor."

It was a complicated ask: a pasteurized, flavorful cheese that pairs well with ginger jam. But this globe-trotting, miraculously pregnant auntie sounded pretty cool.

A moment later, the monger presents a small, familiar-looking wheel. I recognize it as one of the spruce bark-wrapped Vacherin Mont d'Or–style cheeses, but I don't know which one.

"This is Harbison from Jasper Hill," the monger says, waving a hand over the cheese. "It's pasteurized and it's got flavor all day, but it's also pretty mellow and it's not gonna overpower the jam. That ginger's still gonna pop out through the cheese on your palate."

The shop owner smiles as though he might break kayfabe and actually buy the cheese somehow.

"I'll take it," he declares.

"Do you want to, uh, try it first?"

It was an unspoken rule that mongers were supposed to sample each cheese with the customer, so they know exactly how it's tasting that particular day. The monger feared he would lose points for not offering a taste, even though he'd already closed the deal, and even though Harbison came in tightly sealed packaging and is generally considered unsampleable.

Once each transaction is finished, the monger has forty-five seconds to clean up the station for the next person, and then the virtual reality mongering challenge continues apace.

"My first year of CMI, I was so nervous during this part," says Jordan Edwards, the inked-up judge I remember from last summer. I didn't even realize he was standing next to me in the hallway, so intently was I eavesdropping on people pretending to sell cheese to each other.

"How did it go?" I ask, turning toward him.

"I ended up talking about crack dealers in Detroit in the 1980s, the ones that movie *New Jack City* is based on?"

"Wow."

"Guy asked me if Harbison was pasteurized, and I was like, 'Uh, I don't know, let me Google it.' Then I pantomimed typing on a keyboard."

"Oof," I say, shaking my head as Jordan demonstrates his fake-typing.

"I'll never forget the look on his face."

Jordan and I introduce ourselves properly. Like the other judges and former CMI champs Rory and Lilith, he has also moved on from mongering—to wholesaling, in his case. After a minute of conversation, he asks if I want to see something. Of course, I do.

In another room, the main auditorium where the top six mongers will compete in front of an audience tonight, he and Rory are setting up a cheese display more intense than anything I've seen so far in the competition itself.

The display takes up an entire twelve-foot rainbow table, a glorious Mardi Gras float of cheese and pepperoncini, potato chips and charcuterie, watermelon radishes and blood orange slices, all intricately arranged in sections that added up, like Voltron, into a powerful whole. It's a tragedy that in just a few hours, all of it would be reduced to the increasingly familiar grease-soaked brown paper sodden with cheese shrapnel. This work of cheese art wasn't just meant as a decorative addition to the room, though; they were creating this display as practice for the greatest cheese challenge of their lives.

Last fall, Jordan and Rory had competed in a special masters edition of CMI back in Brooklyn. They'd faced off against a formidable group of previous champions to determine who would represent America at the Mondial du Fromage: the world's most prestigious international cheesemongering competition, which takes place every two years in France.

"CMI is like Burning Man, and Mondial is like going to Carnegie Hall," Jordan says, touching up a checkerboard of Gruyère slices with a diamond cutout from each replaced by cherry preserves. "It's super serious, high production. Only two mongers from each country can compete. And it's televised in France, which I'm still trying to wrap my head around."

Jordan planned on packing up as much of the leftover cheese from CMI as he could stuff in his suitcase to bring back home to Chicago, so he could practice carving and cutting and making chain-links out of cheese. I imagined him having to explain to someone at the airport that the reason his suitcase was lumpy with ice packs and smelled like a locker room was because he needed to prepare for an international cheesemongering competition.

Suddenly, all I could think about was how such a competition might work. How would mongers from around the world approach cheese compared to Americans? I decided right then that when the moment arrived, I would head to the Mondial du Fromage with them to watch.

There was probably a law against getting as deep into cheese as I was without visiting France at some point anyway.

BY THE TIME CMI is in full swing, all the competitors seem gloriously, exultantly depleted. A monger with long magenta hair sprays whipped cream directly into the mouth of a new friend with a 1980s Sunset Strip mohawk, like milk from the teat, and then they both laugh, little tufts of whipped cream blowing everywhere. A bunch of the other mongers are drinking beers or cocktails, strolling arm in arm through the great hall that now serves as a gallery display of their cheese creations, observing other people observing their work.

It was about this point in the day that I walked into the Brooklyn Expo Center the previous summer, having no real idea just what the mongers who made it onstage had been through already. Just like last summer, the main ballroom is now an orgiastic cheese free-for-all. The difference, however, as I take a nibbly walk around the maze of tables, is that I now know what to expect from many of the offerings, and I no longer approach each wedge like a pot-committed gambler going all the way in. For the first time at any cheese event I've been to, I'm on familiar ground. I don't have to act like I've been here before. I have.

Jonathan Richardson, who is MC-ing in Adam's place, introduces the six finalists, and they spend the next hour repeating many of the challenges they had performed earlier in the day. After taking so much of it in earlier, it's hard for me to remain hyped for all the cutting and wrapping. The crowd, however, is enthralled. They cheer for every slice and fold like it's a winning touchdown pass sailing toward the end zone. My attention finally perks up when the mongers are each given a beer and asked to name a cheese to pair with it, and why—in only three words.

The three-word limitation challenges the mongers to find the ultimate economy of words for selling a cheese experience. Jill Zenoff, the monger who brought her guitar with her, describes the clash of pale ale and salty, creamy Lunetta as "bright, supple, tangy." Another finalist calls the flavors of Kirkham's Lancashire and Goose Island "tangy meets funky," wasting a descriptive word on *meets* to do it. (Unless I misheard and she meant "meats.") Finally, Alex, who was so impressive during the grading and selection yesterday, brings down the house with his description of a Belgian farmhouse saison paired with Taleggio: "sourdough apple pancake."

"Holy shit!" Jonathan says into the mic, which the DJ takes as a cue to drop a beat.

Sourdough apple pancake. Only three words but packed with so much flavor potential: yeasty, fruity, somehow autumnal. The description sets up both an expectation and an irresistible mystery. Where does the beer end and the cheese begin? Don't you want to find out?

It's finally time to find out the winner in tonight's cheese competition. Jonathan runs down the order of the runners-up, listing everyone except Alex and Jill. The two hug each other in the suspenseful moment before Jonathan announces Jill as the winner.

Jill hoots ecstatically and darts offstage, returning moments later with her acoustic guitar, its ultimate purpose finally revealed. In lieu of a traditional victory speech, she starts gently strumming "Galileo" by the Indigo Girls, singing slightly modified lyrics: "How long will this cheese last tonight? Can any human being tell me if I should eat this rind?"

It's a perfectly summer camp end to a weekend at Cheese Camp.

Months later, I visit Jasper Hill during the weekend the winners from the last few CMIs are also visiting. While Jill flies in from California, Alex doesn't have to travel very far to make it. In the months since CMI, he had moved from San Francisco to Vermont to start working at Jasper Hill.

During the day, we visit the Cellars, Jasper Hill's 20,000-square-foot underground system of cheese caves, built into the side of a grassy hill. Based on the French model of affinage, the Cellars has five caves for keeping different cheeses at different temperatures and humidity levels. From the outside, it looks like the Avengers compound, or any other secret fortress, and has a similar feeling since I have to sign a non-disclosure agreement before entering. Inside is equally impressive. The Clothbound Cheddar cave, for instance, has fifty-foot-high walls full of wheels that are cleaned and turned by a robot the team has affectionately dubbed Turnie Sanders, aka the Swiss Tickler. (Their first choice, Tina Turner, was already taken by another creamery with the same robot.) The smell inside the cave is powerfully cheesy, just the exponential aroma of a thousand herbaceous British farmhouse-style cheddars closely packed together.

Later on, after a dinner of tacos and margaritas, the group of visiting mongers follows Alex and Lilith Spencer back to Jasper Hill's guesthouse. It's no longer winter, but we get a fire going in the pit out front anyway because that's what you do at night in the Northeast Kingdom of Vermont, among the high trees and low cell reception.

Even though it's not very cold, being near the fire feels nice. We have a surplus of snacks Lilith found in the guesthouse pantry: half of the ingredients for s'mores and some Tostitos Hint of Lime chips. Everyone starts sliding marshmallows onto tree branches, while Alex loads the leftovers from a dinnertime Jasper Hill cheeseboard into a pot to roast over the fire.

"These always have way more than a hint of lime," I tell Lilith as we eat chips out of the bag.

"It's a whole thing," she says, moving a loose branch with her foot closer to the chopped-up wood beams and grass surrounding the flames. "You can tell there's a lot of citric acid and lactic acid powders in there."

"It tastes like a thick, creamy lime ranch dip," I add.

"Yeah, or a lime Creamsicle," she says.

Working in cheese production, Lilith is familiar with how different cultures and chemicals impact flavors. It must make it impossible to not analyze all food through that lens. But she can't stop looking at cheese like a monger either.

It would be generous to describe what Alex is making as fondue. With a couple glugs of wine poured in and regular stirring, though, he has created a respectable cheese dip.

What's shocking is what the others appear to be doing with it while I'm talking with Lilith.

"Are you putting cheese on the marshmallows?" I ask.

"Fuck yeah, we are," Alex says.

He tilts the pot of burbling cheese at an angle, as Jill ladles some out and drizzles it over what had been intended as a s'mores-making marshmallow tree branch. I am witnessing a potential future Perfect Bite being born in the wild. Or maybe not.

"That could work!" I say, even though I'm not convinced. In fact, I would've been hard-pressed to come up with two foods that seemed less innately compatible than cheese and marshmallows. But that would never stop me from trying. Cheese people don't avoid trying something because it sounds gross. If they did, nobody might have eaten the mold growing in that Roquefort cave, or those first curds in the desert.

Lilith and I stand up and walk around the fire to where Alex sits and pick up some branches.

"We've been talking through the logistics of Cheesy Rice Krispies treats for a while," Lilith says, lancing her marshmallow and holding it over the fire. "It might be yummy to use Wilde Weide for that, because it has that white chocolaty flavor, you know?"

I'm incredibly flattered that Lilith thinks I might know off the top of my head what Wilde Weide, a Dutch Gouda that Essex St. brings into the United States, tastes like.

Once my marshmallow is lightly toasted, I bring the branch over to Alex who pours a languid deluge of bruised-banana froth all over the puffy cylinder. The cheese weakens the marshmallow's structural integrity right away, so I pluck it off and eat it.

Even before the flavor hits, I laugh out loud at the texture. It's preposterous. Two separate kinds of goo—the sticky-soft inner marshmallow and the milky melted cheese—fusing into a mushy sludge-flood in my mouth. The singed marshmallow skin adds a grainy crisp to each bite, like tyrosine crystals in aged cheese.

Then the flavor hits. Against all odds, the opposing forces work together—the sugary vanilla pulverized into cooperation by nutty umami. I'm stunned.

"It's so wrong, it's right!" I yell.

Lilith nods her head and tries to rush through chewing the rest of her marshmallow.

"There's an aftertaste like a cheese Danish," she says through a full mouth. "Like, the kind that has cheese and the fruit and the powdered sugar on top?"

That's it! That's exactly it. Lilith's perfect description flips a switch in my food memory.

"It's like cream cheese frosting on a hot buttered roll," I say.

"Totally!"

Lilith and I tap our tree branches together like clinked beer bottles. I wish Rachel Juhl from Essex St. were here, so she knew I wasn't always so timid about describing how cheese tastes.

A little later, once everyone gets a bit tipsier, Alex starts putting marshmallows into the reheated cheese sauce to melt and we dip our Hint of Lime chips into the strange stew.

This experiment is an abject failure.

It's in part because the lime flavor is way too, uh, assertive in this context. It shouldn't be allowed within twenty miles of a marshmallow. The problem is also that marshmallows and cheese don't mesh well together in this configuration, either in flavor or consistency. This mush is way too marshmallowy. It had to be just the right amount.

Apparently, outside forces aren't supposed to change cheese; cheese is supposed to change them.

CHAPTER SEVEN

The Trojan Horse Cheese Course

NOTHING COULD HAVE BEEN MORE SURPRISING THAN FINDING OUT I was boring.

When I moved to New York in the early aughts, in my early twenties, I thought of the vast metropolis as my personal playground. My destiny was to prowl the most impenetrable bars and nightclubs at nonsense hours, running up extravagant tabs while talking color theory with Karen O from the Yeah Yeah Yeahs.

What I quickly realized was that clubs are too packed, bars are too shouty, and my favorite nightlife activity in New York was just going out to eat. It was devastating to learn that I was not very cool, but it was an important breakthrough, nonetheless.

Restaurants: I couldn't get enough of them. I loved sliding into immaculate or carefully disheveled spaces, making a mental March Madness bracket of menu options, and rating décor and music choices like a guest judge on *RuPaul's Drag Race*. And the food. Oh God, the food! Coming from Orlando, where I'd subsisted on Subway and considered P. F. Chang's a hot date spot, there was so much I'd never tried before. Tasting new things in new places with new friends was an active, experimental, deeply analog thing to do; a scrumptious exploration with a social function built in. But once I started exploring the cheese world, eating out suddenly took on fresh dimensions. I would walk into a restaurant and wonder, what level of cheese is this place operating on? Are they lactose intolerant, with maybe some salad crumbles and melty sandwich slices but nothing more? Would there be a basic-ass plate with a trio of greatest hits? Or would they have a full-on cheese program, which is every bit as official as it sounds, requiring the careful planning and execution of a secret government project?

The answers begged more questions. If there was a cheese plate, how did they source it? What accoutrement would they pair with it? What wine would we order too much of to wash it down? The surprise and variety of figuring out what went well together was far more fun than just comparing notes on how each other's meals taste.

Going out to eat cheese became its own category of going out.

Over the last twenty years, the line between cheese shop and restaurant has begun to blur. Some shops now serve meals and elaborate boards like restaurants, while some restaurants now sell cheese like retail shops. You could go to a spot like Bedford Cheese in Williamsburg or Foster Sundry in Bushwick, pick out a few cheeses, and get them served on a board packed with pickled onions, blanched almonds, and apple slices. You could go to Murray's Cheese Bar, which is attached to the main shop in the Village, and get Buffalo Cheese Curds and geographically organized cheese flights. You could go to Cave Music every other month at Crown Finish Caves in Brooklyn and eat their cheese in a drafty cave thirty feet underground while listening to a klezmer folk band freak it for a small, enthusiastic crowd. The city was alive with innovative ways to eat artisan cheese in public, which is probably not a prospect I would have found very exciting when I first moved here. How foolish I'd been!

BEFORE CHEESE PLATES became a unifying force in bistros, cafés, gastropubs, and various purveyors of white-tablecloth opulence, there was Laura Chenel's fresh chèvre.

When Alice Waters of the influential California eatery Chez Panisse discovered it in the late-1970s, she found it as tasty as any goat cheese she'd sampled in France. She placed a standing order for fifty pounds a week, and started serving Chenel's chèvre baked and breaded on a seasonal salad—the textural collision of grainy bread crumbs, tender mesclun, and soft, tangy cheese making it a destination dish. Around the same time, French chefs in Manhattan discovered Allison Hooper's Vermont chèvre, but it was the Chez Panisse baked goat cheese salad that got the most press and became a national sensation.

"That was a pivotal moment in American food," says Clark Wolf, a cheese expert and a friend of Chenel's. "It was simple and complex. It was something that, if you knew a lot, you could appreciate the cheese, and if you knew a little, it still tasted good. And that's how things develop in America. Your friend from Manhattan and your aunt from Iowa both love it."

The next significant moment in American cheese at restaurants arrived a few years later, in the mid-1980s, when New York–based chef Terrance Brennan came home after years of working in Parisian kitchens. He returned with a mission: to make New Yorkers as passionate about cheese as French people were about it. Against all odds, he ended up succeeding. For a while, at least.

The chef had been gobsmacked by not only the quality of the cheese he'd found abroad but also how deeply it was ingrained in the culture. Every family meal for staff at the restaurants he worked in had a cheese course, as did every actual family meal he attended when friends invited him into their homes for lunch or dinner. These were no mere cheese plates either, mind you, they were mini-smorgasbords served just before dessert, featuring five or so carefully selected cheeses, along with accoutrements. People simply didn't eat that way at meals in America.

The chef had a tough time convincing the Manhattan restaurateur he worked with over the next few years to implement a cheese course. It was too much to manage. Also, people might not want it. And if they did want it, well, that meant another half-hour or so until the servers could turn those tables over. Unacceptable. It wasn't until 1993 when Brennan was finally in a position to open up his own French restaurant that he was able to realize his vision.

"New Yorkers back in the eighties and nineties, they talked about European cheeses but nobody was doing it right," Brennan tells me over the phone. "Cheese was something you kept in your refrigerator. A cheese plate was just three or four mediocre cheeses coming out of the icebox. No one did anything more over here."

That was all about to change, though.

Brennan started out by sourcing a dozen cheeses for his restaurant Picholine, a tony Upper West Side space with a rosy interior that made it look like the inside of a conch shell. Although it took some deliberation to decide on which kinds of cheese to carry, there was no debate on how Picholine would present them. French restaurants often serve their cheese courses from a cart, known as a *chariot de fromages*, and Brennan wanted to do the same. His cart would be a Trojan Horse from which he could gladiatorially attack the palates of adventurous eaters.

It became almost immediately clear that the initial twelve cheeses Brennan brought in would simply not be enough for his growing fromage obsession. He wanted more, but he was having a difficult time keeping everything else at Picholine humming while simultaneously overseeing an expanding cheese program. As a solution, he bumped up Max McCalman, a food runner who had taken a major interest in the restaurant's cheese, to be in charge of it. Soon enough, the number of cheeses on the cart doubled as the pair got further infatuated with their project.

Brennan's next step was importing another element of French cheese culture to American restaurants: affinage.

A lot of French restaurants and cheese shops have caves built into their cellars for in-house aging. They pick up young wheels directly from producers and wash them in whichever brines or alcohol they want, putting their own unique stamp on the product. If hosting a cheese course was extremely rare in American restaurants, though, an affinage program was unheard of. The humidity-controlled cave Brennan built, which featured special anti-fogging glass windows, was likely the first of its kind in the country. It was a spectacle built into the Picholine experience. Unbeknownst to him, Max McCalman soon acquired the nickname "the Undertaker" among cheese people in the know, because the restaurant's cave looked like a morgue to them, with big steel doors he would toss open to wheel out cheeses in gurney-like fashion.

With the affinage experiment, Picholine developed an allure of further exclusivity in its offerings. You couldn't find cheeses quite like these anywhere else. Brennan and McCalman would do vertical tastings of a cheese at three months, six months, and nine months, a showcase of how their flavors developed over time. The number of cheeses available on each cart gradually crept up to forty as the two turophiles further tested the limits of how much was too much. New York's culinary cognoscenti had no choice but to surrender, and like Chez Panisse's baked goat cheese salad, Picholine's reputation reverberated throughout the country.

The response was, as Brennan recalls, "insane." He and McCalman started selling so much cheese it became a problem. Too many tables demanded the cart at the same time, jamming up orders. McCalman would be presenting and cutting one table's cheese course while several other tables stared daggers at him, willing it to be their turn. The pair eventually had to spring for a second cart. Now, on any given night at the restaurant, it appeared as though two fancy mini-food trucks were competing against each other.

Pretty soon, the traffic would spill far beyond Picholine.

"In New York, It's Cheese-Cart Gridlock," declared a *New York Times* headline in 2001. The piece itself went on to describe the city as utterly infested with chariots of cheese: "As recently as five years ago, most restaurants—even traditional French ones— didn't have cheese courses at all. . . . Now, it's hard to find a place that doesn't."

Picholine's impact on New York restaurants was seismic, and America's other major food cities felt the aftershocks. Cheese-carts started springing up in French restaurants from Chicago to Los Angeles. A lot of eateries that didn't skew so upscale found the cart concept an astronomic extravagance. Instead, they just got whatever cheese they could muster to feed the growing American appetite for fromage, which is how the cheese plate became a staple on American menus. It arrived in tandem with cheese-cart gridlock, and ultimately outlasted it.

Once Brennan saw how influential his cheese project had become, he decided to experiment some more. In 2001, he opened Artisanal, a hybrid bistro and retail spot, which mimicked the dining rooms in French cheese shops where customers could get a more in-depth tasting than they could at the counter. It was another first of its kind in America: a place you could go to eat mind-blowing mac and cheese, and leave with the right wedges to make the dish just as tasty at home. (Which you probably could not.) By then, he had upgraded to five caves—each designed specifically for a different kind of cheese—with a highly computerized cooling system that he and McCalman could regulate to one-tenth of a degree. A couple years later, Brennan expanded his empire ever further with the Artisanal Premium Cheese Center, the hub of his new distribution arm, where McCalman hosted tastings and educational courses for enthusiasts and aspiring pros alike.

Brennan claims that this development proved especially influential.

"Murray's pretty much copied everything we did a year or two later," he tells me. "The cheese caves and the classes? We did everything first at Artisanal."

Brennan's expanding cheese domain coincided with, and probably assisted, the rise of the modern artisan cheese movement in America. He opened his center the same year that Jasper Hill began selling cheese, and the year Rogue River Blue won best in its class at the World Cheese Awards. By then, he had become a celebrity chef, the kind who gets booked on the *Today* show to set a Guinness record for World's Largest Fondue on-air.

Brennan saw himself as an ambassador of America's artisans, and shouted out makers like Jasper Hill, Cowgirl Creamery, and Vermont Shepherd during every publicity opportunity. However, as these producers continued to flourish, Brennan himself decided to get out of the game. Toward the end of the aughts, perhaps not coincidentally just in time for the financial crash, he decided he'd devoted himself too wholly to cheese and sold off his businesses. Picholine and Artisanal stuck around for many more years but by 2017, they had both shut down. At that point, the cheese-cart gridlock in New York had cleared up considerably.

"The era of the French cheese-cart has come and gone in New York," says Liz Thorpe, the cheese consultant and author. "It's not a thing anymore."

Well, it's not entirely not a thing.

RESTAURANT DANIEL, THE double-Michelin star, *American Psycho*–quality, gilded gravy boat on the Upper West Side, is said to have one of the best (and only) cheese-carts remaining in Manhattan. It's about as far away as one can get from CMI, where everyone is working to make cheese more approachable, scrubbed from any association with flouncy upper-crust dinner parties in Mr. Monopoly's penthouse. But maybe there's something to be said for unapproachable cheese.

On the night of our reservation, Gabi and I get dressed up in medium-fancy wedding attire: a dark suit and a tie with little bulldogs on it for me, and a red, sleeveless midi dress with funky jewelry for her. Compared with the other diners, we look like students who won rush tickets to a Broadway show on our big night out.

The plush main dining room could be the cover art for an al-

bum called *Late Capitalism*. Gleaming marble columns and arch-
ways frame the room like relics of the Roman Empire. Tall slivers
of mirror are scattered along the walls, between mood-dimmed
lanterns held aloft by metal branches. We settle into seats with
mahogany leather padding, and brace ourselves for the show.

The waitstaff deftly deposits tiny wooden boxes on the table
before us and scurries away. Before opening the boxes, Gabi and
I look at each other searchingly. I half expect a wren to fly out
and hum the *Game of Thrones* theme song. Instead, it's just the
silverware, which includes a flat, notched spoon that Gabi dubs
a "spife." The servers then proceed to take our order and eventually chauffeur out dishes in perfect synchronization, as though to
avoid the appearance of favoritism between us. The pace of the
meal is novelistic, with the courses coming faster as we go further.
Along the way, there's summer vegetable fricassee, with tomatoes
that disintegrate in your mouth, and stir-fried chanterelles that
taste like brown-butter-roasted ambrosia. The meal is spectacular,
even though I barely have any basis for comparison. Would the
titans of industry and Knicks point guards who eat here all the
time be similarly moved?

Finally, it's the moment we've been waiting for. Our cheese
chariot has arrived.

Pascal Vittu, the maître fromager, looks like a capo in the
French mafia. His slicked-back hair is the color of elephant hide,
he wears a jet-black suit with silver cuff links, and he has heavy-
lidded eyes that have already sized you up and figured you out
long before you see him coming. He pushes the cheese-cart along
the ultrasoft carpeting, as though chaperoning a nervous fashion
model down her first catwalk, greeting several other guests on the
way to our table. The cart itself looks like a fabulous antique but

an antique nonetheless; a rickety, mobile desk, with a cylindric, hinged plexiglass dome above sealing in twenty-five or so cheeses. They all lay across a marble slate set within the top of the cart, unadorned. I recognize some of them—Époisses, with its rippled rind and round wooden container, and the radioactive-orange Mimolette—but most are mysteries.

"Would you like white wine or red wine with your cheese?" Pascal asks in his mellifluous French accent.

"Ordinarily we're white wine people—" I say, getting ready to provide backstory for my choice, but he cuts me off right there to say that he agrees, pouring us each a Riesling.

"So which profile of cheese do you like?" he asks.

"Lately I've been gravitating toward alpine cheeses, but I'm open to anything," I say.

He nods, with a hint of a smile, and then asks Gabi the same question.

"I'm just not a big fan of the washed rinds," she says, an apologetic grimace forming. "I had one last year that almost made me cry. I'll try them, but they're not my favorite."

"I understand," Pascal says, placing his hand over his heart. For a second, I think he and Gabi are going to hug. Instead he grabs a plate and a knife from beneath his cart and starts moving around the cheese like a hunter stalking his prey. His face remains placid as he selects each one, but I can see the computations dancing in his head—which cheese will go with white wine and suit alpine lovers who tend to be washed-rind agnostic?

Unlike at a cheese shop, we have no further say in the matter. We are completely at Pascal's mercy. It was more like getting a haircut than buying from a monger—which is what I would have preferred when I first started going to shops and didn't know anything. Not that I'm opposed to it now.

Finally, he sets down an eggshell plate holding six pieces of cheese, along with a pair of figs and a cluster of white grapes with a light red skin. It looks like a Rennaissance era still-life painting. Some of the cheeses are firm and flat, while others are squidgy and multi-dimensional. There are at least three washed rinds.

Pascal walks us through each, describing them like stops on a tour.

"So, we are in Vermont, with a domestic goat's milk Tomme," he says, pointing at an ivory white diskette. "Milky, hazelnut, and a beautiful mold. Wonderful."

Pascal has actually been on this tour in person, having visited the farm and creamery of every producer whose cheese he carries. The closest stop on this plate is Annelies, an alpine-style private label cheese that Murray's ages in its caves, although it originally comes from Switzerland. I'm surprised how many American cheeses there are on our plate, and also on the cart. At a certain point during his twenty-three years working at Daniel, Pascal realized he could get American-made versions of just about any of the cheeses he loved in France, and started switching over. You'd have to pry French Époisses from his cold dead hands, though.

Once Pascal wheels the cart away, we slowly explore our bespoke plate of cheese. Mixing and matching each bite with either of the fruits on hand leads us to discover that Annelies with fig tastes like a peanut butter and jelly sandwich. It's a hit. Gabi is nervous at first about tasting the washed rinds, but the Riesling cuts the pungency and she almost cries tears of relief at actually enjoying Grayson's buttery paste and sunset rind. Pascal had nailed it.

By the time we finish dessert, I feel not just full but utterly conquered. I'm ready for four servers to gently hoist Gabi and me up in perfect synchronicity, forming a human chariot of sorts, then take us outside and yeet us down the subway stairs.

Having a cheese program as extensive as Daniel's requires a lot of resources, which is why the vast majority of American restaurants don't have them. Instead, many opt for simply putting three to four top-shelf cheeses on a plate, perhaps investing the budget of what might have been a more extensive selection into designing one highly Instagrammable dish that could conceivably become an edible meme. In the years since the heyday of Picholine, the cheese course has broadly evolved from a cart just before dessert to a composed plate available as a starter. However, a new generation of restaurants has taken a more playful approach to cheese overall, instead focusing on the art of the pairing as much as the quality of the cheese.

JUST AFTER VALENTINE'S Day, I get an invitation from Madame Fromage, the cheese guru I'd met in Philadelphia last fall, for her Black Sabbath and Blue Cheese party.

"Let us celebrate the dark days of winter with a feast of pierced cheeses and some heavy metal!" her invite urged. Attendees were to bring their favorite blue cheeses and classic metal records to a Philadelphia bar called Martha.

Rock and roll.

I pick up a Wisconsin triple-mixed milk blue called Ewe Calf to be Kidding, a pun so powerful its creator probably had to apply for a permit, along with a Jasper Hill rarity called Hinman

Settler, which is just their Bayley Hazen Blue but with sheep's milk added to the cow's milk base. ("Not many people got wheels of this," the monger at Saxelby's in Chelsea Market says. "Any cheese dork will probably flip for it.") I pack up the white label cheese with my Led Zeppelin *Physical Graffiti* vinyl and catch a bus to Philly.

In the din of the bar, a long narrow table is covered with more blue cheese than I'd ever seen in one spot, laid out on thick wooden boards, with labels visible by candlelight. It looked as though a gunfight broke out at a wedding, leaving all the fudgy white cake slices riddled with buckshot. Fourme D'Ambert, Blue Jay, Roquefort; all pitted with sapphire pockets of minerally mold. I top the battery-licking spice-shock of Cabrales with a glaze of clover honey, chase it down with hearty oatmeal stout, and let the elephant stomp of Black Sabbath's "Paranoid" trample over me. It's perfectly balanced sensory overload, a controlled detonation. I feel ready to start the revolution, or at least sign some radical petitions.

Tenaya Darlington, aka Madame Fromage, was used to these kinds of wild, music-based pairings. She had published a book with her brother called *Booze and Vinyl*, seeking out ideal combinations of tunes and alcohol, and had recently created a Bowie, Bubbles, and Brie party for a design firm's Bastille Day celebration. Just last month, however, pairings became an even bigger part of her life, with her new role as cheese curator for Tria, a restaurant group in Philly. It's a way to professionally carry out the research part of finding new flavor permutations, which is what she loves to do most—cracking open a bottle with a friend and trying out different cheeses with random items from her fridge until landing on something that clicks.

Searching cheese shops to find bold new flavors already feels like panning for gold, if there were a 95 percent chance of finding gold wherever you looked. Searching for new pairings, though, turns every tasting into a cross-country prospecting adventure. When you find one that works—apricot and Appenzeller, Red Hawk and roasted peanuts—it resonates as a momentous scientific discovery. You want to mass-text everybody the good news.

The search for hidden flavor combinations appeals to the innate part of us that craves variety and the thrill of the hunt. It's the reason kids mix all the different sodas together at Burger King fountains—partly just because they can but also because maybe Dr Pepper secretly goes well with Sprite and Hawaiian Punch, and you could be the baby genius who figures that out. (Those three beverages do not even remotely go together.) Although the ability to detect flavors evolved out of the human need to distinguish whether the mushrooms growing near your Neanderthal yurt were going to kill you, tasting the entire flavor spectrum is a leisurely right humanity has earned and dare not waste.

The playfulness and mutability of cheese in particular is why more restaurants and hybrid shops that specialize in pairings have cropped up in America over the last decade or so. Mission Cheese in San Francisco and Cheese Bar in Portland both build on the Artisanal formula of a sit-down restaurant where you can order a custom board or cheese flight, get wine to go with it, and also leave with a half-pound of Pleasant Ridge. Wine bars have crowded cityscapes for far too long, unchallenged in their dominion of bringing together fermented grapes and fermented milk. It's about time the cheese world turned the tables.

Billing itself as a cheese and wine bar, Casellula is a thirty-five-seat café in Hell's Kitchen, near where theatergoers are constantly streaming in and out of *Juno*, the Broadway musical, or what have you. The menu hits within the same hipster strike zone as many Manhattan restaurants, straddling the line between avant-garde and folksy with items like Mustard Miso Pickles and the Pig's Ass Sandwich. The difference here is that they refuse to dumb down their cheese even a little. That pork butt hoagie comes with cheddar from Shelburne Farm, not "Vermont," and the Reuben has Emmentaler, not "Swiss"; distinctions designed to please those who already know their shit and inspire those who do not to learn more. There's a jewel case of cheese in the center of the room for guests to inspect, an edible jukebox with options from all over the world, spread across five categories. You can design your own flight or you can put yourself in the hands of the maître fromager and get a curated plate of unlikely pairings.

Although she's since parted ways with the restaurant, Casellula is the brainchild of Tia Keenan, a food writer, activist, and author of *Art of the Cheese Plate*. At the time she was opening up the place in 2007, she found the cheese plate options around New York practically identical, comprised of cheese, honeycomb, nuts, fruit, and bread. She had something much wilder in mind.

"I always knew that pairings were an equalizer," Tia says when we meet one afternoon to share a cheese plate at Foster Sundry in Bushwick. "They could make cheese approachable, funny, sexy, titillating. I could take an obscure French cheese that people would be scared to try pronouncing, pair it with a brittle or popcorn, and challenge the whole intimidation factor."

Terrance Brennan and other top chefs had made cheese a fixture in restaurants throughout the city. Tia set out to unleash its full potential. She wanted to bust cheese out of any stuffy preconceptions and make it fun and accessible. Casellula would flip the script on conventional pairings, setting its guests loose inside a digestible jungle gym. It would bypass the tried and true—the nuts and dried fruit of it all—for uncharted cheese territory.

At the time, Tia lived in Jackson Heights, among an international bouillabaisse of restaurants. Every stroll to the subway took her past all sorts of Indian spots and Nepalese joints, the air outside thick with tamarind, curry, and cumin. She was inspired by her surroundings to create pairings with ingredients like wasabi peas, plummy sauces, and seaweed. On her way to work, she'd detect tantalizing exotic spices wafting out of crowded minimarkets and try to figure out what they might be—Tandoori?—and which cheese they might pair well with.

"I was working with forty cheeses and forty ingredients and they could all interact in many different ways," she says as we nibble on the colorful contents of our elaborate plate. "Sometimes this cheese got one pairing and sometimes it got another. It's a lot like jazz. You've got your notes, you've got the rhythm, and you're trying to figure out where you're placing them and how they're relating to the other musicians. When it was Saturday night at 9:30 p.m. and we had a two-hour wait, I felt like John fucking Coltrane."

When I had eaten at Casellula, the maître fromager seemed similarly versed in improvisational bebop: the goaty tang of fresh chèvre duetting with tart raspberry curds, breakfast-sandwich-flavored Belgian sheep cheese grooving with the alt-universe ketchup of carrot puree, a super dense blue locked in perfect textural rhythm with thick squares of brown sugar fudge. I wanted to give the cheese plate a standing ovation and buy its merch.

Back at Foster Sundry, Tia abruptly shushes me at one point

by jabbing a knife toward the section of our shared plate domi-nated by Oma, a washed rind made by Von Trapp Farmstead and aged at Jasper Hill.

"This with the onions," she says.

I don't need to be told twice. I spear some pickled onions on a fork and drape them on a bulging smidgen of Oma. It tastes like pot roast with a briny tingle. It's fantastic.

"Do you just know on sight what goes together like that?" I ask.

"A rich, funky cheese is almost always going to be happy with something citric," Tia says. "But you learn through trial and error, and I have done a *lot* of trial and error."

Although Tia left Casellula a few years before it ever landed on my radar, she still had a lot of opportunities for trial and error as a food writer and the *Wall Street Journal*'s go-to cheese col-umnist. As much as she already knew, which is more than most, she was still out on the hunt, one of the cheese world's master mixologists, chasing her muse and translating the results to the masses. However, she also plants a seed of authoritarian distrust against listening too closely to experts such as herself. No matter what common wisdom surrounds any prescribed pairing, Tia tells me the most important way to know whether a pairing works is if you like it.

PART OF WHAT I'd loved about going out for cheese, and what had drawn me to restaurants over clubs and bars originally, was that there was order to it—divine design. A trusted guide is in charge of the experience in one way or another. Even when you choose your own cheese for a board at Bedford, the monger matches the accoutrements for you. Someone has already searched the sprawling cosmology of pairing possibilities and found just the right thing.

All of the tasty pairings I'd found for myself over the last few months were ones I'd stumbled across by accident. If you're eating artisan cheese all the time, you'll inevitably come around to trying Gruyère and M&M's together, that's just science. What I hadn't done is curate a cheese experience for someone else the way so many maître fromagers and mongers had done for me. I wanted to cosplay as Tia Keenan or Madame Fromage and apply some trial and error. I called an emergency meeting of the cheese-tasting club I'd put together months earlier. Our mission? Create the ultimate cheddar and wine pairing.

By now, through volunteering a lot at Murray's, I'd absorbed some of the agreed-upon pairing principles: shortcuts for making choices in an untamable cheesescape. It turned out many of the rules around which wines and cheeses might be friends could apply to actual friendships.

There was the idea of putting like with like, the magnetic pull of complementary flavors and textures reflecting simpatico energy at each other. You pair a cheese that has a strawberry note with a wine that has one too and watch them hit it off like strangers at a party once they realize they listen to the same true crime podcasts.

People who are too alike, however, run the risk of destroying each other, as demonstrated by every *Fast and the Furious* movie with both Vin Diesel and the Rock. Sometimes it's better to just let opposites attract. A sweet Riesling cuts the footy aroma of Époisses, for instance, like a real Hobbs and Shaw situation.

One of the most common guidelines is "what grows together

goes together." It's like how children end up becoming best friends just because they live on the same street and won't be able to drive anywhere by themselves for many years. When a cheese and a wine both come from the same region, they're imbued with the same terroir, or taste of place. They either have naturally complementary flavors from sharing microbes and fauna, or they enjoy the benefit of people in the area having learned over many years how well they work as a team.

When I start to set parameters for our pairing project, narrowing down the wines is an ordeal. One monger seems offended when I ask which ones go best with cheddar, since there is no all-purpose pairing that works across the entire cheddar spectrum. I might as well ask someone at an Opening Ceremony store to help me find "clothes." After doing some research, I settle on three options: a vintage port, an oaky Chardonnay, and Chilean Cabernet Sauvignon.

Cheese Club had convened several times since our inaugural outing, filling the back corner of Brooklyn's Crown Inn with a collage of questionable aromas. Following the first couple of meetings, I'd settled on five to seven cheeses as the ideal number for a group tasting, so of course I end up with nine cheddars.

Everybody sits clustered around a barge of tables in the back, where I've laid out roughly five pounds of cheese across several different cutting boards in neat rows of cubes. We all have three glasses of wine in front of us and tauntingly empty plates. We are ready.

It's a revelation to discover that some wines and cheeses truly do not mix. It's not that any of them are straight-up revolting. Nobody spits out a viscous mist of cheddary vino at any point. There's just no spark sometimes, two entities coexisting with zero connection, like a party guest with whom you run out of things to talk about right away.

But then there's the port, that charming friend who seems to get along with everybody. It amplifies the sweetness of the cheddars that have a caramel note, and its fruitiness brings a nice counterbalance to the ones that pack a horseradish punch. But it seems to go best with the only cheese that can match it in richness. After trying twenty-seven permutations of cheese and wine, the port with Flory's Truckle is our consensus pairing.

I feel woozy with the excitement of the find. Or maybe I'm just drunk from all the wine. Either way, I now know that as much as I love the order of having curated cheese experiences, I just might enjoy the chaos and uncertainty of being on the other side of curation even more.

CHAPTER EIGHT

The Succulent Funhouse

SOUTH BY SOUTHWEST IN AUSTIN, TEXAS, IS THE URGENT CONVERGENCE of absolutely everything. There's a film festival, a music exhibition, a thunderdome of interactive brand activations, and a lollapalooza of TED Talks. For ten synergistic days a year, Austin becomes the only place in the world where you might find Jordan Peele, Alexandria Ocasio-Cortez, Billie Eilish, and the CEO of a lifestyle coworking space that offers gamified cardio, all in the same pop-up interview junket/cantina. Attention is the coin of the realm here, and you have no idea how much you have to give until you find yourself in a seller's market, the subject of an oversaturated bidding war. Whatever project anyone is boldly launching this year, you, lucky you, can be among the first to experience it, possibly in the form of an Experience, which is when paid actors help you perform a real-time commercial, perhaps inside of a steampunk labyrinth constructed by Amazon Studios to promote its new limited series. The air is thick with ideas, desperation, and barbecue. Everywhere you turn, someone has taken great pains to place something in front of you, something to look at, something to feel, something so immersive you forget where you are but not so immersive that you forget to bleat about it on social media, where the attention you're paying might multiply exponentially. By day, the streets are clogged with fleets of lanyard-wearing creatives on Lyft-branded scooters and electric JUMP bicycles from Uber (free to unlock; then fifteen cents per minute), which they leave on street corners in spontaneous scrap heaps. At night, it's Diet Mardi Gras, with rogue musicians and street teams warbling and flyering, respectively, the same lanyard-wearing creatives, now medium-drunk, hightailing it to an *Entertainment Weekly* party where an augmented reality app sponsored by Tinder can make the reunited pop-punk band onstage appear to be whichever age you'd prefer them. It's a chance to lose yourself and find the next big thing and the thing after that while getting thinkfluenced by global professionals.

All of this feels deeply antithetical to cheese, a food that's been on-trend for centuries. However, to ignore that cheese is now competing for your attention in the same brave new world that spawned South by Southwest would be as naïve as purchasing gas station boner pills—and probably just as effective. Since whatever artisan cheesemakers have been doing to get their names out there had been eluding me all these years, I wanted to find out more about just what it is they do to market themselves.

Cheese has relied on the dark arts of marketing ever since it spread far enough around the world that some towns began to have more than one cheesemaker. In seventeenth-century England, for instance, a savvy producer started using annatto, the seeds of a Brazilian tree, to give their Leicester cheese an electric orange hue that made it stand out on a crowded shelf. Modern cheese, though, needs bolder ideas than a Crayola makeover to break through the clutter. It needs the marketing of today—a psychological funhouse full of trick mirrors that distort your perception, unsteady ground that keeps you on your toes, and sudden bursts from compressed air jets just to mess with your mind. South by Southwest is a place where brands can actually construct that funhouse in a physical space, and that's why Dairy Farmers of Wisconsin has brought Cheeselandia to Austin.

Dairy Farmers of Wisconsin is a marketing entity, funded by the state's farmers, that promotes their products collectively. If you are aware that Wisconsin has great cheese and plenty of it, and has been making it since before Wisconsin was even a state, that's probably at least partly due to them. The organization, formerly the Wisconsin Milk Marketing Board, has been around since the 1980s, when it enjoyed a boost from its California counterpart's ridiculously successful Got Milk? campaign. Now, one of the group's main goals is to graduate people beyond just knowing that Wisconsin is the cheese capital of America, into knowing by name several specific producers that carry the Proudly Wisconsin label.

Enter Cheeselandia, a campaign the group mostly conducts on the internet, but which it's taking offline and into the meatspace today.

A massive line has formed outside the ballroom in the Marriott on East Second Street, near Willie Nelson Boulevard. It's a fundamentally disorganized line, single file in parts and chessboard-packed at others. Like nightclub bouncers at capacity, the gatekeepers up front only let new people in at the pace the guests are leaving, which they seem as reluctant to do as Adam and Eve leaving Eden. I knew that whatever lay beyond the congested entrance would be yet another room full of seemingly unlimited high-octane cheese. Unlike all other such rooms I'd been in recently, there were no ticket-buying curd nerds or competitive mongers here. This time, the crowd was comprised of suggestible experience-seekers who randomly got sucked into a cheese-vortex at an innovation festival. Many of their jaws hit the floor the moment they walk in.

Cheeselandia looks like a cross between a state fair and a traveling circus, set in the heart of a fictional town that worships cheese. Rows of red and yellow flags hang from either side of the room, between booths that look like midway games, but instead offer fresh curds and Italian-style cheeses. Manning the booths are members of the Dairy Farmers of Wisconsin comms team, or mongers they've recruited during their travels, all wearing carnival barker outfits: straw hats with black bands, candy-striped shirts and red polka-dot ascots like cartoon hobo bindles. On the back wall, above several fondue pots simmering like unoccupied Jacuzzis, WISCONSIN CHEESE is spelled out in light bulbs, impossible to miss. In the center of the room, beckoning photos from every angle, is a Ferris wheel, each compartment holding huge hunks of Pleasant Ridge, Marieke Gouda, and Red Rock, a cheese so phosphorescent orange (thanks, annatto!) it has the vibrancy of a Rothko painting. Each of the wheel's cheeses has a prize ribbon affixed to its name tag because they've all won major cheese competitions, and those name tags carry a newly revamped Proudly Wisconsin logo, which has been subtly tweaked into a ribbony shape to incept the idea of award-winning cheese into potential buyers' heads.

The buffet table surrounding this centerpiece contains even

more Wisconsin gold, stacks of full wheels surrounded by tributaries of cheese chunks. I taste cheese as perfectly balanced as a tightrope walker, cheese that keeps as many flavors going at once as a juggler's clubs, ghost pepper cheese as hot as a fire-breather, and a playfully puckish blue-cheddar hybrid as surprising as a water spritz from a clown's lapel flower. *Step right up, folks. Hurrah, hurrah!* Every inch of this ballroom may be infused with a suggestion of spectacle, but the cheese is a spectacle all its own.

"Have you ever seen so much cheese before?" a woman with severe magenta eye shadow and Wednesday Addams braids asks a guy wearing fringed camo shorts showing off winter-pasty calves.

"Never," he answers, without looking up from his phone.

The average person has never had occasion to try 150 cheeses in one go before. Every time I've been in such a situation, I've been surrounded by non-average people—the kind who probably have a favorite type of mold. (Team *Geotrichum candidum* over here!) The Cheesemonger Invitational crowds are psyched to try certain cheeses and maybe to talk with Jasper Hill honcho Mateo Kehler; their general enthusiasm blends into the chumminess that comes from being surrounded by other cheese people. Rarely are they stunned, though, since they know what they're walking into. A lot of people here raise their eyebrows when they see the giant mountain of cheddar on a wood crate at the front of the table, individual curds jutting out like so many carbonite-frozen Hans Solos. The same palpable delight spreads across one face after the next, skipping only the occasional seasoned South by Southwesterner who has already been to the circus and just sees all this as another free lunch.

"Ladies and gentleman!" roars a man going full P. T. Barnum in a lion tamer's top hat and red jacket, standing in front of a cardboard cutout of parted red curtains. "Now presenting 2019 Cheeselandia State Fair queen: Miiiiiiss Bubbly!"

From behind him emerges a platinum Disney Princess with a fake block of cheddar fastened to her head. She's dressed in a polka-dot ball gown, cradling a bottle of champagne with red satin gloves up to her elbows. Hovering all around her dress is a bell-shaped cage holding dozens of full champagne flutes in orbital rows. She looks like a mirage that the cheese-loving pirate from *Treasure Island* might have imagined before young Jim Hawkins showed up.

"Welcome to Cheeselandia, where dreams of cheese become reality!" Miss Bubbly says in a voice as squeaky as fresh curds.

She smiles magnanimously, pulling focus from the Ferris wheel to become the most photographed element in the ballroom. As the crowd applauds, a harried man in a wireless headset discreetly stomps a patch of Astroturf in place a few feet away from Miss Bubbly, lest anyone see the fantasia's fragile seams.

Cheeselandia is a pop-up extension of Dairy Farmers of Wisconsin's ambassador program of the same name. Members from the organization comb the country in search of people excited about Wisconsin cheese who might be willing to get their friends excited too, perhaps by throwing a Wisconsin cheese–themed party at home. It has the ring of a multilevel marketing scheme, except instead of ripping off your friends and neighbors, you're giving them a casual cheese seminar while stuffing their faces. Over the past year, the organization received hundreds of applications from forty-nine states, then carefully selected one hundred of the most promising candidates, and shipped them all the ingredients for cheese bacchanalia. A rectangular flat screen hanging on the wall near the entrance here at South by Southwest is divided into sixty cubes, each displaying a group awkwardly gathered around a cornucopia of Wisconsin's finest—a mix of unsure faces and cheese-eating euphoria.

"Do you want to host a cheese party with your friends?" a radiant Dairy Farmers of Wisconsin person asks a woman in a sushi-print button-up, gazing at the barrage of images.

"I don't know if I have enough friends to host a cheese party."

"Well, that doesn't sound very exciting!" the recruiter responds, because, really, what can you say to that.

"Eh, I'm not mad about it," the woman in the sushi shirt says, shrugging, and joins a crowd nearby observing a man in a porkpie hat performing a trick involving three foam cheese balls.

It always feels like something is about to happen, like those red cardboard curtains are about to part, revealing a high-dive into a kiddie pool, or an REO Speedwagon concert. After Miss Bubbly's exit, like clockwork, the Italian-style booth switches signage (LET'S GO, ITALIANO! replaced by FEELING BLUE!) and the samples on offer change accordingly. The cheese cauldrons of Lake Fondue, which now have a mashed-potato consistency, are refilled to a bubbling froth; the baskets of dippable, buttery pretzel bites beside them also replenished. If you stay here long enough, you can see the wires undergirding it all, like *Westworld* resetting itself at the end of the day. But you're not supposed to stay for that long. This isn't meant to be an oasis outside of time like Las Vegas, but a brief stop in a pew at cheese church, from which you emerge, born-again.

Hanging around all afternoon, though, like an immortal on earth, it doesn't seem to be working out quite that way.

"This one's pretty good," a sunburned dude in a leather vest says to a friend, pointing to a wedge-stack of the cheese he's currently chewing.

That's Pleasant Ridge Reserve, you fool! I want to shout. *Of course, it's pretty good! Pretty good cheeses taste like dogshit next to it.*

But how would he know that?

I realize suddenly just how far removed from the target audience of this sort of thing I've become. I've already internalized the breakthrough Cheeselandia is designed to inspire. I've already throw a cheese party with my friends once a month. I am a walking ambassador program; a manic cheese preacher.

Will anyone here experience their own epiphany today, rather than a brief, delicious respite from the full-court press of brand Experiences? Sure, they may download the Cheeselandia app, and briefly use Chee-Harmony to get matched with their perfect cheese (the one I get, incorrectly, is Havarti). They may walk over to the Swag Station and type on an iPad the answer to the question "After what you've tasted today, how likely are you to recommend Wisconsin Cheese to somebody?" in exchange for a branded backpack. But will they ever actually fill that backpack with Wisconsin cheese, beyond the stray chunks some of them snatch from the table today? For every person I overhear at a booth asking whether the farmers in Wisconsin actually make their own cheese, or what the blue stuff in Blue Jay is, there are at least two who simply heard there was a bunch of free cheese in a hotel near the Google Fiber mixer.

I try to imagine how these people will remember their time in Cheeselandia. Personally, I've always been distrustful of events that ply me with free food and alcohol in exchange for my data or a social media shout-out. What am I providing that justifies what they're spending? However, South by Southwest is nothing but lavish free experiences, one after another, each trying to outdo the last in a bid to plant flags in the limited real estate of your brain. Everybody here knows what everybody else wants from them and they don't care. It's out in the open. It's part of the promise. It's a parade of otherworldly delights, until you no longer remember your own name, but hopefully remember that cheese you liked at Cheesetropolis or whatever.

"Ladies and gentleman!" the barker announces again. "Now presenting 2019 Cheeselandia State Fair queen: Miiiiiiss Bubbly!"

Applause rings out as the cheddar-headed Champagne Barbie enters the room once again for a whole new set of faces. People are just beginning to fish the phones from their pockets to take photos as I turn away and exit the succulent funhouse.

THERE'S AN ADVERTISING term for a sight so potent it gives viewers a serotonin spike. It's called the Cheese Pull.

Fade in on a pizza pie, fresh from the oven, steam vapors whispering through the golden-brown splotches in a glistening mass of mozzarella. A spatula slides under a particularly tempting piece. Zoom in on the gooey gravity battle between the rogue slice and its home. The stretch of it. The tension. The sense-memory of how satisfying it is to clip those clinging cheese ropes with pincer fingers and eat them; a pure, greasy gush of molten cheese-lava. Cue salivation.

The Cheese Pull is a trigger for ancient urges. Our dumb lizard brains can only process it with the kind of internal scream of need that consumer culture thrives on. It's another funhouse mirror that reflects the part of yourself that only desires one thing, and don't you want it right now?

It's such a visceral visual, the term *Cheese Pull* has become industry standard for any image that creates a primordial itch in need of instant scratching, like the sizzling head on a just-poured beer, or a luxury car wrapped in a giant bow, I guess, if you're rich and also pathologically basic.

Since that money shot of pizza cheese has become marketing shorthand, it should be no surprise that a lot of marketing in the cheese world is heavily visual. But while statewide organizations like Dairy Farmers of Wisconsin exist to spread the good news about artisan cheese, most individual producers don't have the budget to bring on creative agencies. Luckily, a typical day at a creamery, especially a farmstead operation, is chock-full of Instagram catnip. It's all over the place, in freshly made wheels, rows of aging cheeses in ripening rooms, or cows on pasture being silly. At some point in the last few years, many creameries—big and small—realized they were sleeping on a marketing opportunity. They started blasting out photos on social media, letting fans peer into the process, and gaining thousands of followers along the way. They also started sending wheels to influencers like That Cheese Plate or Cheese Sex Death whose followings dwarf their own.

While images go a long way online, what goes even further is letting the cheese speak for itself: giving people a chance to taste and buy it. Cheese influencers can help out that way, too, by doing sponsored tie-ins. Cabot might stage a pop-up event where That Cheese Plate creates custom cheese-by-numbers plates for visitors to fill in using Cabot cheeses. Cypress Grove or Barely Buzzed might send Cheese Sex Death a bunch of wheels to use at one of her personality-driven pop-ups. (More on that later.)

But one surefire way to get a lot of people to try your cheese at once is by getting a booth at a cheese festival.

Over the past two decades, more and more cheese-producing states have spawned festivals, giving makers a chance to share their cheese and tell their story to thousands of eager eaters. The Oregon Cheese Festival, which takes place just a few days after Cheeselandia, is the next available opportunity to see one for myself.

I should have known that the person who started the festival, the same person who created Rogue River Blue, the first cheese that really blew me away, came from a marketing background.

Nearly twenty years ago, David Gremmels made the wild decision to uproot his life completely. The then-ponytailed hippy had recently fled a marketing gig with Sundance and bought a studio space in Oregon's Rogue Valley, which he planned on turning into a wine and cheese bar. While formulating the menu, he visited Rogue Creamery one day and met Ig Vella, whose father originally opened the creamery in 1933. All David wanted was to carry some of Ig's cheeses at his would-be wine bar. Somehow, Ig talked him into buying the entire creamery.

"I feel like I paid too much for it," David says, telling me the story when I meet him at his creamery. "But it became my life and my passion and my community, so I would gladly have paid double what I did if I'd known what it was leading to."

David is wearing a blue dress shirt and a lightweight insulated jacket with his name monogrammed over the chest pocket. He has a trim silver beard with short, wispy brown hair, and he peers out at me through rose-gold, low-bridge eyeglasses that seem to filter everything as happy news.

Out in front of the creamery, a long line of cheese junkies has formed—families, couples, and solo rollers—even though the festival has yet to begin. The line is so crowded that some of it spills off the sidewalk into the bike lane, all leading to a white welcome pavilion in the distance. A woman on a Segway rides by urging bike lane dawdlers back on the sidewalk where perhaps they might want to take a picture with David's antique Dodge B-series pickup truck, painted the same royal blue that graces all of Rogue's branding, and bearing its logo.

David, of course, designed the logo himself: the silhouette of a cow jumping over a crescent moon. Setting aside the logic of a helmet-less cow loose in the lung-rupturing vacuum of space, it's an industrial-strength sticky image, and a timeless one at that. I'd have believed it was either already there in 1933 when the creamery first opened, or that David created it last week.

"A crescent ascending moon is good luck and good future. It brings people together," David says, as we examine the logo together in front of his creamery.

"It had nothing to do with that nursery rhyme?" I ask.

"Well, I wanted something that really appeals to all ages," he says, not missing a beat. "And no one ever forgets their nursery rhymes."

David says everything with a pleasing, languid drawl, as though he were constantly receiving a deep-tissue massage. I'd have thought his demeanor was a put-on—that nobody with as much on their plate could be so celestially mellow—had I not spoken to him on the phone previously.

A born showman turned cheesemaker with an air of almost narcotizing tranquility, David is the exact average between P. T. Barnum, Willy Wonka, and Mr. Rogers.

Early into owning the creamery, David threw the first Oregon Cheese Festival as a way to drive business during the harsh winter months, when sales were typically at their lowest. People might not venture out into the frigid air to stop by a cheese shop, but a festival, well, that was something to plan a day around; a place to bring the kids. David invited five neighboring cheesemakers along, and they all sold out every last scrap of cheese that they brought. On David's suggestion, they ended up forming the Oregon Cheese Guild, an organization meant to create more awareness of local producers, and to bind those producers together, sharing in their respective victories and miseries. David and the Guild continued throwing the festival every year at Rogue Creamery, growing it from a dozen vendors at first to more than 120 in 2019, with friends flying in from areas as disparate as Utah and Vermont.

"It's like our homecoming," David says, as we head toward his creamery.

Excitement for the festival has been building around town in a palpable way for weeks. David found a banner promoting it at his gym yesterday, and his trainer made him do burpees in front of each letter. A Lyft driver mentioned the event to me, unprompted, on the way over. It's the kind of enthusiasm David is only used to seeing at Cheese in Bra, the festival in Italy that's so massive an entire town gets swept up in it.

"All the hotel beds are full, and all the restaurants are full," he says. "I went to my favorite place to get an egg pie in Ashland this morning, and they said, 'David, we're sold out.'"

"If you're gonna be denied an egg pie, that's a pretty good reason," I say.

It's impossible to tell where the creamery's rustic-chic ends and the just-plain-rustic begins. There's a long, corroded trough out front, filled with prickly plants, bordered by old-timey milk jugs. A sign above the rusted metal awning features a faded mural of tree-filled mountains, with a brick of cheese rumbling up from the ground inexplicably. A welcoming sandwich board near the recycle bin bears a long message that ends with a perfectly zen, perfectly David aphorism: "Take your time, there's no clock, cheese never sleeps."

Inside the shop, there's a wide selection of cheeses, local and otherwise, but one case is completely full of Rogue cheese wheels, big as throw pillows, in color-coordinated packaging that makes you want to collect them all. I follow David through a door festooned with a Holstein cow's Rorschach splotches and head down a corridor toward the creamery.

Once David found himself the sudden owner of a cheese factory, nearly twenty years ago, he and his partner at the time, Cary Bryant, began to experiment beyond Rogue's original Oregon Blue. Tom Vella, the creamery's founder, is rumored to have created Oregon Blue by smuggling home some *Penicillium roqueforti* directly from the Roquefort caves in France. It was that kind of fearless dedication David wanted to emulate, but within the boundaries of the law. He surveyed the market obsessively and tried to fill the gaps of what was missing. When chefs started asking for a blue cheese with smoky flavor, unlike Lisa at Bohemian Creamery, he gave them exactly what they wanted, inventing Smokey Blue. Even before that, though, just after taking over the creamery, David began playing around with what would become Rogue River Blue.

"I could spend all day in this cave," David says, taking a deep breath of ammonia-infused air as we enter the Rogue River Blue cave, both of us decked out in head-to-toe protective coating.

The sterile room is filled with hundreds of fresh, doughy cheese wheels, splayed out across plastic sheets on metal racks, leaking their leftover whey. Royal blue air ducts hang overhead, foreshadowing the invisible culture lurking within these wheels that will one day riddle the cheese paste within them.

When David took Rogue River Blue to the American Cheese Society's annual conference and competition in 2003, while coming off of a ten-day juice cleanse, he passed out samples from his backpack like a mid-aughts rapper handing out mixtape CDs. The cheese was still missing something, though. David had received some complaints from buyers about the crumbly, dirt-colored rind, which tasted great but was not aesthetically pleasing, and which the tightly wrapped foil peeled right off anyway. David suspected there had to be a way to not only preserve the rind but make it (and the entire cheese) more enticing. He looked to a cheese from Capriole in Indiana called O'Banon, which was covered in bourbon-soaked chestnut leaves. It made the cheese look like a gift begging to be torn open, and it informed the taste as well. David set out to find a similar wrapping for Rogue River Blue. He went to nearby Eden Farms vineyards with a wedge of his cheese, and spent a day tasting it with different grape leaves, looking for the right match. The leaves from Syrah grapes proved most impressive, so David pulled the trigger. He soaked the leaves in pear brandy, to help with the rind preservation, and started coating his cheese with them. Almost as an afterthought, he sent a batch of the brand-new, leaf-laced Rogue River Blue to the World Cheese Awards that year.

David was just as shocked as the rest of the world when his blue won best in its class, the first American cheese to ever place in the competition.

When the first order from Neal's Yard Dairy in London arrived shortly after, David did not quite know how to legally fill it. At the time, a health certificate for raw milk cheeses heading from the United States to the European Union didn't even exist. Mass shipments of artisan cheese at that point only went the other way. David had to spend the next four years working with the FDA, Neal's Yard Dairy, and Whole Foods to set up the paperwork to sell Rogue River Blue overseas.

David's efforts to make one of his cheeses more presentable ultimately offered a lot of people around the world their first-ever taste of American artisan cheese.

When I start to take a picture in the cave, I try to get as many wheels in my photo as possible, to remind myself later of the enormity of this room and the sheer number of birthday-cake-shaped wheels. David has another idea, though.

"You might want to get this angle, kinda just like such," he says, gently art-directing my photo to capture only one quadrant of the room, pushing in on a wheel so that the rack it's resting on makes a *V* across the frame.

Zooming in this close, all the salt clinging like clumps of crushed ice on that first wheel really jumps out, making for a way better photo than I'd had in mind. Click.

"Now that's a beautiful picture right there," David says proudly over my shoulder.

After the tour is finished, David has to get going. He's spending a substantial chunk of the next two days ferrying friends to and from the airport, and he's currently in danger of running behind on shuttle duty. We say our goodbyes, which are short-lived since we will see each other at several more cheese events throughout the year, and I head out to explore the festival.

Beyond the welcome area, inside the big tent, it feels like I'm back in a funhouse again, or like I never left Cheeselandia. There's an air of whimsical celebration, combined with an urgent inflaming of urges and a dash of claustrophobia. Vendors line the walls, offering not just cheese but everything you might ever want to consume with it, and other vendors are stationed across from them, making a narrow walking perimeter throughout the tent. There's a line going either way on both the outer and inner rim, like several drunken competing congas, so I scoot through the sea of bodies, saying, "Excuse me, sorry" so many times it starts coming out as one word, *Skewsmisari*. Once more unto the cheese, dear friends.

Every maker from David's guild is here, and all their cheeses are vying for my attention. Some of them scream at me, like a black truffle chèvre log that's bold and brassy as a Liza Minnelli one-woman show; some of them draw me in with a whisper, like the washed rind called Maia I have to strain to hear beyond its muted funk, until the taste of ham crepes and buttered carrots breaks through; and some of them just bewilder you until you can't resist filling in the curiosity gap, like Face Rock's Vampire Slayer, a cheddar so garlicky I feel bad for anybody who tries to talk to me next. Eventually, I'm burped out of the initial tent onto a gravel-covered yard with a rainbow caravan of food trucks bearing Peruvian and Argentinian cuisine, all in the shadows of the snowy mountain peaks in the distance.

The state fair vibes here are more than a promotional concept, as they were in Cheeselandia. There's an actual petting zoo at the high school across the street, a face painting station for kids, and a motorcycle raffle right next to the Krav Maga place. All that this festival is missing is Sarah the "Cheese Lady" Kaufmann, the Michelangelo of cheese sculptures, who attended the last two years. Sarah is known for turning mammoth mounds of block cheddar into larger-than-life renderings of Mickey Mouse, Meredith Vieira, or the melting Nazi from the climax of *Raiders of the Lost Ark*, their features rendered in ever-edible bas-relief splendor. She calls her services "shoppertainment" or "theater in retail," and huge crowds form at grocery store openings and dairy industry events to watch the high-wire act of excavating crocodile teeth from a cheese block, as if from an archaeological dig site.

In her absence, the greatest cheese spectacle here is the taste of Oregon's cheese, which this festival has given a spotlight—the same way Rogue River Blue threw an international spotlight on American cheese altogether.

A COUPLE MONTHS after the Oregon Cheese Festival, a woman in Chicago created the most audacious experiment in artisan cheese marketing history.

It was more ambitious than when Tillamook cemented the company's birthday as National Cheddar Day through the official calendar registry.

More momentous than when Jasper Hill launched a slice of its Bayley Hazen Blue 100,000 feet into the atmosphere, using a weather balloon and some GPS tracking software.

Far racier than the exuberantly wholesome Cheeselandia.

The woman behind the event is Erika Kubick, the influencer better known as Cheese Sex Death. Erika had thought a lot recently about expanding her brand beyond the internet. She was already selling merchandise for her goth-tinged cheese blog and had actually seen someone wearing one of her Cheese Slut T-shirts on Tinder. She also made herself available to lead Cheese Church, a private tasting in her own inimitable style, and offered custom Raclette parties, personal shopping, and cheese tours. But what she really wanted to do, what might answer all her cheese prayers, was to put on a cheese-themed burlesque show.

Tonight, she is debuting the very first edition of *Strip Cheese*, a show that sold out so quickly she had to add a second performance for later tonight, which also sold out. Although technically *Strip Cheese* is only marketing the concept of cheese itself, and the Cheese Sex Death brand, Erika lined up sponsors for it, and they're being represented here as well.

"So, Emmi and Cypress Grove know they're sponsoring a burlesque show, right?" I ask Erika, who is wearing thigh-high boots and a matte-black short skirt.

"Oh yeah," she says. "They're always jazzed about my more unique events."

It doesn't get much more unique than serving cheese out of a coffin with a plastic skeleton inside it, a bowl of olives precariously balanced on its pelvic bone.

There could be no more fitting venue for a Cheese Sex Death experience than the former funeral home we're currently inside. Although Charnel House in Logan Square had long ago been converted into a performance space, dark vibes remain everywhere—from the grimy, fossil-gray facade, to the rows of no-frills foldout chairs parting the parlor like the red sea. The coffin, which fellow Chicagoan and CMI champ Jordan Edwards had been driving around in his van all day, only enhanced the darkness. You could practically smell the embalming fluid.

Guests soon begin to file in, looking alternately like members of a 1980s speed-metal band reuniting for the money in 2019, and thrift-store-raiding roller derbyists. Nearly everyone is wearing black, but their mood is far from funereal. There's nothing but smiles on the Raclette line, where Erika and two friends—both in Cheese Slut T-shirts—scrape the gooey surface of an Emmi donated Tête de Moine wheel onto waiting pretzel bites as each new person comes by.

As it gets closer to showtime, Erika realizes the stage should probably be protected by a tarp. She dispatches a Raclette friend to Loew's Hardware, which only has tarps in bulk. That's okay, though. Erika is pretty sure this is going to be a "tarps in bulk" kind of night.

I couldn't quite anticipate what kind of burlesque show has a splash zone, but soon enough a zaftig vixen in full beat and *Flashdance* legwarmers is chomping down cheddar while two women spray her nearly nude body with Easy Cheese. Now I understand.

Erika wisely recruited her friend, fellow former monger and self-proclaimed "comic stripper" Florence of a'Labia, to host and help curate the show. In a skintight fluorescent pink dress with matching beehive wig, and armed with an astonishing number of cheese puns, she holds the audience's attention hostage in between sets.

"What's a stripper's favorite cheese?" she asks, waiting for a beat and then delivering the punch line: G-string cheese.

Before the rowdy crowd can even stop groaning, she has another one locked and loaded.

"What's a cheese slut's favorite sex act? Fromage à trois."

With the audience still laughing, she introduces Indianapolis' Jezebel Sinfull, who has prepared a conceptual piece set in an Italian restaurant. Jezebel starts off seated at a red checkered tablecloth, which matches her magenta pixie cut, a server shaking a green cannister of Parmesan on her pasta plate with the bored indifference of someone miming masturbation. As soon as the song "Mambo Italiano" kicks into high gear, Jezebel flies to her feet, the tablecloth revealed to be part of her dress, detachable at the thighs, and starts removing clothes. The server promptly fetches a big silver bucket of Parm and starts sprinkling it on the guests, until she gets down to spaghetti-and-meatball pasties, at which point, she purrs, "When!"

Never before tonight has the connection between cheese and sex appeal been so crystal clear. The performances are goofy, leaving the audience laughing way more than they're wolf whistling. But the come-hither stares and satisfied looks on the performers' faces, which usually only register in one context during a burlesque show, now share another one entirely. It was a Cheese Pull the likes of which the world had never seen before, one that gave new meaning to the phrase *food porn*. This is what's really lurking behind almost all cheese marketing, behind almost all marketing altogether. This is what's splashed across the master blueprint of the funhouse. Everybody wants to be fully satisfied in every primal way, and sometimes it's hard to tell one hunger from another. This show gives everyone permission to acknowledge something we might not otherwise: that the cheese button in our brains is right next to the horny button.

The show reaches its climax with an unexpected celebrity animal cameo. Right This Way Robbie, a performer decked out in a spotless white suit and tie with a bullet-smooth head and mascaraed lashes, starts off singing "O Sole Mio" in classically trained operatic swells. Unlike at a typical opera, however, Robbie is singing to a single Cheeto he's plucked out of a bowl, seated on a table covered in white cloth. Although he gazes tenderly at the cheese puff throughout the song, his mouth keeps inching closer to it, as if magnetically pulled by temptation. First, he takes little nibbles, then he devours the treat . . . only to find Cheeto dust sprinkled on his immaculate white outfit. With a panicked face, but still singing, Robbie starts removing one orange-tainted garment after another, before disappearing behind the table momentarily. Suddenly, a gritty punk version of "O Sole Mio" rings out, and Robbie emerges, pantsless, in a Chester Cheetah face mask, romping all around the stage. For the grand finale, he dumps the bowl of Cheetos on the floor and does a full-frontal flip on top of its contents. The audience erupts.

I imagine Erika talking with Frito-Lay about sponsorship. It would probably be a very short conversation. *A smug talking cheetah wearing sunglasses and shell tops but nothing else? Fine.* Give him a suit to take off, though, and suddenly he's not "on-brand." They'd never go for it.

Leave it to the artisan producers to help make cheese dreams become a reality.

CHAPTER NINE

Playing with Your Food

ACCORDING TO LEGEND, ON A STARRY NIGHT, DEEP IN THE ENGLISH countryside of Somerset, over the plot of land where Camelot once stood, exploding cheese rained down from the sky.

The only witnesses to the bizarre event were those responsible for flinging the cheese unto the heavens, before it returned to the earth in charred shards. They were guests of world-renowned cheddar producer Jamie Montgomery; industry friends invited over to kill their dead cheese, the cheese that had betrayed them. Anyone who'd produced an unsellable wheel was encouraged to stuff that wheel full of napalm, load it into a trebuchet, and catapult it far above the grassy hills of the sprawling Montgomery estate in North Cadbury. No pictures exist of the fiery sky-curds descending. Video of the demolition was strictly prohibited. What any camera would have captured that night, though, is a perfect expression of how it feels when the cheese you poured your heart and soul into doesn't return the favor.

Cheese recipes aren't born fully formed; they're honed, tweaked, and beta-tested, over months and often years, until the proper path reveals itself, invariably with many wrong turns and detours along the way. Sue Conley and Peggy Smith came up with Cowgirl Creamery's Red Hawk by accident. Cypress Grove's Mary Keehn conceived of Humboldt Fog in a dream. Whatever the genesis of any cheese, in between the moment of inspiration and its arrival in a display case (or the swinging arm of a trebuchet) comes a lengthy research and development phase. It was curiosity that drove the mythical Arabian merchant to eat primeval goo out of his calf's stomach-flask, but it was research and development (R&D) that evolved those raw materials into the stuff of Guy Fieri's Trash Can Nachos.

Songs work the same way. The history of music is littered with great songs that almost went in different directions during the R&D phase. Listen to the early demos of Nirvana's "Smells Like Teen Spirit," and you'll hear what we know in hindsight were the wrong lyrics and arrangements. Had one decision gone differently, nineties kids would have all been singing "I'm a liar, and I'm famous / Here we are now, entertain us" like idiots. Lucky for them, Nirvana had super producer Butch Vig around to help figure out that song, and lucky for everyone else, cheesemakers have the Center for Dairy Research (CDR).

Located in the heart of cheese country, at the University of Wisconsin–Madison, the CDR is a place where cheese problems are solved. It was founded in 1986 during a period of immense milk surplus in America, as a means of expanding the possibilities of what to do with it all. A decade later, around the time the cheese-cart had migrated from France to New York, the focus at CDR had shifted to specialty cheese. Since then, many award-winners have emerged from the vats in their pilot plant. The CDR helps makers either perfect new cheeses or improve the ones they already have. If a legacy artisan producer finds unexplained cracks in their paste, or a major conglomerate's mozzarella starts melting into plasticky nubbins like Shrinky Dinks, the CDR is their savior.

Another thing the CDR does is educate. Beyond teaching the milky arts to university students, they also host short courses where Whole Foods mongers get whisked off to Wisconsin for a week of immersive cheese-learning. Since I was already going to Wisconsin to tour the CDR and pay a visit to Andy Hatch at Uplands, I asked if I could get in on the next cheesemonger *rumspringa*.

However much you've heard about Wisconsin's obsession with cheese, double it and you'll still be way off. Cheese is deeply embedded within Wisconsin culture. It's abundantly available everywhere, along with foam cheese hats—in cowboy, baseball, and construction worker variety—keychains, paperweights, footballs, dice, coasters, and fridge magnets. Wisconsin is America's Dairyland, as the license plates proudly proclaim. It's the only state with its own official microbe: *Lactococcus lactis*, which is essential for cheesemaking. Jim Gaffigan, the arena-touring comedian who has literally written more cheese jokes than he can remember, tells me that he credits marrying a Wisconsin woman with awakening his love of cheese. Everyone in Wisconsin seems to adore the stuff, aside from vegans and dairy farmer offspring experimenting with low-effort rebellion. Sure enough, less than an hour after my plane touches down in Madison, I'm walking down Willy Street eating cheese curds right out of the bag, on my way to visit a cheese shop called Fromagination, where I pick up a hunk of cheddar old enough to get its learner's permit. This is a cheesy utopia.

Any college campus in farm country is bound to look a little different from most others. Driving around the University of Wisconsin–Madison, I pass the usual libraries and cafeterias, but also signs for MEAT AND MUSCLE LAB and BUCKY'S BUTCHERY. I half expect to pass one for TAXIDERMY WORKSHOP, the logical next step, but never do. Things only get stranger when I enter Babcock Hall, which looks outwardly like any other building on campus. In the lobby downstairs stands some antique cheese-making equipment whose provenance or utility are impossible to guess, an acknowledgment of our pioneer past from those shaping the dairy future. Walking the second-floor hallway, the smell of grass and dirt hangs in the air, but when I peer into a lab to try and find its source, all I see is a metallic cluster of what looks like ghostbuster containment units. I get turned around for a moment, until I locate a sign for the CDR and a trail of cartoon cows plastered to the floor that point the way there. At the reception desk, next to a sign-in sheet, sits a wicker basket holding a rhomboid wedge of grocery store cheddar, along with some Ritz crackers. During every subsequent visit over the next few days, a different greeting-cheese appears in the same spot, presumably in lieu of peppermints.

The Whole Foods mongers gradually pile into the lecture hall in room 201, ready to kick-start a week of cheese education. They have come from all over, and don't seem to have much in common beyond the fact that their team leaders have nominated them to take the Certified Cheese Professional (CCP) exam at the American Cheese Society conference later this summer, and they've accepted. The next few days pass by mostly in a water torture drip of cheese knowledge no human should ever possess, although I'm excited about my new superpower of ruining people's nights at any party in the future.

This cheese smells like feet, someone might say before eating a piece of Taleggio.

Well, that's because it's made with a bacteria called B. linens *that grows especially well on human feet*, I could respond.

I love Parmigiano-Reggiano even though it tastes kinda like baby vomit, someone else who wasn't privy to that first exchange might say.

That's because it uses an enzyme called lipase *that's found in human breast milk. You have a lovely home, by the way.*

As many revolting factoids as I pick up that week, the instructors also help solve some long-lingering cheese mysteries.

"I want you to squeeze this curd that's just a couple of hours old and see if you can squash it," says Dean Sommers, who is not actually a dean. He then clenches his fist around a Nerf Cheeto and shakes it at the sky. All the Whole Foods mongers follow suit with their own curds.

No one can do it. No matter how hard we squeeze, the curds restore to their initial shape, like memory foam mattresses.

"These fresh curds haven't yet been through proteolysis, the breakdown of proteins over time," Dean says. "They're still at peak elasticity. That's why fresh curds squeak. It's the proteins at their strongest pushing against your teeth as you bite into them. Give it a try."

I'd heard so many times that fresh curds squeak, but still had no idea what that actually entailed. Never had I bitten into curds early enough to experience the fabled squeak for myself. When I bite into this one, though, a sound fills my head like a rubbed balloon or a persistently cleaned window. Because the sound arrives with the motion of every jaw-chomp, I can *feel* the noise, as the rock-and-roll scientists in Quiet Riot once implored us all to do.

After the third day's morning lecture, we finally get to go down to the pilot plant.

An assembly line of safety gear sits on a table in the break area and we trudge around it, donning transparent white ponchos, red hairnets, oversize goggles, and booties along the way. Once we're shielded from bacteria, or rather our bacteria are shielded from the cheese, we head downstairs in a single-file line like an elementary school fire drill.

The pilot plant is a vast forest of chrome metal machinery; vats, tubes, and gauges in every direction, with pipes running the length of the building in rows above us. It looks like it's all one interconnected, milk-powered Rube Goldberg machine that somehow ends in cheese. Each device is shaped like either an iron lung or a teakettle big enough to crush a car. The hiss of steam punctuates an insistent clanking that follows us past signs for MILK BOTTLING, PASTEURIZER, AND CREAM SEPARATOR. The windows that make up much of the eastern wall consist of small cubes, an Excel spreadsheet of light flooding through them and onto the red-tile floor, where there's always a cascade of soapy, sanitizing water to almost slip on. After scrubbing up at the hand-washing station midway through the room, we head just beyond the ice-cream-making area, where a jet stream of welcome vanilla wafts into my nasal passages. Up ahead, everyone else is gathering around four deluxe washing machine–size vats.

These are the experimental cheese vats, where much of the CDR's research is tested. The technicians can use them to make up to four batches simultaneously when testing out a hypothesis on a company's cheese, tweaking some variable in the recipe for each one, and comparing the results afterward. The vats are all currently in use, and each at a different point in the cheesemaking process. FRESH MOZZ is written in green marker on the rim of one—which has a giant, motorized paddle inside, working the milk like an electric eggbeater.

"Feel free to get your hands in the vats," says Andy Johnson, who is wearing a blue hairnet like the other dairy techs, marking themselves apart from the Whole Foods crew in red hairnets, like Bloods and Crips. "If you see us doing something and you want to do it, just get us out of the way and you can do it yourself."

Several of the mongers lock eyes at this news, as though silently planning a coup.

The techs start making cheese, which is a slightly more straightforward job than what they normally do here each day.

Sometimes Dean or Andy will get a call from a cheesemaker with a problem and know right away what's causing it. That's what happens when you have as many accrued years of dairy crisis management as they do. Other times, some of the techs instead pay an on-site visit to perform analytical testing. Perhaps the flavor or texture of a cheese is off because of a sanitation issue on the farm or in the cheese plant. The CDR staff pokes around like cheese detectives, trying to find the contaminating culprit. If they can't solve the problem this way, the techs troubleshoot ingredients in the experimental vats at the CDR, based on their analysis.

When they're not solving dairy problems on demand, the CDR crew is anticipating future issues and testing out theories. Recently, they've been working on a project to extend the fridge life of mozzarella up to a year, in the event the supply chain demands it. (Normally, if you haven't eaten the mozzarella in your fridge after six weeks, that ship has sailed.) So far, they've gotten up to nine months and no further. But the dream of calendar-year mozzarella lives on.

My fellow red hairnets rotate from one vat to the next, tracking the various stages of cheesemaking as they happen concurrently. It's like watching big news breaks across four TV screens, each with a different network reporting on a different element, all at once. Andy Johnson pours the coloring agent annatto into a cheddar vat. It makes a bloody swirl in the center of the milk, as though a shark attack has just occurred below, and then the entire vat turns the exact orange of Muenster rind.

"Stick your fingers in and make sure it's the correct firmness," Andy Johnson says, a few minutes later.

Pretty soon, all the mongers are sticking bare hands into vats, willy-nilly. When I put my hand in one, it leaves a Hollywood Walk of Fame imprint in the cheddar, which means it's ready for the next step: cutting the curd. Andy slides into the vat a cheese harp, which is basically a large square-metal tennis racket. He then asks for volunteers to cut the curd. The monger standing next to me, whose lab coat hangs past her arm like a wizard sleeve, offers her services. After Andy gives her the nod, she thrusts her phone in my hands so I can film her expertly pushing the harp forward, flipping it, and dragging it back, with no overlap on her previous cuts. Cloudy pockets of whey billow up from within the cut spaces.

By the time the whey flows out of the vats through a filter bucket and gushes into a floor drain, leaving a tenth of the vat full of curd, I'm getting kind of hungry. Luckily, I don't have to wait too long to taste the fruits of our labor. Andy instructs everyone to dump large slabs of mozzarella curd into a kind of mini-thresher placed over its vat. The cheese comes out on the other side in damp mozzarella-thumbs. Andy pours salt and hot pepper on them, and then a few of the mongers and I reach into the vat and start rubbing in the seasoning. It feels like shaking hands with a bunch of freaky thumbs all at once. They're delicious thumbs, though, and I eat way too many of them.

It's become clear over the course of this week that the CDR staff can make cheese look or taste just about any way they want. They are mad cheese scientists using bacteria to Frankenstein flavors in unlikely combinations. Sure, sometimes they have to work on problems like trim loss, which means reducing the amount of cheese wasted during an industrial company's slicing. Other times, the "problem" is just that a company wants its cheese to taste more awesome—extra buttery, perhaps, or more caramel-like. At that point, the CDR techs tinker with different starter cultures and enzymes to reverse engineer whatever the maker wants. In fact, they also work with the companies who *supply* those dairy cultures and enzymes. Many of the more popular ones of the past thirty years were first tested in the CDR pilot plant.

The techs can perform honest-to-God cheese miracles. They can pull out good bacteria from raw milk cheese and slip it back into pasteurized cheese, which has all the bacteria heated out of it, to retain a passable impression of terroir. They can add *Lactobacillus helveticus*, what's known as an adjunct culture, and create a sweet and fruity note, which explains why a lot of American cheddars taste like candy.

Depending on the style of cheese the CDR is working on, it may take up to nine months or more to age out and run sensory trials. In one recent case, it took three years.

Paula Homan, one of the owners of Red Barn Family Farms

in Wisconsin, wanted to create a new American original, one with the flavor profile of Parmesan and the creamy texture of a young Gouda, but with the tyrosine crystals that develop with age in both. In other words, kind of a tall order. Paula met with the CDR team, though, and they worked backward to figure out what kind of culture cocktails might produce the hybrid cheese she had in mind. What they came up with is Cupola, a nutty marvel of cheese science.

People throw the word *pineapple* around a lot to describe cheese flavor, but I have seldom tasted a pineapple note as pronounced as the one in Cupola. This, of course, is intentional.

"We were trying to develop that toasted pineapple flavor," Paula tells me over the phone one day. "And the reason the process took so long is because we had to get the culture just right to achieve that."

The CDR team tried out a lot of different ideas for the initial batches, using the experimental vats and conferring with Red Barn's preferred culture company. Once they arrived at a recipe and began producing wheels that were on track to develop into Paula's concept for Cupola, Red Barn's resident cheesemaker started making batches at their own creamery. A lot of back-and-forth followed. *Should we try lowering the salt? What about raising the pH level?* As is always the case with cheese, the ultimate test was time.

"We would taste it around six or seven months and think, 'not too much going on here,'" Paula recalls. "And then it could happen within a few weeks. All of a sudden, those cultures would go to work and achieve just what we were looking for."

A couple of months after my visit to the CDR, at the same American Cheese Society conference in Richmond, Virginia, where the Whole Foods mongers finally take their CCP exam, Cupola goes on to win best of its class during ACS's judging and competition portion: the Oscars of cheese.

The CDR aims to please and more often than not, their aim is true.

Once the cheesemaking demonstrations are over and the activity around the vats dies down, our focus turns to the nearby string cheese machine. Instead of spitting out little perfectly formed missiles of low-moisture skim mozzarella, the machine emits a continuous stream through its nozzle like a frozen yogurt dispenser. This is incredible news to me. The tyranny of pocket-sized string cheese has gone on for too long. Have the machine plop out a coiled pile on a plate and hand it over!

While I'm too sheepish to ask for such a favor, the next best thing is about to happen instead. We're taking a run at the CDR record for longest continuous string of cheese.

Andy Johnson asks everyone to form a circle around the make area. A couple of the mongers almost slip on foamy water and curd residue as we fan out beyond the vats.

"The record is three loops around," Andy says, catching the first toothpaste-like burst from the nozzle. "But there is some dispute about that."

The cheese is super thick, closer to python size than POLLY-O. It swoops in between each person as they pass it on, like a birthday banner. Everyone squeezes the cheese string during each handoff, leaving behind clenched handprints. The process is not orderly at all. If we were firemen trying to transport a hose up a ladder, the building would definitely burn down. Fortunately, we're not, and all that burns is the shared dream of making CDR history. The cheese string barely makes one revolution around before the monger who'd been so dexterous with the cheese harp earlier lets her end of the hose fall to the floor.

"I didn't see anything, keep going!" a monger with an extra hairnet over his pointy goatee calls out, but it's too late. Andy nods to one of the techs, who turns the machine off.

Soon, everyone is walking around carrying intestinal tubes of string cheese and grinning ear to ear. Some of the mongers gnaw on it or make rubber band balls of cheese knots.

"When you're done playing with your cheese, head over here for Colby," Andy says, as three mongers attempt to jump double Dutch with a length of cheese rope.

It's physically impossible to stop playing with this much cheese, even if sooner or later, we must. The more I thought about it, though, I realized that the CDR is a place where scientists play with cheese every day. They might be solving technical problems for individual producers or huge corporations, but the techs also spent plenty of time chasing their own private cheese muses. They fiddled with formulas to produce certain flavors, monkeyed with milk to make creamier textures, and puttered with proteins to enhance elasticity. Play was inherently an important part of the process. The field of dairy science was one big salty sandbox.

AFTER MY TIME in Madison is over, I head out to Dodgeville to meet Andy Hatch of Uplands, one of the cheesemakers the CDR has helped a lot over the years.

To buy the farm, colloquially, means to die, but buying a farm was all Andy ever wanted.

The pastoral fantasy of life as a farm owner appealed to him as a Wisconsin teenager, but after years of actually helping out on dairy farms, he became convinced he'd never scrape together enough capital to make it a reality. Fresh out of college, he was working for a local corn breeder when an unexpected opportunity arose. His boss's father-in-law passed away, leaving behind a widow who needed urgent assistance making cheese in Norway.

Andy thought the corn breeder's idea for him to fly over and help out sounded like an adventure. He had no idea his whole life was about to change.

Although Andy grew up surrounded by cheese, he had to travel to a Norwegian fjord before he started thinking about becoming a cheesemaker. He liked the work, he was good at it, and he had a head for the science undergirding it all, but more importantly, it made him realize he could make cheese in a way that increased the value of the milk. His eyes weren't filled with dollar signs, but he thought cheese might just be his ticket to eventually owning a farm.

He was right.

As I park in the pebble-strewn dirt driveway at Uplands, a herd of mixed cattle walks by in a squiggly line from a nearby barn. It's hard to overstate the vivid, eye-popping green of the pasture grass they walk along, and the severe jut of the hills in the distance. It's a kind of green I've only seen in the high-definition shimmer of peacock feathers. Rising above the roof of the dairy is the same kind of navy-blue feed silo that appears up and down Wisconsin backroads and highways so often that it seems like the silos grow naturally from the ground.

"Would you mind putting on the crocs?" Andy asks, once I walk through the doorway.

Just behind him, a pair of perpendicular shoe racks barricades the rest of the office. The bottom row of each rack is filled with white sanitary Crocs, which I exchange for my black high-top Adidas before hurdling over.

Andy has an angular face, tired eyes, and naturally tousled brown hair. A swim team coach's whistle begs to hang on a lanyard around his neck, in a way that is hard to articulate. He just radiates knowledge and patient encouragement.

Inside his office, a banjo hangs on the wall next to a window looking out on the Uplands plant, where all the machines are currently turned off.

"Want some toast? Butter toast? Cheese toast?" Andy asks, clearing a Neal's Yard Dairy tote off a seat at the kitchen table for me. A few minutes later, he slides over a piece of toast with three Dorito-size strips of Pleasant Ridge melted over them, sprinkled with pepper, on a water-stained metal plate. The cheese is melted to transparency, the tips of each piece running over the crust. It tastes amazing. Later, the CMI champ, Jordan Edwards, would chide me for turning down coffee since Andy is known to serve his guests creamy, cow-to-jug raw milk.

Above the window into the make room hang framed glamour shots of both Uplands cheeses, set against stark black backgrounds, the gooey Rush Creek paste dribbling out of its rind. Although Pleasant Ridge is the more famous, more award-winning cheese, Rush Creek is the only one of the two that Andy created himself, and it's the one that allowed him to buy the farm.

After a few years of working at Uplands, Andy realized that original owner Mike Gingrich was missing out on an opportunity. Uplands made their alpine-style Pleasant Ridge on the same schedule as the Swiss cheesemakers who bring their cows up in the mountains over the summer to feed on high-elevation pastures. Later in the year, though, when their barn-bound cows were subsisting on hay, Uplands had been selling off all the fattier winter milk they created instead of turning it into pudgy Vacherin Mont d'Or like the Swiss cheesemakers did. Andy had spent time in Europe apprenticing for a Mont d'Or producer years before and knew how it was made. If he could just get the young cheese to cooperate with America's sixty-day minimum raw milk restriction (it usually sells in Europe at half that age), he'd really have something.

In 2009, Andy started making trial batches and had to feed most of them to the pigs. Fairly early into running variations on the dozens of departure points in the process, he felt like he'd nailed the flavor of the cheese. The problem was the texture. Vacherin Mont d'Or is very much a texture-based cheese. If it wasn't custardy smooth, it would be as useless as crunchy grits or spoonable steak. Andy was having a difficult time getting the paste to stay soft for as long as he needed without it getting chalky or gummy. Something had to give.

"I assumed it would be mostly ripening techniques that got it out over sixty days," Andy says as I eat my cheese toast. "It actually turned out every little thing you do in the vat has implications months down the road and into the ripening."

The following year, Andy made four thousand prototypes of his take on Vacherin Mont d'Or and only ended up feeding about a quarter of them to the pigs. It was a huge leap forward. Along the way, he had regular conversations with Mateo Kehler from Jasper Hill, a friend who had already cracked the sixty-day code with a similarly silky winter milk cheese: the ACS Best of Show champion Winnimere. Mateo even flew out to Wisconsin and assisted Andy in some early batches of what became Rush Creek

Reserve. Outside of a facility like the CDR, this is what research and development in the cheese world often comes down to: just two friends hunched over a vat together, trying some shit out.

Andy also talked about his ripening issues with Soyoung Scanlan, a piano-playing scientist who owns California's Andante Dairy. Soyoung is a highly regarded cheesemaker and an eccentric who claims to have slept in her cheese cave overnight in order to experience the change in humidity. When Andy asked for her advice, she encouraged him to shift his thinking altogether, offering metaphysical prompts like, "Pretend you're the cheese and you've just been salted: How do you feel?" Andy tried everything.

All the effort it took to clear the sixty-day hurdle proved worth it in the end. Andy debuted Rush Creek in the winter of 2010, and it was an instant hit. Hot on the heels of this success, he teamed up with Scott Mericka—a dairyman who started running the farm at Uplands around the same time Andy came on— and together, they bought the farm.

IT'S A BUSY day for Andy Hatch. After working the vat this morning, and having lunch with me, he's giving a talk to some food students later this afternoon at Riverview Terrace, a restaurant at Frank Lloyd Wright's estate, Taliesin. Finally, he has tickets tonight to see the cellist Mike Block perform at nearby Hillside Assembly Hall, which Wright also designed.

Andy, who plays mandolin in a band called the Point Five, had a plan to lure Block back to Uplands and entice the virtuoso to play cello in his cheese cave. If there's a hidden agenda, it's that Andy hopes to get a nifty video out of it that he could use to promote Rush Creek in the fall. But mostly, he just thought it would be cool to listen to professional cello in a cheese cave. He even found Block's contact info online and reached out.

"He said, 'Let's talk later,'" Andy reads off his phone, shrugging. "Probably wants to make sure I'm not a weirdo."

"If he turns down a cheese cave gig, he's the weirdo," I say.

With no last-minute guests, Andy and I head into his cave.

Affinage is the part of artisan cheesemaking that most closely resembles taking care of a baby. You have to wash it (in brine or alcohol) and guide it (through physical rotation) to ensure its proper development. Gradually, you do less and less as the cheese internalizes and builds on the early care you put into it. And then, at a certain point, you have to just get out of the way and hope for the best.

Well, that and you also have to scrape off mold and mites as the cheese ages, typically something you don't do for children.

Before we move into the cave, where some of the wheels Andy made two years ago are still developing, he takes me to a nearly empty ripening room that he'll start loading up as he gets deeper into Pleasant Ridge production season this summer. There's a rack in the center with only two trays, each containing a monster wheel as wide as a manhole cover and thick as a mattress.

"What happened here?" I ask.

"We make a couple of these each year for my kids on their birthdays," Andy says, a faraway smile on his face. "I started when they were born and now it's just a tradition."

Although he's a year or two younger than me, I suddenly wish Andy was my dad. I want to wake up on my birthday and watch him make a wheel of cheese that I could also use as a flotation device in the unlikely event of an emergency.

Next to the mega-wheels stands a nearly empty rack with one lone tray holding a pair of blonde, peach-rimmed wheels.

"Those are sheep's milk," Andy says, gesturing at the mystery cheese. "I have half a dozen of those wheels aging as a kind of experiment."

This is huge news. Large-font headline stuff. Uplands Dairy is testing its third-ever cheese—and using sheep's milk to do it! What if it ends up spectacular? What if it misses the mark? It was all very exciting, even though I only first heard of Uplands less than a year ago.

"I just got off the phone with Murray's the other day and they were drooling at the prospect of us doing a sheep cheese," Andy says. "I don't know, we'll see."

That's the hard part about research and development—the "we'll see." Maybe Andy will be close to officially unveiling the third cheese from Uplands by the time this book comes out. Maybe he'll have abandoned the idea. Just like with all things cheese, only time will tell. For now, Andy will continue his sheep project by talking through his issues with the CDR, and by making experimental batches with a nearby friend, Chris Roelli, who has experience with sheep cheese. Years ago, the two freestyled on Chris' vat one night and ended up with an early version of his award-winning cheddar-blue hybrid, Dunbarton Blue. Helping Andy now is Chris' way of returning the favor, although he'd have probably still done it anyway.

As Andy is trying to crack the sheep code here, far away in Vermont, Andy's friend Mateo Kehler of Jasper Hill is currently deep in the research and development stage with a new animal of his own: goats.

Last fall, the Kehlers bought a herd of two hundred from a

Vermont goat farm and poached a husband-and-wife goat farming team from Cypress Grove in California. A herd this size wouldn't produce enough milk to make a lot of typical goat cheeses, but there was practically no end to the kinds of mixed-milk cheeses they could make by combining it with their cows' milk. As the goats were set to arrive at Jasper Hill's new farm, about a month from the time of my Wisconsin visit, the Kehlers asked everybody on staff to start brainstorming ideas for potential new cheese projects. Soon enough, everyone at Jasper Hill began listing off every crazy goat cheese they ever wanted to make—and ended up trying out dozens of them. There was a goat Tomme they had to abandon after it proved too much hassle. There was a firmer washed rind that didn't work out either. Ultimately, the team honed in on three ideas: a blue, a washed brick, and a Raclette-style cheese. Although so far, only these three are ready for retail, Jasper Hill is still playing around with other ideas. And there has been talk about eventually expanding to include sheep cheese, too.

The experimental spirit of research and development hangs in the air wherever raw milk cheese is aging. Each batch has a unique microbial makeup, so the potential for variation is high. Whether it's a prototype cheese or a long-established one, whoever's aging it has to keep checking back in with regular tastings to make sure it's developing along the path it should. Performing affinage is like piloting a ship that way. If you're off by a degree now, you could get fully lost somewhere down the line.

The Pleasant Ridge cave at Uplands is an austere white room full of metal racks holding cocoa-brown UFOs of cheese on wooden boards. The racks all have tags hanging off of them listing the day of production—when each one set off on its course. Although the wheels might be sellable at seven or eight months,

Andy lets some of them continue aging for two years or even longer. If the flavor is still developing, why stop it? The trick is to pinpoint the exact moment the flavor has reached its apex in complexity and sell it just before then—a sense that only comes with years of affinage experience. At a certain point, holding on to a wheel of cheese any longer goes from improving it to denying the world a finished work of art.

Andy and his team come in here every other week to taste each batch. Well, unless the ammonia is too strong that day, in which case they do it out in the office.

"If we have a boring cheese, we would say it's 2-D: two-dimensional. It exists on a flat plane," Andy says as we examine a wheel from last July, the leathery potato skin rind riddled with pinprick perforations. "We talk about shapes. Are the flavors round? Jagged? Is something like sourness poking out? That's probably going to get worse with age. But if everything is in proportion, even if it's very reserved, you can afford to wait and watch it unfold some more."

Over the course of watching flavors develop for months and sometimes years, Andy and his team can't help but form favorites. The racks of Pleasant Ridge in this cave may all look the same, but Andy knows that if he's having people over for a party, he's whipping out Batch 858—his secret stash.

I ask to try some 858 because, like, imagine if I didn't.

Near the back end of the Pleasant Ridge labyrinth, Andy finds the rack of Batch 858 and thrusts in his trier—a steel bicycle pump handle with a long, fluted edge for sampling cheese from deep within a wheel. Every batch has one wheel just for tasting as it ages, and you can tell which one it is by all the holes with moldy rind growing over them. Andy hands me a porcelain cylinder of the cheese, and I warm it up in my hands to get it to what room temp would be if we weren't in a chilly cheese cave. I take a sniff, and it smells like Pleasant Ridge. I take a bite, and it tastes familiar but fresher, like burrowing deep into the source. The texture has just a little more give than usual and the flavor is . . . *wow*. It comes on slow. A flicker of sweet citrus fruit, a drip of salty ham grease, a wave of milky butterscotch. It shouldn't all work but it does. It tastes like a juicy Hawaiian pizza. It's solemnly delicious, like I should cover my face as I eat it.

Andy takes out a plug from the wheel one rack over, the next day's batch, and hands it to me. This one has an extra upper register of sweetness, but it's a little flatter on the savory notes. It feels like it's hitting different parts of my tongue than the 858 did. What a difference a day makes, as they say.

Some of the racks nearby have little white tags with names written on them. These wheels are headed to the cheese shops who cared so much about selection that somebody from the store came out to Wisconsin to spend an afternoon in this cave, sampling wheel after wheel until finding the one they wanted. I understand their motivation. Ideally, I would camp out here overnight until finding my personal favorite, but Andy still has a busy day ahead.

The cellist Mike Block, whom Yo-Yo Ma has called the "ideal musician of the twenty-first century," wasn't going to make it to the Uplands cave after all. Not that Andy holds that against him.

Before heading to the concert later tonight, he invites me to tag along and I happily accept.

Hillside Assembly Hall, where the show is held, is part of a complex of buildings in Taliesin that includes designs from throughout Frank Lloyd Wright's career. Block begins his performance by playing a six-hundred-year-old song, the oldest piece of music ever composed for the cello, and follows it up by playing one of the newest: a pizzicato number he is still working on. He smiles more confidently during the second number, performing in a theater built by the greatest American architect of all time. When the show ends, after the applause fades and we all file out, Andy corners Block in the lobby and presents him with a gift—a wedge of Batch 858—from one artisan to another.

Perhaps it would provide the ideal nourishment as he finishes developing his new song.

CHAPTER TEN

Tour de Fromage

ABOUT AN HOUR INTO MY RED-EYE TO PARIS, THE FLIGHT ATTENDANT brings over a meal that includes a plastic-sealed nugget of industrial French Emmental. Even though it tastes like diet air, I appreciate the gesture of it—like getting lei'd on the plane to Hawaii but for visiting France, that historically aromatic cheese Xanadu.

I was headed to Tours in the Loire Valley to link up with Team USA for Mondial du Fromage. Before the international mongering competition kicked off this weekend, however, I would spend a few days in Paris, unhinging my jaw like a python and eating my way through the cobblestone streets I'd been led to believe were paved with cheese. After a year in continuous awe of America's artisan offerings, I'd finally get to experience firsthand some of their most pivotal influences, in their natural habitat, and eat raw milk cheeses legally too young for America. I was headed to the same city where generations of gallivanting yankees had their own cheese epiphanies before me and returned home, changed.

I'd been to Paris before, but only once, briefly, and many years ago. Somehow, cheese hadn't really factored into that trip, which was mostly spent eating budget baguette sandwiches in between walks to and from museums. Looking back now, as I sat in the metro, studying an ad for shortbread cookies "made with real Comté AOP (Appellation d'Origine Protégée)," going to France without eating any cheese seemed like going into the ocean without getting wet. *How had I even done it?*

France is the top cheese-consuming country in the world, with a hefty fifty pounds per-person yearly average that makes the Unites States' rising thirty-five look like grated Parmesan particles in comparison. Paris alone has at least two hundred cheese shops. Indeed, there are no less than three of them within a fifteen-minute walk from my Airbnb, which is located—like every place else in this city—steps away from a random whimsical carousel.

In the cafés strewn throughout Paris, all the chairs at the outdoor tables face the street, sometimes in rows: an audience to the grand show of quotidian city life. As I stroll around, dodging rogue cyclists and busking accordionists, I'm more interested in the theater of cheese; the staging at shop counters, the performance of mongers, and the dramaturgical nourishment of the cheese itself. Each shop pulsates with possibilities. Piles of Couronne Lochoise, a powdered donut of lemony goat's milk, sit next to stacks of heart-shaped Neufchâtel, soaking in the open air. So many cheeses on display are compact and grabbable, intended for eating in one ambitious session, or perhaps as an afterthought, in the case of the goaty gumdrops called Aperobiques. American shops are under FDA orders to keep most cheeses covered in plastic, which can be like going to sleep at night without taking off your makeup, in terms of clogging pores. Here, mostly only feet-fragrant washed rinds like Époisses and Soumaintrain are kept under wraps, for everyone's protection, while quarter-wheels of Comté sit unencumbered on top of the counter. Some of the shops do away with the familiar, front-facing case altogether, though, displaying their wheels on wall shelves like designer handbags. If the cheese isn't hovering up there, it's laying inside a thick glass dome, or spread out in neat heaps across a waist-high counter, a vision of endless abundance and playful variety. Cookie dough rolls of Buchette de Manon; pistachio-snowballs of Mystère de Chèvre; a sheaf of bloomy rinds meant to look like the Eiffel Tower but which instead appear decidedly scrotal. They're all so neat and unsullied. I'm almost shocked when I remove one from a pyramid arsenal of its identical brethren and it doesn't auto-regenerate like a digital simulation.

Some of the mongers receive me like I'm the only obstacle preventing them from going home for some 1:00 P.M. wine: stingy with samples and visibly rushed. Others much less so. I walk among the wall displays at Fromagerie Laurent Dubois, which looks like a hole in the wall from the outside but is intimidatingly elegant within, until a monger finds me.

"What is the wildest cheese you have?" I ask.

"Come with me," he says, without hesitation, in heavily accented English. He's dressed in head-to-toe black, has eyes the deep ocean blue of Stilton mold, and seems so confident about his choice, I would follow him into battle if it meant coming out on the other side with whatever cheese he had in mind.

"This is very . . . particular," he says, producing a round of cheese wrapped in thin wood, the rind on top like uncooked bacon. "You can't really find it anywhere. It's a cheese from Bourgogne that we wash here with sake, so it's floral on the outside and inside it's very vegetal."

Sold! I grab the sake-washed Soumaintrain, which smells

like old bananas but tastes beef-brothy, along with a cake slice of Roquefort intercut with stripes of quince preserves that sparkle in the sunlight. The fridge at my Airbnb is starting to look like it belongs to a Make-A-Wish kid whose dying wish is French cheese.

I eat cheese almost exclusively, as much of it as I can, only occasionally switching to salad out of guilt. I eat compact briquettes of moldy goat cheese from a Japanese shop called Salon du Fromage Hisada. It's spicy and tangy with a texture so dense my teeth leave perfectly formed imprints in the top and bottom after each bite. I eat a hunk of Brie de Meaux split open and stuffed with cream and walnuts like a jelly roll. I eat a slim disc of Brie de Melun that hits like a double-hoof cow-kick of zesty mac-and-cheese flavor. I go from shop to shop, a cheese-seeking missile, past neon-lit salons pumping daytime disco, past the high-ceiling ground floors of Haussmann-style buildings, open to every cheese experience, to the point where I enter a space called Royalcheese only to realize it's a clothing store for guys who still use Axe Body Spray.

Since only 5 percent of the cheese in France is sold in cheese shops, I start invading grocery stores too. Every single one of them, no matter which part of the city, has enough variety to rival any Brooklyn cheese shop I've set foot in. Some of them have cut-to-order stations like at Whole Foods, others have precut wedges in sections labeled CHÈVRES and BREBIS—whole categories instead of one option of each. It's a stunning mixture of AOC-protected cheeses alongside industrial versions: Gorgonzola slices, shredded Comté, Camembert d'Isigny with a Mickey Mouse insignia, and Saint Agur packaged in a promotional tie-in with *Top Chef*.

The radical difference between what "grocery store cheese" means here and back home cements for me how truly far America has left to go in cheese culture, despite everything else.

Knowing that Madame Fromage had just spent some time in Paris, after hosting a Cheese Journeys tour through the United Kingdom, I'd called her up before my flight and pressed her for tips. The recommendation she pushed hardest was a guided tasting with someone called Le Cheese Geek inside of a cheese cave. It sounded perfect. I scheduled a session for my last day in Paris.

Although there's a back room where cheese is actually aging, the whole cellar at Saisons Fromagerie is technically a cheese cave. As I descend the creaky staircase, behind a middle-aged Swedish woman with choppy blonde hair, I have to watch my head or risk bonking it on the low, arched ceiling. It's drafty down here, a welcome reprieve from the surging summer sun.

"Thank you everyone for joining me and trusting me in the cave," our host says once everyone is huddled around a table. Fabrice Gepner has a baby face, lightly dusted with stubble, and a mop of springy curls on top. He graduated from a Parisian mongering school a few years ago and started his cheese career in the caves at Fromagerie Laurent Dubois, washing and turning and brushing wheels all day, a nursemaid for cheese. Once he'd had his fill of an affineur's quiet solitude, he'd struck out on his own, starting a business conducting cheese tastings. It appeared to be going rather well.

"Why don't you tell me your names and your relationship to cheese?" he asks with a soft, raspy accent.

First up is Ingbritt, the flush-cheeked Swede I'd followed down the stairs. She's one of four tourists in Paris for the week, the only English speaker among a group that includes her parents and a rugged-looking man in a wholly unnecessary scarf. Seated beside them is a timid German student named Nikolaus, whose glasses seem in permanent danger of sliding off his face, and who wants to know about cheese history. Next up are two Americans.

"Hi, I'm Cristi," says a redhead in a peasant dress. "I work for a cheesemaker in the United States."

All four Swedes make a surprised *ooh!* over their new friend from far away, but they can't possibly be as surprised as I am.

Cristi doesn't just work for any US cheesemaker; she works at Spring Brook Farm in Vermont, makers of Tarentaise, an American take on the French alpine cheese, Abondance, and 2017's Best of Show winner at ACS. Tarentaise is American prestige cheese, and Cristi has brought along a pound of it as a gift for Fabrice, who thanks her profusely.

Although she's in Paris visiting her friend Amanda, currently seated next to her, Cristi is actually on her way to Mondial du Fromage in Tours to watch some friends compete. I tell her I'm going there too, after my introduction, and we quietly high-five across the table.

Once the tasting begins, Fabrice frames each cheese like a stop on a French tour—"and now we are going to the Loire Valley, where some of you are heading this weekend"—pairing them all with appropriate wines, a selection of accoutrements he'd plucked from around the city, and three separate breads. After each leg of the trip, he invites his pupils to talk taste.

"It's a bit fudgy," Cristi says after biting into Brebis d'Estive, a washed rind sheep cheese that tastes like the musty basement level of a toasted caramel pretzel.

"What is *fudgy*?" asks Nikolaus, a German student.

"There's no fudge in Paris?" Cristi says, smiling incredulously.

Fabrice does an apologetic half shrug with his face.

"It's dense," he explains.

"Like peanut butter?" Nikolaus asks.

Ingbritt looks like she's trying to decide whether any of this is worth translating to her companions. We then spend minutes discussing the ingredients, uses, and textural properties of fudge. I'd heard *fudgy* used to describe cheese so many times, but never thought about whether it would travel. As we move on to the next cheese, I hope Cristi didn't accidentally suggest to this group that fudge is an American staple eaten with every meal.

Next, Fabrice places two runny wedges with rinds like powdery white fig skin on our plates. One has yellow—almost golden—glossy paste; the other is much paler. Both are shaped like the state of Oklahoma.

"Here you have two cheeses with the same name," Fabrice says. "One is raw milk Camembert de Normandie from the only farmstead producer left in the world, and the other is a pasteurized Camembert I got at the supermarket. See if you can find which is which."

The wheels he's cut from offer clues. The yellow one is bright at the cream-line and doesn't run so much as dissolve into buttery foam, the rind collapsing inward. The paler piece maintains its form perfectly, though, so it must be the pasteurized one.

I try the small nub of what I'm pretty sure is grocery store cheese first and it tastes pleasantly bland, a functional brie for an office happy hour.

I try the yellow one next and it tastes like mealy onions, bitter and sour. Somehow, it tastes like the color yellow. As I chew more, I now only taste cow. Then more cow. So much cow. It's as if I've entered a cow's asshole, mouth-first, and kept going until my face was inside its face and its saliva my own. It's not an especially pleasant sensation.

While Fabrice goes on about the potential extinction of authentic farmstead Camembert de Normandie, I feel like an ugly American. Apart from the novelty of having tasted a rare twenty-eight-day-old French cheese on the brink of collapse, I know in my heart which of the two options I prefer.

The final cheese we try is one I've had many times before: Marcel Petite Comté. Fabrice again passes out two pieces to each of us. One is aged ten months and the other thirty-six months. They look exactly the same—gorgeous almond-colored rind bordering a paste-like milk and honey—except the older one is flecked with clusters of crystal bombs.

The thirty-six-month tastes like vanilla apricots with a faint undercurrent of brisket—the kind of bold, complex flavor-orgy I love in alpine cheeses. The younger version is far less pronounced in any direction.

"I don't love the ten-month," Cristi says. "For that age, it's really underdeveloped. I mean, the Tarentaise I brought is the same age."

"Should we try it?" Fabrice says, picking up his pound of Vermont bounty and swiveling to face the group. The rind on the Tarentaise is the same burnished brown as the Comté, but the paste is slightly brighter.

"Is that your cheese?" Ingbritt asks.

Cristi nods.

"Could that cheese compare to this one?" Nikolaus asks, fixing his glasses again.

"We're going to see," Fabrice says.

There's an air of anticipation bordering on tension in the drafty cheese cave. Everybody straightens up a little, looking on as Fabrice applies a thin knife to the Tarentaise.

"To be fair, it has traveled in a suitcase from the United States," Cristi says. "So, just keep that in mind."

Ingbritt quietly says something in Swedish that definitely contains the word *American* and it makes her scarf-strangled cohort's eyebrows go squiggly.

The cave is silent as we taste. Everyone appears intent on getting as astute a flavor diagnostic as possible, eyes darting around the room.

Fabrice speaks first: "It's very good!"

It is. Tarentaise tastes like hazelnut soufflé with a gritty crystal crunch. The Swedes and Nikolaus all make *yum*-type appreciative vocal noises as well.

"Grainy and buttery . . ." Fabrice continues, possibly to himself, examining the wedge in his hands as he chews.

"Thank you for bringing it," Ingbritt says, raising the rest of her cheese as if to toast.

"Thank you for trying it," Cristi says.

"It's really nice," Nikolaus adds.

"Tell everyone," Cristi responds, a joking-but-not-joking glint in her eyes.

We continue eating cheese and chatting amiably until it's time to leave the cave, bellies full, cautiously mounting the steps under the drowsy haze of several glasses of wine. On the way out,

I say goodbye to Fabrice and promise Cristi I'll look for her at Mondial du Fromage, where I hope her American cheesemonger friends fare as well as her American cheese did here.

THE MOST SALIENT news out of the Mondial du Fromage press conference in Tours, at least to me, is that the event has a press conference at all. I have no idea what the ringmaster, Rodolphe Le Meunier, is saying in rapid-fire French, but I'm surprised a throng of reporters is here to cover it.

Le Meunier stands before a plexiglass podium in the middle of Les Halles marketplace, a shadow-bar from a four-quadrant skylight cutting across his tan, stubble-sculpted face. He's wearing a crisp white chef's jacket, French flag colors running around the collar in thin stripes. The baseball roster of mongers to his left are wearing similar jackets, but their collars are plain. They all stand, arms clasped in front like natural athletic cups, behind a buffet table diorama of a cheese planet, Le Meunier–branded wheels sitting atop Le Meunier–branded wax paper. In addition to being a restaurateur, fromager, affineur, and a brand unto himself, Rodolphe Le Meunier is an MOF—winner of the almost solemnly prestigious Meilleurs Ouvriers de France, a competition for talented craftsmen across a variety of fields, held every four years since the 1920s. Ambitious artisans with skill sets as varied as graphic design, hairstyling, and cheesemongering all attempt to prove their mettle as MOFs, with the winners feted in a victory ceremony at the Sorbonne, the president of France in attendance. It's a prestigious honor and an instant ego-inflater; a James Beard Award on steroids. Years after winning his MOF title in 2007, Le Meunier started a competition of his own: this one. By then, he had already served as a judge at the first Cheesemonger Invitational in New York and attended similar contests in Japan and Belgium. With the creation of Mondial du Fromage in 2013, though, he provided a higher height for the winners of those national titles to reach—the title of Greatest Cheesemonger in the World.

A few French words from the press conference register in my monolingual ears. I'm pretty sure Le Meunier is explaining the format of Mondial, which is so complicated I have trouble grasping it in English. To wit, there's a written test, a blind taste test, a cutting-the-right-weight test, an oral presentation—with each contestant rhapsodizing on a favorite cheese for five minutes—and only *then* comes the confusing part: five separate, simultaneous feats of fromagineering and presentation, including a themed "plateau" (an ornate tabletop display) and a sculpted cheese. Perhaps it's just one of those things that only makes sense while it's actually happening, like role-playing game rules or paradigm-shifting magic mushroom realizations.

Not twenty minutes ago, I was eating lunch with the mongers at Rodolphe's nearby bistro, [R], those heavy jackets slung over the backs of their chairs in the oppressive June heat until the last possible second. Only two entrants per country are permitted in the competition, and I had spent much of lunch trying to figure out who was from where. Team USA, of course, consists of Rory Stamp and Jordan Edwards, both of whom I'd met at the San Francisco CMI, and who are accompanied by their coach, Adam Moskowitz, unusually subdued through most of the meal. This is the third time Adam has shepherded American mongers to the competition. Last time, one of them was Lilith Spencer, who ended up not placing, although another monger, who Adam has since had a falling-out with, came in third. Sitting near us was the violently jet-lagged Cesar Olivares, representing Mexico, even though he lives in California; Nick Bayne, a former theater actor from the United States who now lives and mongers in the United Kingdom; and Andy Moulton, a prematurely silver-haired Canadian. The lunch tables weirdly broke down along gender lines, like a shy middle school dance. Although a man representing the Netherlands sat across from Adam, the competitors to the left were all women: one from South Korea, two from Japan, an Australian, and a Frenchwoman.

Some of the competitors had won mongering competitions in their home nations, the way Rory and Jordan had each won CMI. The others had needed to justify their Mondial-worthiness with a curriculum vitae detailing at least three years in the industry, photo evidence of having created an elaborate ten-cheese platter, along with an explanation of why each piece was chosen, and audio testimonial from one hundred satisfied cheese customers. (Okay, that last one is made up. But it's barely an exaggeration.) Now, the esteemed cheesemaster behind the event brings everyone who made the cut up to the stage and introduces them to a crowd that includes the mayor of Tours.

Jordan Edwards mirrors my own blank face as Le Meunier's front-rounded vowels and guttural *r*'s bounce off his uncomprehending ears, but Rory beams and reacts to everything exactly as the crowd does. I'm not surprised. Over lunch, he'd spoken fluent French with the server and appeared to know absolutely everything about wine.

After Le Meunier brings Rory to the podium, the host jumps in the air to briefly bridge the full-human-head distance in their respective heights. Few applaud the American stranger besides me and Adam, who is filming the moment with heartfelt dad-pride. Both Japanese mongers, Tomoko Kasseki and Hiroko Suzuki, get a bit more fanfare, accompanied as they are by a familial entourage. Evert Schonhage, the gray-bearded Dutchman, receives the most walloping applause, having competed here twice before. The crowd seems most hesitant of all to welcome Jordan, perhaps because his head is shaved close to the scalp and he has tattoos all over his face, wrists, knuckles, and ears. Le Meunier must sense their discomfort because he gestures vaguely at the ink applied to the front and sides of Jordan's head and says, ". . . but fromage!" A few approving *aah*s arise in response, which are ill-gotten because Jordan doesn't have any cheese tattoos. He has the words STAY FREE in an orbital curve just beneath his left eye, a gentle reminder never to go back to jail, but nothing related to cheese.

After the press conference, the competitors have an hour to run around Les Halles in a supermarket sweep to find all the products they need for tomorrow. Once everyone scatters and floods the market, Adam and I look at each other and silently agree to take a stroll together.

"It's gotta be pretty exhausting to do CMI so soon after this," I say. It's an unsubtle way to fish for a reason he hasn't announced the summer edition yet.

"I'm not doing it this year," Adam says. "There was some trouble with the date for the venue I wanted, and if I do it at my warehouse now, I need to get a permit of assembly, so . . ."

He dismisses the idea with an over-it hand wave.

"I don't feel like doing it, anyway," he says, turning to face me, little sprigs of gray in his auburn beard scruff. "I don't feel like being here now, if I'm being honest. I'm struggling, dude. If these tariffs pass, I'm fucked."

For a long time, it had felt like I was living in a parallel America, the United States of Cheese. It was inevitable, though, that at a certain point, the anarchic un-reality of the Trump era would become impossible to ignore, even in the cheese world. Over the course of the year, Wisconsin alone was on track to lose 10 percent of its dairy farms. Many had already been struggling to begin with, but the president's tariffs on steel and aluminum triggered retaliatory tariffs on American dairy products from Mexico, Canada, Europe, and China. (Within the next two months, Trump would bestow $22 billion in relief to American farmers, without congressional approval, widely perceived as a bribe to prevent those farmers from blaming him for their misfortune.) Where the president's actions finally threatened to hit home the hardest for cheese shop owners and importers like Adam was in the latest development in the fifteen-year fight between the United States and United Kingdom over aircraft subsidies. The continental pissing contest was somehow poised to culminate in a wave of tariffs this fall that would jack up import prices on Parmigiano-Reggiano and untold other European cheeses by 100 percent or more. When Adam told me about his fears, it was the first I'd heard of the impending tariffs. They would soon become a topic of constant conversation in the cheese world.

After a few minutes of wandering around the marketplace, a camera crew from the press conference flags down Adam for an interview. His face instantly flips from combat-haunted Vietnam vet to game-show-host-back-from-commercial. I stand by an auto-misting display of cooked sea snails on ice and watch Adam tell a woman in a flight attendant kerchief and updo about the importance of breaking down geographical barriers in cheese.

ADAM HAS A small towel draped over the shoulder of his suit jacket like a basketball coach as he hauls ass down the highway the following morning, on the way to the competition. I briefly wonder if, in the event of a Team USA victory, instead of a cooler of Gatorade, we could dunk a bucket of whey over his head.

"It's your time to shine, boys!" Adam yells as we pass beneath the arched red entranceway into the expo center, pounding the steering wheel with the flat of his hand.

"What did they say on that show, *Friday Night Lights*?" Rory says. "Clear eyes, full hearts, can't lose?"

"I don't know," Jordan says. "I didn't watch that shit."

Techies drive by on golf carts, barking into walkie-talkies on the way to the exhibition hall where the trade show part of Mondial is happening. The competition will play out instead in a natural light-free warehouse on the far opposite side of the massive property. We flash our lanyard badges at a security guard and enter. I'm already beginning to sweat as we weave between stacks of electrical equipment and pallet jacks, and cross a vast empty space, before finally reaching a cliff-face of bundled speakers and slip through a set of black curtains.

On the other side, it looks like the ideal setup for a hyper-efficient director to film several episodes of *Iron Chef* simultaneously. There are eleven monger stations spread across three rows facing the steel bleachers where an audience will soon materialize. Each station consists of a mini-fridge and trash stand fenced in by perpendicular tables covered in tightly clamped black cloth. The side tables are mostly empty, since this is where the cooking and prep will take place, while the front tables already contain some preliminary setup for the over-the-top plateaus the mongers will soon be crafting. The competitors' names and home countries are clearly visible on banners hung over the edge of each front table. Lest anyone have trouble reading them, a giant screen in the center of the curtains, flanked by thin scaffolding towers of flood lights, is set up to broadcast the event.

Rory and Jordan quickly find their stations and do some last-minute prep for their plateaus, awaiting the official start of the event: a written test.

"What cheese are you doing your oral on, Jordan?" Andy Moulton asks from one station over, gently lacing purple flowers through a triptych of wooden fences.

"Marcel Petite Comté, baby. What about you?"

Andy walks over holding a knife and a lactic slab of ghostly white paste with a Manchego arrowhead rind. It's a sheep cheese called Zacharie Cloutier from his native Toronto. Nick and Rory notice this exchange and wander over right as Adam and I do too, like we've all heard a dog whistle. Rory brings with him a piece of the cheese he's presenting, Old Goat from Twig Farm in Vermont, whose rind has the color and dexterity of the lunar surface.

Andy and Rory proudly distribute thin slices to everyone in the semicircle on this game show set. Nick brings over his cheese too, the beloved British farmhouse cheddar Kirkham's Lancashire, and even though everyone here is already familiar with it, we all accept slices anyway because it's very tasty.

Rory's cheese lives up to the name Old Goat only too well, while Andy's has a sumptuous mix of flavors, like salty lamb chops cooked in brown butter and plums. It's fucking amazing.

"That's the truth!" Jordan says, pointing at Andy's cheese.

Adam and I nod as I strategize how I will steal a piece of this cheese from Andy to bring back to Gabi, my salty queen. I can see the gears grinding in Adam's head too, calculating the potential for importing Zacharie Cloutier into America. No matter what else is going on, he remains ever on the hunt for the next hit.

Rory asks to examine the bigger piece, and Andy happily hands it over.

"I've never had this before," Rory says, turning it over in his hands with scientific curiosity.

"I have," Nick says.

"Not at this age," Andy says. "This wheel's super killer. It's eighteen months. They usually sell at six, but I hit up the maker and she sent me this."

Nick's face betrays a minor tremor, as though he didn't realize he was even allowed to present a rare cheese. Still, he compliments Andy's find and everyone drifts back to their workstations.

There is hardly a crowd to speak of when the competition kicks off a half-hour later with the written portion, but one dedicated group has taped a Japanese flag to the bars at the front of the bleachers in a show of support. After Rodolphe Le Meunier wishes the contestants good luck, the DJ cranks up AC/DC's "Thunderstruck" to pump up monger adrenaline, and we are rolling.

The written test is followed by a blind tasting. Judges in gray chef's jackets drop off bento boxes with four rindless rectangles at each workstation. Without rinds, which offer huge clues to a cheese's provenance, the mongers can only assess based on texture, taste, aroma, and some undefinable sixth monger sense. On the big screen, Rory breaks a piece in half, sniffs it, and chews, tilting his head thoughtfully as if listening to a seashell for sounds of the ocean.

"That's Catherine Fogel," Adam says, nudging me and pointing toward a stout, clipboard-toting judge in a flowy white blouse. "She's the toughest judge in the game."

Fogel is giving Nick the hairy eyeball as he prods a piece of cheese with his finger. The other judges are also closely observing, just in case one of the mongers has invented and snuck in an app that can digitally taste and identify cheese like Shazam.

There's a brief break between the cut test, which follows the blind tasting and the oral presentation, so Adam and I head backstage where he can pep talk Team USA.

"We gotta talk about that taste test," Jordan says as soon as almost everyone is in the greenroom, which is just four prefab walls around one of the warehouse's docking ports. "Number one was Taleggio, right?"

"Without a doubt, Taleggio," Cesar says. "That one was a gimme."

"Not Taleggio," Evert the Dutchman says, rifling through a blue cooler of bottled waters and juice. "Quadrello di Bufala."

Everyone contemplates the possibility for a moment, and then Rodolphe Le Meunier glides into the room with the kind of pumped enthusiasm that can only be expressed via air guitar, which he strums once he reaches the head of the table.

"Don't worry, I am more stressed than you," he says, picking up on the energy in the room.

With his million-dollar smile, Le Meunier doesn't look very stressed, especially next to Nick, who is pretty sure he accidentally sliced his cut-test cheese in quarter-pounds instead of quarter-kilos and now looks as though he's just seen a ghost and that ghost was himself.

Rodolphe runs down the order for the oral presentations, which are about to begin, and glides back out of the room. As all the mongers start looking at their phones or handwritten notes, mouthing the speeches they've prepared, Adam and I leave them to their studies.

"Moo baa maa," Adam says on the way out.

"Moo baa maa, brother," Jordan says back.

No matter how much they've prepared, I doubt any of the first-timers are truly ready for the oral presentation. When it's Rory's turn, he stands facing a firing squad of judges right in front of him, the newly filled-out audience in the bleachers beyond, and those watching the telecast from home. He looks like a witness about to be interrogated in a high-profile murder trial.

"Trois, deux, un," Le Meunier says and Rory begins. He leads the judges on a poetic expedition through the area in Vermont where the Twig Farm's cheesemaker practices his craft.

"Here, on the legendary pastures, wetlands and wild fruit trees, simplicity takes priority over novelty, and the cheesemaker stands on the shoulders of giants in European tradition," he says.

Rory is using the same skills he regularly puts to work creating sensory programs and marketing materials for cheesemakers. Part of his job is teaching clients to tout their cheese as a taste of place, a culinary translation of geographical character and identity. The client he's representing now, though, isn't Twig Farm: it's America. Rory is making the case for American artisanship to a panel of international judges, in flattering language they can't misinterpret or dismiss out of hand. Their response, for the moment at least, is inscrutable.

"I'm worried about Jordan," Adam says, when Jordan appears in the wings before his turn. "I think the face tattoos may be a problem."

It is far too late to start considering if this is a problem.

Jordan comes in a little too hot, his words jumbling together, but finds his rhythm soon enough. He has cleverly divided the different "parts" of the Marcel Petite Comté into the parts that comprise beef—the nose, the middle, and the heel—and he's prepared samples of all three.

"Each part can stand on its own, but they're all parts of something bigger than themselves," Jordan says. He then invites the judges to start with the nose, the piece representing the part of the cheese furthest from the rind.

There's a problem, though. Fogel refuses to accept any cheese directly from Jordan, instead signaling some unseen figure off set to bring her the mother wedge. The other judges follow suit and wait as well, lest they ingest whatever has spooked Fogel.

Jordan valiantly gets through the rest of his speech, while the whole squadron of judges takes turns sniffing his cheese wedge. A cameraman locks in and captures it all at close range, so the entire spectacle plays out on the big screen. Fogel seems to suspect that Jordan smuggled his cheese into France inside a suitcase, rather than what really happened, which is that he visited a shop in Paris whose owner let him inspect all the Marcel Petite wheels in their cellar before selecting his favorite.

"That was rough," Adam pronounces when it's over.

As the sun finally makes its presence fully felt in the inadequately air-conditioned warehouse at noon, and the crowd expands substantially, the main portion of the competition begins. The DJ plays "Thunderstruck" again and nobody at all seems pumped this time.

Over the next four hours, the mongers will have to prepare the following: a cheese plate comprised of five unknown cheeses, six identical dishes that utilize Gruyère in just about any fashion, a creative cold dish involving Époisses—although in current conditions, no plate of cheese in this warehouse could be considered "cold," which certainly does not bode well for how things are going to smell in here shortly—along with a giant cheese plateau on the theme of the "Originality of the Cheesemonger," and finally a sculpture that demonstrates both cutting skills and general cheese ingenuity. The judges will rate each element up to two hundred points by some byzantine rubric that includes categories like "quality organoleptic wedding." Afterward, presumably, everyone will collapse on the floor in a deep, dreamless slumber for a couple of days.

"They come here with their own culture, their own approach to the cheese, their own recipe," the announcer says, dreamily. "It's like we're visiting eleven different kitchens in eleven different restaurants in nine different countries."

A half hour into the cheese-construction, Cristi from Spring Brook Farm arrives. It already feels like weeks have passed since we met in a Paris cheese cave, but it has only been two days.

"What did I miss?" she asks, grabbing a spot on the fast-filling bleachers.

I give her a rundown of the events so far, filling her in on the main cheeses the mongers will have to use in their preparations.

"It's a miracle the entire place doesn't stink of Époisses in this heat," I add.

"Give it time," she says.

The mongers are subject to constant video scrutiny, the footage on the big screen forever flitting from one of them to another. Since each has their own internal schedule for getting everything done within four hours, they're all working on different things at all times. Cesar is mushing up what looks suspiciously like tuna in a cup for one of his dishes while Aurore from Australia uses a pen knife to carve a kangaroo into the paste of a hard cheese for her sculpture. Each time I look at the rubble on any given mon-ger's display table, their plateau has taken slightly more shape.

Everyone has interpreted the theme, the "Originality of the Cheesemonger," in different ways on their plateaus, and loosely at that. Tomoko Kasseki from Japan is lining up thick-cut Gruyère slices like a phone's reception bars across a plexiglass terrarium. Nick Bayne has laid out elements of an English garden, like card-board plant pots and a bright blue watering can, with wedges of cheese everywhere, including one hiding in a teacup. Rory has a mysterious, elegant setup—a gold chandelier dripping with fake diamonds, stacks of cheese rounds sitting on a red velvet cloth. It's all meant to evoke Salvador Dalí, in a way that only fully becomes clear when he hangs up a clipboard that reads, "What would Dalí do?" Jordan, meanwhile, has put together glass trays full of empty Pabst Blue Ribbon beer cans and a cactus pierced by metal, thorn-like prongs with tiny plastic skulls at the ends. I don't hold out hope it will make more sense when it's finished, but no one could rightly say his display *doesn't* express the originality of the cheesemonger.

The heat has now become a full-on problem. It's so hot, my eyelids are sweating. Everyone in the audience uses complimentary copies of *Profession Fromager* magazine to fan themselves, while the competitors quietly suffer under the blazing studio lights. Nick ducks down and sticks his head into the fridge at one point, pretending to look for something but staying down there for way too long. Rory discreetly wipes his face while cleaning his sta-tion and a nearby judge glares at him. Jordan hits a breaking point and makes a run for the bathroom, only to be blocked by a judge. Jordan manages to out-juke him, though, and disappears through the black curtain, returning minutes later with a wet towel wrapped around his scalp like a sushi headband.

The judges come by at odd intervals and whisk away completed dishes made of Gruyère or Époisses. Jordan had made a Gruyère pad thai dish at CMI once that was well received—a balanced flavor that was also cheese-forward—so his Gruyère dish is similarly Southeast Asian–influenced, with green curry and coconut sitting over herbs. Rory meanwhile is finishing up making a walnut-phyllo faux-bird's nest with a quenelle egg of Époisses—complete with orange rind "yolk"—atop a mustardy frisée salad. The closest I get to these dishes is the giant TV broadcasting close-ups, but I can practically taste them through the screen.

When AC/DC's "Thunderstruck" plays for the fifth time, Adam's face falls into his hands.

"I gotta do something about this," he says, bolting up and stalking off toward the DJ booth.

He can't help himself. It's not just that he hates hearing this song again, or that he knows he'd make better choices than the closed loop of loungey French covers of Metallica and Tears for Fears we've been cycling through—although he *does* know that—it's the lack of curation. The idea that the cheese spectators in the stands could be having a slightly better time but aren't being properly looked after. It grates on him. After a brief exchange with the DJ, Adam eases into the booth, headphones on, spinning chill French dream pop. He looks more comfortable in that booth than I've seen him look at any point on this trip. Although he's wearing a suit instead of a cow costume, he seems to have slipped back a little into his usual Mr. Moo mode from CMI. Pretty soon, he grabs a microphone from the booth and goes all the way.

"Is this possible?" he says, causing all the mongers who know him to look over. "Mongers: when I say Moo Baa Maa, you say Moo Baa Maa."

All the competitors shout Adam's barnyard chant back at him all three times he leads them in it, even the ones who don't speak English.

"Merci beaucoup," he says afterward.

When he starts interviewing contestants at their stations, though, he's apparently breached some unspoken rule of decorum and one of Le Meunier's minions signals him to stop. Adam reluctantly relinquishes the mic, along with his DJ-ing duties, and goes back to the stands.

Inevitably, the heat has overpowered the cheese displays as we come to the end of the fourth and final hour, unleashing their full aromatic fury. The smell of chocolate, cold cuts, and elderly testicles vie for dominance as the clock counts down the dwindling seconds.

Then it's over.

All the mongers finally take a breather. One by one, they look around and admire each other's work, each plateau a cheese wonderland in miniature. If the displays at CMI had a playful science fair flair, many of these tableaux looked like professional architecture, the kind of constructions that require blueprints. There were Gruyère dollhouses, cheddar castles, stairways of Comté, and crinkle-cut Mimolette tree-forts. There was Japanese minimalism, French elegance, and American entropy. Mondial du Fromage promised a world of cheese and the mongers had delivered.

The heat wreaked havoc on many of the plateaus, but it had inadvertently added extra flair to Rory's Salvador Dalí offering. A bloomy rind had ruptured and exhaled its entire gooey contents down a plastic staircase, like the melting clocks in the artist's most famous work.

Rory continued the art theme beyond the Dalí tribute with his sculpture portion, carving a piece of Gruyère so the rind formed a small frame for a "painting" of a piece of cheese against the bright yellow background of Gruyère paste. It was a tribute to René Magritte's "This is a Piece of Cheese," a painting of, yes, a piece of cheese, stored in a museum under a glass serving dome.

It was a sly tribute to cheese as its own form of art. However, there was one plateau that expressed Rory's message even more concisely.

Evert, who finishes an hour before everyone else, has made both a work of art, and a commentary on cheese as art. His pièce de résistance is a backlit matte-black painting frame, with an elegant, three-dimensional abundance of mostly French cheese bursting through. The frame simply cannot contain it. Cheese is meant to be eaten, not merely admired, so Evert's spills out of the painting and into reality, a Neufchâtel heart appearing to knock over a nearby wineglass in the process. It's simple but brilliant, and with a message that resonates.

Evert is the winner of Mondial du Fromage, with the French monger Virginie Dubois-Dhorne and Japan's Hiroko Suzuki taking second and third place. Later on, Rodolphe reveals that Rory came in fourth and Jordan sixth. So close, yet so far away.

As we're loading up the car to leave, Nathalie Vanhaver, the Belgian judge who won two years ago, stops by with her husband.

"You going to the reception?" Adam asks her.

"Fuck reception."

Everyone agrees there's no reason to spend more time today doing anything even remotely associated with cheese.

"It's a pity you didn't get to explain your plateau," Nathalie says to Rory. "It was beautiful, but nobody understands."

Rory leans against Adam's car in silent disbelief as she walks away.

"Salvador Dalí is the most European thing I can think of," he says a moment later, eyes agog.

On the gloomy ride back to the château Adam rented out for the trip, I think a lot about just what had happened today. Rory had demonstrated the similarities between American and French cheeses, our shared respect for age-old tradition and the mutual feeling of connection to the land. Jordan had brought the rebellious spirit of artisans experimenting in a country that didn't see tradition as immutable law. They were two sides of the same coin, the duality of American cheese embodied. Whether either of them came back next time and won, it was maybe enough for now that they had been here at all.

At the airport the following day, I am forced to dump out the ice packs cooling all the cheese I'm bringing home. Apparently, ice packs can only be used for medicine and the authorities have determined that cheese is not medicine. (Have they even *tried* cheese?) Hopefully, all the air flowing against the fuselage will keep my lactic bounty cool in the overhead bin.

As I wait online, I prepare to follow the advice everyone has given me about returning to the United States, and declare my cheese at customs. I think about everything else I would like to declare, too: that I secretly prefer predictable grocery store Camembert to nearly extinct farmhouse Camembert de Normandie; that just because the same traditions have kept certain cheeses alive for centuries doesn't mean they can't be updated with the times; that slavish devotion to the past can't dam the raging wa-

ters of the future; that establishing America's cheesemaking abilities over the past two hundred years should be at least somewhat
as impressive as the French preserving those abilities for the two
thousand previous years; that American cheese cannot and will
not remain underrated forever.

Instead, when I get up to the customs agent, I simply declare
that I have cheese in my bag.

"Is it for me?" she asks, raising an eyebrow.

"Uh, no."

"Then why do I care?"

With that, I sling the bag of temporary souvenirs over my
shoulder and head home.

CHAPTER ELEVEN

The Cheese Oscars

IT'S THE WORST DAY OF THE YEAR. SAMANTHA GENKE HAS TO DECIDE which of her babies is her favorite.

The cheesemaker from Boxcarr Handmade sits in her North Carolina creamery with her brother, Austin, and the rest of their team, surrounded by samples of all their work: runny Robiola and creamy Cottonbell filling the room with their fragrances. Everyone takes bites from several batches and talks about flavor, texture, which cheeses might travel best, and all the barely perceptible elements that make one batch better than its nearly identical twin. Finally, they decide on which pieces they'll submit to the American Cheese Society's annual conference and competition, and Samantha goes home to pour herself a big glass of wine.

All around the country, artisanal cheesemakers at every scale are performing a version of this same ritual, the larger ones choosing from a far bigger pool of product and the smaller ones training apprentices to hold down the vat for a few days while they pry themselves away.

The ACS conference is the biggest week of the year in American cheese. It's when makers, mongers, distributors, farmers, shop owners, dairy scientists, food writers, marketers, and random cheese obsessives all collide for a week of workshops, parties, tastings, dealmaking, and maybe passing the CCP or T.A.S.T.E. exam, all the way through to Saturday morning's Butter Brunch and the curtain-closing Festival of Cheese. It's like simultaneously experiencing all of high school at once: classes, hallway gossip, prom, SATs, a job fair, and the ten-year reunion. Not to mention, of course, that there's also an awards show: the Oscars of cheese.

ACS is held in a different city each year, and this time it's Richmond, Virginia: beloved birthplace, I'm pretty sure, of race cars and cigarettes. I fly in on Monday to observe the judges at work on Tuesday, but the Greater Richmond Convention Center has been abuzz with cheese activity since receiving day late last week. That's when all those mightily fussed-over, hopefully unbruised competitive wheels begin arriving, and the great sorting of 2019 gets underway. Dozens of volunteers have to organize twenty thousand pounds of cheese on hundreds of racks, assigning each cheese a code to ensure anonymity in the judging, before a designated "cooler captain" escorts the cheese into one of five massive refrigerated trailer trucks to keep it chilled. Considering that there are more than two thousand cheeses, butters, and yogurts in contention for 127 award subcategories, this part of the competition is like a clerical Olympics in its own right.

Different cheeses need different amounts of time to reach room temperature, so the volunteers follow an algorithmically determined schedule for precisely when to haul each one out of the truck to get it to the judging area in optimal condition. If a fresh mozzarella and an aged cheddar came out at the same time to go to the same judge's table, for instance, it could be catastrophic.

The first thing I notice upon entering the judging room in the convention center is that it's frigid, in stark contrast to the late-summer Virginia heat. This is by necessity, since the optimal condition for eating most competition cheese, but not all of it, is "unmelted." The judges sit in groups of two, both wearing lab coats, which look cozy in the cold. Next to each table is a metal rack holding heaps of cheeses in plastic-covered squares, balls, mounds, lumps, and wheels on top of wax-papered trays. High above the racks, the ACS planners have brought in chrome towers with bonus floodlights aimed directly down at each judging table to eliminate any chance of shadow on the cheese. No blemish or flavor crystal will go overlooked.

The ACS relies on a buddy cop comedy–style teaming of technical judges with aesthetic judges—an erudite egghead to dress down a cheese for its defects (the bad cop), and a cheese-slinger with street smarts to size up its desirable attributes (the good cop). All that's missing is a poster of the pair standing back-to-back, each casting a thumb at the other like, "You mean I gotta work with *this* guy?" It's instantly obvious in each pairing who is the aesthetic judge and who is the technical one. Anyone with silver hair and a flinty stare who looks like they may have *PhD* in their name is always the technical judge. The guy with the ponytail or the woman with pigtails is always the aesthetic. Luis and Carlos certainly fit this mold.

Luis Jiménez-Maroto is a food scientist at the University of Wisconsin–Madison, whom I recognize from my visit to the Center for Dairy Research. Carlos Souffront is a longtime monger and current wholesaler who deejays on the side in San Francisco. (You can and should check out his SoundCloud.) Luis has jet-black hair and a chin-strap beard; Carlos has a two-inch flattop, a tight fade, and a muscular mustache. Guess which judge is which.

Like everyone else, Carlos and Luis' table is entirely covered with knives, cheese, and shuffled papers, which Carlos pushes out of the way to make room for the next specimen.

The cheese comes with no designation beyond its category, in this case Asiago. Each judge picks up their respective wheels and examines them, like children trying to decipher a wrapped Christmas present. They've already formed expectations based on appearance and their years of personal experience with Asiago.

They know it's going to smell briny, so they take bunny sniffs and big fat whiffs to confirm.

Check.

They also know the taste is going to smack of electro-shock acidity, so they take a bite . . . and share a confused look.

The judges are generally discouraged from talking, although many of them do carry on sotto voce conversations during the seven to ten minutes allotted for each sample.

"This doesn't really have the characteristics of an Asiago," Luis says in a sprightly midwestern accent. "Even if it was young, you'd expect some *lipase* activity going on. This one has none. But it's a pretty good cheese."

Carlos nods as he chews.

"It's moreish and delicious," he says with some bass in his voice, pausing to swallow. "Actually, I think that's the only cheese today I didn't spit out."

In most situations, adults only tend to spit out food if it's revolting. When judging forty-eight cheeses per day for a competition, though, spitting out one's food is just self-care. There are only so many pieces of cheese the average person can consume in a row before getting too full to go on. The alternative is to chew each cheese just enough to capture its essence before ejecting the expectorated remains into a Kentucky Fried Chicken–sized white spit bucket. Wine judges tend to do the same thing when tasting, but the process is much easier on the eyes. The discreet spritz-stream of gently used wine into a spittoon is the height of elegance compared with the slovenly plop of a cheese judge's bucket-spew. Sometimes it looks like a Roman vomitorium in this room.

The other danger for a judge, besides getting too full, is flavor fatigue. Constant cheese weakens the ability to distinguish nuances, so judges need the occasional palate cleanser to reset their taste buds. In the back of the room, there's a table full of well-known flavor-rejuvenators: cantaloupe and honeydew, crackers and ranch dip, all sorts of crudités. Some judges chomp on bread in between cheeses to sop the butterfat off their tongue and teeth, while others chew pineapple in an effort to erase the taste-memory of a strong flavor. (It doesn't always work.)

Luis struggles with finding a constructive way to let the cheesemaker know he or she has made a fine product that has been entered in the wrong category. As bad cop, he starts each cheese with a perfect score of fifty, deducting points in different sections for each defect. Good cop Carlos has the opposite task: starting with zero and assigning points for the cheese's positive qualities. Ultimately, the cheesemaker ends up with a possible hundred points and two separate score sheets that explain how the judges arrived at their numbers. It's the kind of feedback cheesemakers find useful—an anonymous expert assessment. For some of them, the prospect of getting judged this way is far more important than the competition itself.

Sometimes the judges come across cheeses they know well, removing the anonymity part of the equation. While the ACS strives to eliminate bias, prohibiting anyone who has worked directly for a producer from judging, inevitably some judges end up evaluating cheese made by friends. When that happens, any judge with integrity views it as a chance to give their friend the same fearless feedback they'd offer in an email, rather than dap them up with an automatic perfect score. To critique a friend's cheese honestly is an act of love.

While Luis soberly assesses the defects, Carlos gets a little more detailed and flowery in showering praise. Next to the listed descriptions for a washed rind cheese's aroma, he writes *dirty diaper nose on the rind, buttery on the inside,* which is apparently a plus, because he gives the aroma three out of three points. In the *Additional Comments* section for the washed rind, Carlos adds, *perfect cheese for the stinky cheese lover. It's very sexy. Cut in half, hot and baked, topped with a little white wine and breadcrumbs equals date night!*

Once the judges get through all the subcategories, the first-place winners are put in the same room to be evaluated all over again. At that point, each judge individually picks a winner—not necessarily the technical best so much as a personal favorite, the cheese that most sticks in their memory. The head of the judging committee then tabulates all the scores and reveals the Best of Show winner later in the week during the Cheese Oscars.

Every so often, the judges uncover some Holy Shit cheese that seems destined to leapfrog the two thousand other anonymous offerings and enter the running for Best of Show. When that happens, whoever tastes it might gather some nearby judges to bask in its superior flavor.

Of course, sometimes it also goes the other way.

"I've never seen anything like this in a goat cheese before," a judge near the front of the room says, with the excitement of an astronomer discovering a new star. "You've got to taste this."

A small crowd of lab coats forms around a fresh goat cheese that looks perfectly normal but sends convulsions through the faces of all who try it.

"Holy shit, what happened here?" a bad cop says.

"It tastes like rotten old mutton," a good cop responds.

After briefly talking through the possibilities, they reach a consensus. Some auto-oxidation occurred during pasteurization, probably followed by some unknowable outside stressor. It's a domino effect that leaves the cheese the worse for wear as it ages. One can only imagine what this wretched fresh cheese would've become if allowed to flourish into its final form. Days later, there will be whispers of a cheese nicknamed The Squid because its mold had become liquefied and squirted out in a most unfortunate geyser. For now, though, this ungodly goat cheese is the unofficial Worst of Show at ACS. And anyone who understands and appreciates the full spectrum of cheeses is just about as interested to taste this one as they are the eventual winner.

IT'S EARLY ON Wednesday morning, but the convention center is already at full-tilt boogie. The lines at the multiple registration booths look like graphic equalizers at a constant thrum. Just beyond them, a trade show is underway that will last the entirety of the conference. The screech of friends ecstatically greeting each other melds with the muted murmur of impromptu business meetings near cardboard cutouts boasting DualTemp Clauger industrial refrigeration and hygienic air control. Everywhere I go, cheese people from the past year appear like *Star Wars* Force ghosts. There's Andy Hatch taking Advil for an earache. There's Madame Fromage at the booth where her friend Mike Geno is showing his cheese paintings, the ones ACS commissioned him to paint of last year's top three winning cheeses. There's Doug Jacknick, Adam's point man at Columbia Cheese, handing me wrapped samples of some new Spanish product from Quesería Cultivo out of a fully stocked cooler he's dragging along. Nobody can seem to get very far in the fish tank flow of familiar faces without giving a dozen hugs and getting into a thousand conversations, identical giddy gridlocks at every turn; Amish beards are indistinguishable from hipster beards, and *Kate Plus 8* haircuts blur with the Megan Rapinoe ones. At no point during the next few days does the excitement level ever dip below a seven.

Some of the excitement today, however, is pure nerves. More than a hundred people are about to take either the Certified Cheese Professional exam or the T.A.S.T.E. test. The first one measures a monger's knowledge, establishing a base familiarity with regulations, pairing, production, and affinage—basically, every aspect of the industry. This is the test the Whole Foods mongers I met in Wisconsin a couple of months ago were studying to take. Last year, the ACS also implemented its second level of certification, the T.A.S.T.E. test. It's a way for CCPs to quantify their sensory skills and prove to prospective employers that they can run a research and development tasting for a creamery or source cheese for an importer—mostly by spotting defects.

This exam is also apparently a way for one cheese enthusiast writer to gauge how much he's learned about cheese in the process of gaining over twenty pounds in a calendar year.

On my way up to the conference room where the T.A.S.T.E.

test will be held, I pass a woman with a blonde pixie cut maniacally running up and down the stairs. Having exorcised her jitter demons, she soon joins me and the other test-takers.

Behind all the desks, in the back of the room, a squad of volunteers in blue *Virginia is for Cheese Lovers* shirts stands in front of a table with about a dozen defective cheeses. Over the next four hours, they will be handing us samples so we can decipher each specific problem. That's right, we'd be eating bad cheese on purpose. Like lunatics.

To prepare for the test, I'd perused the official ACS lexicon and become familiar with many of the ways that cheeses can go foul. I'd also visited Murray's one day and asked whether any cheeses had gone off recently. The monger on duty smiled cordially and disappeared, returning a moment later with an ammoniated bombshell of thermonuclear cat piss.

"Enjoy!" she said and did a little curtsy.

I most certainly did not enjoy. In fact, I couldn't even bring myself to taste it. Why bother? I already knew its defect. (A terminal case of being "the Devil's cheese.")

Before getting to the tasting portion of the T.A.S.T.E. test, we must first partake in an olfactory workout. A monochrome rainbow of plastic ramekins runs across each desk, filled with cow's milk of varying viscosity and brightness. Each of them, labeled A to J, has been spiked with a single substance we have to uncover through smelling, and smelling only. (DO NOT TASTE is stamped in red cautionary letters across the lime-green score sheet.) The milk looks fairly harmless, if a little yogurt-like in parts, but who knows what nostril-assaulting evil lurks within.

The clock strikes noon to the pop of fifty plastic ramekins opening and we are off to the races.

My instant thought on sample A is vinegar. I look at the list of additives, though, and vinegar isn't there. Shit. Stewed cabbage jumps out as a possibility. I open and close the lid a few more times, as though maybe that will jog my brain. All it does is make my nostrils feel inflamed. Stewed cabbage it is.

Sample B just smells putrid, so of course it's the one I spill all over the tablecloth and also my hand. Amazingly, *putrid* is one of the listed options, but so is *rancid*.

Which horrible thing is it?

It seems to me that if you're ever in a situation where you have to know for sure whether a cheese is specifically putrid or rancid, your only concern should be burning it all down.

I pick up the next cup warily and, praise be, it smells like toasty, unmistakable hazelnut. Under the circumstances, this counts as going on vacation.

There's a Windex-y scent in the subsequent cup that I know must be ammonia, followed by ramekins that smell like horseradish, caramel, and something I can only describe as "under Band-Aid," although that's not on the list. I get stuck on a scent so subtle I can barely tell whether anything has been added at all. Maybe scanning some deep cuts from the listed options will help. Does this smell *catty*? Is it *sweaty*? Oh God, did they put human sweat in there? Or *cat sweat*?! How is that even possible?

I hit a wall of frustration and nasal distress after a while and head to the palate-cleansing station to the left of the long defective cheese table. A deep whiff from a ramekin of coffee beans hits me like a mochaccino sledgehammer to the face, a hard reset.

I'm ready to power through the rest of the aromas.

We've been going nearly ninety minutes when I finish the first part of the test. Now it's time to taste the mutant cheeses.

I have a number two pencil, a spit bucket, and a bunch of paper plates. Let's do this.

Here's how this test works: We pick up a piece of mystery cheese from the volunteers at the back table and bring it over to our desks for evaluation. Upon request, the volunteers will gladly hold up and display the wheel the piece came from like an auctioneer's assistant, so we can get a better look at the rind or larger surface areas. The level of assessment here is much more expansive than the milk test. Each cheese has its own score sheet, with four categories of defects—*Appearance, Aroma, Texture,* and *Flavor*—but different sets of descriptions. Unlike the milk test, we can check off as many words from each list that fit whatever nightmare we're experiencing.

The first thing to evaluate is appearance. Does the cheese have *rind rot*? A *rough surface*? *Immature mold*? Sounds like kind of a bad boy. Maybe I can change him.

Next is aroma. The list includes attributes like *buttery, herbal,* and *pleasantly fruity*; options for defects are *ammoniated, atypical,* and *barnyard*. How is "barnyard" a defect if so many people love a goaty stinker? They probably just mean for us to check off that word when it's a cheese that isn't supposed to taste barnyardy. The unexpected barnyard. A barnyard ambush.

The list for texture includes defects like *gummy, uneven ripening,* and *corky*, which apparently is when the cheese is too firm.

Finally, there's flavor, which promises to be a real roller coaster. We'll either ascend to the island paradise of *toasted/caramel, citrus note,* and *tangy finish*, or be cast down into a flaming pit of *whey taint, old milk,* and *unclean*.

The first cheese is from the category of *fresh, unripened*. It's smooth and creamy—possibly a mascarpone—and doesn't appear defective in any way. I leave the *Appearance* section on my Scantron empty. Aroma is milky and promising, so nothing doing there either. Texture is a bit gummy, so I check that off. The taste is kind of flat. Lo and behold, *flat/lacks characteristic flavor* is an option. Okay, one down! Perhaps my spit bucket would end up being merely decorative.

Next up is *Emmental-style with eye formation*, or what I used to refer to as Swiss cheese. It looks like melted plastic at the bottom. A definite defect. Is it *mottled*? *Seamy*? Does it have *dead/dull eyes*? I check the first two. The smell is nutty as all get out, as if someone cracked open an almond-nitrate popper directly beneath my nostrils. *Maybe this one only has appearance issues*, I think for one fleeting moment, before tasting it and seething at the sad naïveté of "two seconds ago me." It tastes like sulfur that, itself, has somehow gone off. Like deviled eggs that have sat in the sun too long before falling into a jar of year-old mayonnaise. Ahoy, spit bucket!

I feel like we should all be screaming. Instead, it's dead-quiet. Someone sneezes and it's an event. Reluctantly, I turn my dead/dull eyes to the next cheese and crack on.

By the time I go back to the table for my last piece of cheese, I am worn down and weary. I've tasted things no man or beast should. Weaving through the other test-takers doing "the Thinker" pose while staring at the wheel of ungodly cheddar a volunteer is holding up, I arrive at the washed rind. As soon as I see the moist, spray-tanned, pug forehead–like, gefilte fish juice–covered crime scene, I want to mark off *apocalypse* in the *Appearance* section of the Scantron, even though that's not an option.

"Hit me," I say to the volunteer.

This cheese looks so bad, I'm shocked it only smells the regular amount of cow patty *à la* jock strap. When I taste it, I'm so relieved I don't keel over and die right away, I underestimate what's coming. This one is a grower. It performs a glorious diarrhetic pirouette on my tongue, and then I wash it away with a slice of pineapple and get the hell out of there. It's over.

Down the hall, in a grand ballroom, there's a post-test reception with an overflowing buffet. It's the first unlimited cheese event of the week. Even the guacamole has cheese in it, which I'm not sure is even legal, mold glinting in the goop-like emeralds.

I put some on my plate in case it's secretly great. (It is.) Every wheel of cheese, though, looks untrustworthy after what I've just been through. Any one of them could be an imposter.

AT NIGHT, THE cheese freaks take to the streets.

There are suggested icebreaking events like the Cheese Crawl, a tour of taverns where local producers sample out their cheeses to ACS guests. All the bars fill up with mongers double-fisting drinks to decompress. They've finally taken the CCP exam. They can feel the memorized percentage points of certain dairy temperatures draining from their brains like whey out of the vat.

Everywhere, people are catching up after brief hallway encounters earlier in the day or week.

How are things?

You know: busy, cheesy.

Nobody seems to be speculating about who will triumph at the awards show later in the week. There's no conjecture about whether this year's batch of Pleasant Ridge has what it takes to win Best of Show for the fourth time. Cheeses tend not to have Oscar buzz. What people do seem to be talking about is the impending tariffs on imported cheeses, a subject that has only heated up in the almost two months since I first heard Adam Moskowitz mention it in France. It remains both a hot topic throughout the week, the subject of circulated petitions, and something people are actively avoiding.

Things get a little rowdier at Midnight Mongers, the annual cheese-themed karaoke outing.

Now, when you hear "cheese-themed karaoke," it probably sounds like a light lift. With just a tiny adjustment, that Ashlee Simpson song becomes "Pieces of Brie" and Marky Mark is singing about "Gouda Vibrations." But nobody here would dare. That's for amateurs. These mongers take their karaoke very seriously and approach it with technical rigor, preparing fully altered lyrics, rather than one tweak of the chorus.

Tom Perry from Shelburne Farms in Vermont goes first, performing Cardi B's "Bodak Yellow," as it's never been heard before.

Said little calf, you can't suckle me
If you wanted to
This expensive, this is grass-fed, this is yummy juice

He's reading lyrics off his phone, and he's just miles behind the beat, but the words I can make out over the sound of cheese people cheering are pretty clever.

Another monger named Tina Mooney does "Your Own Personal Cheesuz" by Depeche Mode, a three-by-three grid of TVs just behind her tuned into SportsCenter.

The main event, though, is when Julia Gross, a Joan Jett acolyte in a short skirt and studded leather belt, rounds up a group of her fellow cheeseheads and launches into N.W.A.'s "Fuck tha Police," remixed as "We Got the Cheese." She clutches her mic and screams her lyrics with undeniable stage presence. Tomorrow, Julia will lead a session called "Why Is This Cheese So Expensive?"

which she bills as "an Eva Perón–like rant about class warfare in cheese." For now, though, she is a karaoke queen.

Every night of the week, people splinter off into groups and explore the further reaches of Richmond, past the historic Carpenter Theater, which looks like a nuclear-powered church, and over to GWARbar, where fake blood splatters the floor and you can order the Baconecutioner; you can go down the rabbit hole at an *Alice in Wonderland*–themed pop-up bar, with its felt-topped toadstools beneath a deranged Cheshire cat exhaling dragon-plumes of hookah smoke in a mural. Getting swept up into one of these outings, you might meet your new best cheese friend or someone to share your hotel bed with or even your next employer. The lifehack for clout-sharks trying to see and be seen, though, is to stake out a prominent perch each night at the Marriott lobby bar, the low-key epicenter of conference schmoozing, where the biggest names in American cheese eventually breeze through for some unwinding. Catch them at the right time and they might invite you to dinner with a formidable group of makers and distributors and who knows who else, wedging open the door to so many social and career possibilities.

The morning sessions become more poorly populated throughout the week as people wake up increasingly hungover. This is, after all, a working vacation for a lot of people. Some of the four hundred or so volunteers—offering their services in three- to eight-hour shifts at a time in exchange for getting to attend the convention for free—always seem to be up early in their blue T-shirts, pushing racks full of wrapped cheese down yet another hallway.

One session I attend on Friday morning, the day of the award show, calls into question how I've tasted every piece of cheese I've ever had.

Russell Smith is an Australian sensory expert and a veteran cheese judge. At some point in his twenty-five years of flying around the world for competitions, he noticed all the judges were saying different things about the same cheeses. These weren't just subtle differences either, like whether a cheese tasted of pink salt or sea salt, but rather differences like whether it tasted salty or not salty. Russell realized that most people, even cheese experts, have different thresholds for detecting certain tastes. He disappeared down the rabbit hole of flavor science for a while and emerged with a surefire way to prove it.

"How Sweet Are You?" is the workshop Russell uses to teach cheese judges the inner workings of their own taste buds. He also teaches it to random conferencegoers at ACS each year.

When I walk into the conference room, a man with a sheep's wool mane and caterpillar eyebrows is standing in front of a flip board that lists alphanumeric combinations, as if keeping track of a game of Battleship. On the other side of the room is a table full of red Solo cups, like the world's sloppiest game of beer pong. It is entirely unclear what is about to happen.

"We're here bright and early," Russell says in his Michael Caine brogue, "because your palate gets fatigued throughout the day and it's better to start fresh."

One of the central tenets of the workshop is that the modern world is a flavor minefield for the discerning palate. Russell spends several minutes going over just some of the ways our taste buds are constantly under siege from forces attempting to corrupt them into dullness.

"Every cigarette kills your palate for forty-five minutes," he says. "I've eaten at restaurants before and could tell just from taste that there were too many smokers in the kitchen, and they were over-seasoning everything."

It's not just smoking or prolonged exposure to daylight that threatens palate purity, though; there's also just the general curse of living in the United States, the sweetest place on earth, where everything from bread to yogurt is generously blessed with sugar. Americans are so weaned on corn syrup—from the moment we get our first fix in the flavor compounds of mother's amniotic fluid, according to Russell—that apparently 25 percent of us can't even detect bitterness at all. This is a huge problem for Americans who fancy themselves cheese connoisseurs, and also those of us just trying our best.

"If you find you're really sensitive to bitter compounds, you'll be tasting a cheese really differently than someone who isn't," he says. "It's all about understanding your palate."

Everyone attending "How Sweet Are You?" is about to understand their palates, with extreme prejudice. Russell has placed increasing doses of certain chemical compounds in five rows of water cups, one each for salt, sweet, sour, bitter, and umami. None of the flavors are labeled, though. Instead, each cup has A1, A2, A3, and so forth scrawled on it in Sharpie, with the amount of the unnamed flavor increasing in the cups with higher numbers. As we drink from each one, we have to note at which point in the sequence the flavor registers on our sugar-savaged tongues. The cups are only a quarter full—or three-quarters empty, depending on how sweet you are, emotionally—but there are seven or eight to try for each flavor.

I start running through gauntlets of red Solo cups—

essentially a capsule version of my experience of college, but with water instead of keg beer. It's not until I get to A6 that I realize there is definitely salt in this water. By the time I finally detect the bitterness in E7 a few minutes later, I have never been more well-hydrated in my entire life. It feels like a secret psychological experiment about bladder control, to uncertain ends. Incredibly, nobody excuses themselves to the bathroom for twenty minutes. After the first person goes, though, it's like a dam burst and people keep rushing out and back in for the remainder of the workshop.

"Let's see where everyone is tasting," Russell says once most of us are back at our seats, the courtesy water bottles in front of us now a cruel joke.

He asks for a show of hands to see how many people detected each flavor at which point.

Almost immediately, I start lying. Most people in class detected each flavor by the third or fourth cup while I am stubbornly stuck at the sixth or seventh each time.

Here it was; undeniable proof that all the Tabasco sauce I sloshed on salads and the York Peppermint Pattie flavor bubble gum I chased it with, had taken its toll on my tongue. The way I taste cheese is officially way off from the way most people do; immune to subtlety. If I were a monger, I would have to explain my impairment to customers in the name of full disclosure. *Had I just been subconsciously pretending to taste some of the notes I thought I had in the past year? Or were some of my terroir tour guides just that convincing?*

After spotting defects in cheese earlier this week, I've now spotted one in myself. I'm the unreliable narrator of my own cheese story.

I no longer know anything for sure except that I definitely have to pee again.

WHAT DOES ONE wear to the Oscars of cheese?

For the most part, pretty much whatever they were wearing that day.

The first person I see on my way into the auditorium sets the tone for tonight's award show. It's ZZ Top–bearded Peter Dixon, dressed like a wastrel in north-of-the-knee cargo shirts, a ratty brown T-shirt, and sandals. If I didn't know he was one of the world's most celebrated cheesemakers, I might think he just wandered in off the street. Some people have donned nice dresses and spiffy suits, but Peter Dixon's no-fucks-given approach is de rigueur tonight. The ACS award show is proudly not a black-tie affair.

I've invited myself along with Madame Fromage, and together we circulate among the cheese industry glitterati, hobnobbing near the entrance. Many of the people I've met and spent time with over the past year have popped up over the past few days but now they're all here—in line for the same cash bar.

"This is so exciting!" Tenaya gushes, as we walk past a red-carpet step-and-repeat, where Mario Lopez's cheese world counterpart is conducting interviews.

The audience is fragmented along territorial lines. Representatives from the occupying forces of California, Wisconsin, and Vermont stand sentry among the rows of padded chairs, holding up tiny state flags to guide latecomers. Tenaya and I wander around until we find her people, the Philly crowd.

The Oscars usually start out with a bang, Best Supporting Actor, teasing the false promise of a speedy show, rather than the actual three-hour slog before all the big awards spill out in a thirty-minute sprint to the finish line. I wonder if the ACS awards will be that way, with Best Cheddar right out of the gate, and then wall-to-wall esoteric subcategories of yogurt for hours. Soon, the murmuring drone of conversation tapers off as the competition chair takes the stage and greets the audience. Behind him is a table where others from the committee stand, ready to hand out awards, in front of a wall of heavy curtains.

"Alright, let's get started with the ceremony," the announcer says with little fanfare. "Subcategory RC, in third place: Organic Valley Salted Butter."

Before the eager applause dies down for this very first award, here comes the second-place winner, and then the top spot. The announcer wastes nary a single breath before moving on to the next subcategory (RO: Unsalted Butter with or without cultures made from cow's milk), reading off the award winners like the names of students in an overcrowded graduation ceremony.

It seems I may have taken the whole Cheese Oscars thing a little too literally. There are four hundred awards for all the top-three winners in 127 subcategories. If ACS attempted to stir some "and the nominees are"–style suspense, we'd be here until the Butter Brunch tomorrow morning. Instead, the announcers take turns yelling names as a nonstop onslaught of jubilant winners enter, stage right, to pick up their certificates. People in the audience shake their flags whenever a hometown team wins, and then it's on to the next, again and again.

I struggle to work up much enthusiasm for the winning yogurts and butters, whose names flash by on the big screens on either side of the stage like an exercise in speed-reading. I start to get excited, though, as some cheeses win their categories and become Best of Show finalists. Tarentaise from Spring Brook Farm, the American cheese that surprised everyone in a Paris cheese cave a couple of months ago, wins American Made / International Style, edging out Rupert Reserve from Consider Bardwell, another knockout cheese. Stockinghall Cheddar, a Murray's cheese that frequently appeared on plates when I volunteered at tastings, wins its category, too, and moves on as America's top cheddar. Extra-Aged Pleasant Ridge Reserve wins in its subcategory but doesn't move on to the next round. The further along we go, the more it becomes a nail-biter.

Just when the Oscar comparisons appear to have run their course, the "In Memoriam" segment starts. Photos fly by, commemorating those the cheese world lost this year, alongside bullet points charting a life lived in dairy, all while "In My Life" by the Beatles plays. A lot of people in the audience take this opportunity to mournfully inspect their phones.

It's a rocky transition from somber memorial mode back to the name-yelling again, but the announcers stoically roll with it and, after a stunningly efficient hour and a half altogether, which feels somehow both too long and too short, we arrive at the Best of Show winners.

"This is too much pressure," Madame Fromage says, doing spirit fingers with both hands.

The second runner-up is a brand-new cheese, Aries, made by an outfit called Shooting Star Creamery. People in the rows nearest us are simultaneously clapping and looking around with "what the fuck" faces. Nobody seems to have heard of Shooting Star, the recently launched project from the fifteen-year-old daughter of a married couple who owns California's Central Coast Creamery.

In the number two spot is Professor's Brie, a cheese created by the grocery store chain Wegman's with the help of Old Chatham Creamery. Team Wegman's is positioned near the front of the stage, all shaking the big red Wegman's balloons they've brought for just such an occasion.

Finally, it's time to unveil this year's Best of Show cheese.

"Congratulations, Murray's Stockinghall Cheddar!" the announcer says.

Although the applause that follows is bog-standard enthusiastic for the final award in an awards show, buried within it is an off note of surprise. It wasn't the kind of joyful surprise when an underdog triumphs, like the infamous *Moonlight* fiasco at the Oscars; nor was it the kind of outraged surprise when a deserving contender is robbed, also like the infamous *Moonlight* fiasco. This one was more like when the killer is revealed at the end of a thriller and it's a marginal character whose identity wasn't properly seeded throughout the film. Not only was the winner a cheese most people in the room hadn't tried before—Stockinghall Cheddar is an exclusive at Murray's Manhattan shops and online—but also the victory was a lot to wrap one's head around. It was the first time a collaboration between a creamery and a retail shop had taken Best of Show at ACS, and with a similar team-up claiming the runner-up spot to boot. Murray's has been cave-aging young cheeses since 2011, while Wegman's followed suit in 2014. The idea of cheese shop affinage in America had started with bringing in European cheeses and aging them in caves, until the cheese shops doing so realized they could just find a creamery and *create* cheese that stood up to French standards. Now it had all come to fruition. They had officially imported the European style of affinage and translated it on a mass scale.

They'd Americanized it.

BECAUSE THE ONLY way to cap off a cheese award show is by tasting as many of the winners as possible, the last day of ACS is a Herculean taste-a-thon.

The day begins with the Butter Brunch, where last night's victorious spreadables sit on edible display in a grand banquet hall. Even though I now worry I am unable to taste cheese the same way most other people here do, thanks to my blown-out sugar-junky palate, I'm ready to be dazzled. The boringness of hearing the winning butters announced at an award show is inversely proportional to how much fun it is to taste them. School-bus-yellow domes of cultured butter, ramp-riddled sheep cheese, Bulgarian yogurt from California; they're all here, in overflowing scalloped bowls or condensation-soaked carafes, surrounded by placards noting which awards they've won, along with trays of kaiser rolls and Wheat Thins and other humble Ubers to Flavortown. I try mascarpone that looks like frosting and tastes like fluffy sweet-milk; ivory white goat butter, which has a smooth non-Crisco-y mouthfeel and a low grumble of animal flavor; honey and sea salt fromage blanc, whose pretzel-cheesecake punch nearly makes my knees buckle. My plate is awash with so many blots of white, yellow, pepper-speckled, shiny, thick and gray-salted butters, it's impossible to remember which is which. And what's this? An entire table of stracciatella and crème fraîche that I somehow missed? Almost everybody leaves at the same time, just after my discovery, so I raid the table, abandoning all protocol and just dunking crackers straight into ricotta di bufala, accidentally dipping my messenger bag in a bowl of salty butter in the process, leaving be-hind a greasy permanent reminder of the moment I got a glimpse of an as-yet-unexplored corridor of Dairy Narnia.

The Butter Brunch spread, though, is nothing compared to Saturday night's Festival of Cheese.

This was it: the most primo cheese buffet I'd ever seen. It was the cream of America, the fat of the land, inventively displayed on tables strewn throughout a big sterile room with a high ceiling and shiny marble floor.

"Let's go find the award winners!" Tenaya shouts when we arrive, her gray fanny pack jingling slightly as she speed-walks toward the center of the room.

Her hurry is prescient. Within minutes, the place is jam-packed with cheese-gawkers surrounding every square inch of fermented milk, piling their plates up indiscriminately. Many of the makers who have come by to taste each other's cheeses do an Irish goodbye to avoid high-velocity mingling and fleshy traffic.

Cheese is everywhere, in every style I could ever want and many of which I've never had. Linguini-like mozzarella mini-whips you might serve to some lucky eight-year-olds. A blue with a gorgeous fish-scale rind that I imagine eating on a yacht. A ma-ple brie that looks like it was summoned from the forest floor in a folktale ceremony I want to be a part of. And even though I know I should only save stomach space for heretofore unexplored cheeses, I can't resist taking a piece from a Jenga tower of Taren-taise. I load it all onto my Millennium Falcon–shaped plate, with thumbholes cut out for easy holding, and move along.

"Wanna do blues?" Madame Fromage asks. "Wait, no—cheddar, then blues!"

I look around at everyone in the room and admire what

they've all built together. Snooty connoisseurs could hold their noses up or bury their heads in the sand, but there was no honest way to deny American artisan cheese had come into maturity. Here, among this ridiculous spread, was a trip around the world through the prism of America, where makers had figured out how to faithfully replicate, innovate, and evolve the history of cheese. The ancient traditions had survived and now existed alongside new ones, like dinosaurs and Neanderthals negotiating a truce. And all in the country responsible for inflicting Velveeta upon the rest of the world.

We head to the room where ACS is selling cheese, which has already been strip-mined of award-winners, leaving behind mostly just block cheddar. There's nothing Tenaya or I would feel remiss flying home without, so we head back for a last hurrah at the Festival of Cheese.

Pretty soon, we run into Julia Gross, the heavily tattooed monger who'd rocked it at Midnight Mongers a few nights ago. I mention that our hopes of bringing home any festival favorites had been dashed.

"You know what you do?" she says, and then makes a gesture like she's swiping cheese off of a table. "I mean, wait until the very end—you don't wanna be disrespectful to the makers—but then you go for it. All this stuff is going to the pigs anyway."

I consider walking out with a pocket full of Taleggio and quickly decide against it, even though it would be less sad than the fate in store for the cheese. While some of the unused goods in an event like this go to charitable organizations, they can't give away any cheese that's potentially been in contact with finger-poking humans.

All those wheels carefully selected by the teams at each creamery, all the energy and hopes invested in them, all of it is now destined to be fed to pigs.

And the tragedy is the pigs would never know they were eating some of the best cheese in the world.

CHAPTER TWELVE

The Cathedral

ALL GOOD THINGS MUST COME TO AN END. EVEN CHEESE.

Just as empires rise and fall, sometimes cheeses go extinct. Out like a light.

Some get lost in cheese wars, like the recent battle between authentic Camembert de Normandie and its industrial counterpart, which threatens to wipe out the last remaining farmstead producer.

Others get lost during wartime, as several British cheddars did in World War II after the British government streamlined cheddar production in the name of rationing.

It's proteolysis on a grand scale—proteins in cheese are always breaking down, and so are we.

During a lovely panel at ACS, Alyce Birchenough told the story of becoming Alabama's first licensed farmstead cheese-maker, along with her husband, back in 1985. The pair intentionally neglected to grow the business of their Sweet Home Farm and instead enjoyed a fulfilling life among the animals they looked after, along with their friends and the community. Now that the pair is getting on in years, they're winding down operations. They want to continue making cheese for as long as possible, but they know they can't do it forever.

"A lot of people ask us about our exit plan," Alyce said during the panel. "And right now, it's just death."

That which dies in the cheese world doesn't always stay dead, though.

Époisses was also nearly eradicated in World War II until, a decade later, a couple of its fans found someone familiar with the manufacturing methods and brought it back to life. (Even if some people would argue it doesn't necessarily smell that way.) More recently, the Slow Food movement started a program to protect and promote ancient cheeses, bringing them back from the brink whenever possible. The Slow Food Presidia began in 1999 when a young producer tracked down the recipe for Montébore, a then-extinct cheese that looks like a multistory wedding cake, and resurrected it after nearly twenty years in the ether. It's one of the many rare or endangered cheeses Slow Food ushers out at Cheese in Bra that connects cheese lovers with the long arc of history.

If you ask anyone who works in American artisan cheese where in the world they'd most like to visit—which I have done, a lot—many of them will say Cheese in Bra. It's an international celebration in a remote Italian village, gathering together the most venerated cheesemakers alive, some of them bearing cheese that's impossible to find anywhere else on Earth.

The year is wrapping up, winter cheese is coming, and I am off to Italy.

Cheese in Bra throws down the gauntlet on casual cheese lovers by being very hard to reach. Lyft is impossible—there is no rideshare here—GPS is spotty, and good luck getting a cab to the tiny town in Piedmont from the airport in Turin or Milan. Gabi and I drive our rental down narrow mountain roads with hairpin turns, barely avoiding tipping over the edge and crashing into the most lovely vineyard a mile below, while some maniac in a Fiat behind us is making emphatic, lewd hand gestures because we won't go faster. As we get closer to Cheese in Bra, we hit bumper-to-bumper festival traffic in between a series of roundabouts in place of stop signs. Just outside of town, we pass a blasphemous McDonald's, and the drive has been so nerve-wracking I almost want to stop in and stress eat some spite-fries.

The first Slow Food Festival launched in 1999, the same year as the Montébore resurrection. Only fifteen exhibitors participated but the festival still managed to bring in 150,000 visitors, ensuring that Slow Food would hold it every two years thereafter. Word of mouth about Cheese in Bra quickly reached the American artisan cheese community, and by 2009, makers like Cowgirl and Rogue Creamery were flying out for a rare opportunity to share their wheels with the rest of the world. What they found was a festival like none they'd ever experienced back home, a four-day fiesta that lasted from 10:00 A.M. until 10:00 P.M. and unofficially continued way later than that.

It's not just one area in Bra that celebrates the festival, it's the entire town. Slow Food's red snail logo hangs in foamy spirals from seemingly every clothesline, joining together brightly colored townhouses. A hungry crowd spans in all directions across the stone tile streets, while a vendor floats an inordinate number of balloons for sale and a guitarist in a bowler hat walks around on stilts. It looks at first like the kind of anonymously European scenery you half expect to see Jason Bourne run through before scaling a drainpipe onto a terra-cotta rooftop. Then I wonder if we've entered a parallel dimension that revolves entirely around cheese. We pass by metal sculptures of cows dancing on cheddar, spot jumbo wheels of Grana Padano in the street, holding wood pallets in place to form a bike rack, and finally, we come across a true cheese bonanza.

Familiar fumes of baby vomit and foot sweat hit as we near a line of pointed white tents. The smell is so strong that even if Jason Bourne had been chased through the rest of town without realizing he was in the middle of the world's largest cheese festival, he'd have inevitably caught on by now. The white tents hang over individual food stands on each street, selling raw cow sausage—an ancient Bra delicacy—or buffalo ricotta ice cream with dark Ecuadorian chocolate nuggets. But the nucleus of the festival is made up of four pavilions, each taking up an entire block, all connecting to form one remarkably powerful cheese quad. This is where we spend the bulk of the next seventy-two hours.

The tents in the International Market and on Presidia Street contain so many cheeses I've never seen before. Some of them have unfamiliar names or are stacked in odd rockpile formations, but still fall into standard cheese categories. Others are utterly unrecognizable as cheese. They're indigenous remnants of the distant past, resistant to the full throttle pull of history. There's cheese that looks like burned bread loaves, but tastes delicate and floral; cheese that looks like it was buried in the ground, but packs a primal milky blast of purity; cheese that actually *was* buried in the ground, part of a centuries-old tradition meant to deter thieves, and has a bitter cocoa flavor that lingers like an early spring cough. As I taste them all, I feel unstuck in time. A lightning bolt hits inside my head, flashing a hazy rotoscoped image of earlier civilizations who ate cheese that looked this way and who didn't think there was anything strange about it because there wasn't. Maybe the way cheese looks now, sleek and burnished, is actually the strange way, and we've drifted further from God's light. I don't know. I'm just a person who only recently learned about cheese, coming from a country that only somewhat recently started producing it, visiting a land where it's been perfected over millennia. As I ruminate on my personal link to that shared past, the sound of Italian DJs spinning Selena Gomez and Marshmello brings me back to now.

Finally, there's Affineurs Alley, the section of the festival that Neal's Yard Dairy established, bringing together international cheese houses with an emphasis on aging and selecting. Neal's Yard is heavily integrated into the festival. The one bit of after-hours scuttlebutt I've caught since arriving is that the Neal's Yard party is not to be missed. I'm determined to get invited.

As we enter the tent, one of the first people we see is Madame Fromage, leading a group of tourists on a Cheese, Pray, Love–type journey through the festival. She's scribbling notes on a pocket-size pad while the tour group tastes spicy-sweet Gorgonzola dolce from Luigi Guffanti. We pass by a Belgian booth hosting the makers behind OG Kristal, the first cheese Adam Moskowitz ever gave me to taste. I pester them to sell me some, but it's a pasteurized cheese, and Slow Food officially restricted the festival to only raw milk cheeses in 2017, so they can't sell me any. Then we reach the American Cheese Company section, where a lot of familiar faces are stationed. American Cheese Company originally consisted of Jasper Hill, Uplands, and Rogue Creamery, but has since expanded to include Point Reyes, Vermont Creamery, and Spring Brook Farm. Cowgirl and Cypress Grove used to have stands here, too, but when Slow Food phased out pasteurized cheeses, those creameries had to stop participating in the festival.

David Gremmels appears at the side of the pavilion, wearing his royal blue Rogue milkman hat and shirt, with a bowtie like an explosion of phosphorescent confetti. He's just come from a tasting session that paired a thirty-year-old sherry, the oldest he's ever sipped, with Rogue River Blue, which he's just officially debuted for the season at his booth.

"It's tasting really good this year," he says, taking a deep, meditative breath.

During breakfast at our Airbnb this morning, Gabi and I met a fellow lodger also heading to the festival. He told us that two years ago, he'd tasted Rogue River Blue here in Affineurs Alley and bought a kilo—that's what he called it, a kilo—to bring back to the shop he ran in Belgium. It wasn't for selling, just something he kept aside to sample out to his best customers.

At first, I was flattered on behalf of David, and America by extension, that Rogue River Blue had become this man's secret stash. But then he told us that he'd also received some yak cheese recently from a friend in Nepal, and I realized he held the two cheeses in equal standing. They were both exotic curios.

I decide not to tell David this story.

"Are you going to that Neal's Yard Dairy party?" I ask, blatantly fishing for an invite.

David's eyes turn upward as he appears to weigh the question.

"You know, I might not go," he says, putting a thoughtful hand to his chin. "I'm gonna see where the day takes me. But you should go."

"We would," I say, "but we don't know where it is and we're not invited."

David laughs at our predicament.

"Well, it's actually Giorgio Cravero's party," he says. "If you haven't had his Parmigiano-Reggiano, you really have to. It's divine."

"Oh, I've had Giorgio Cravero's Parmigiano-Reggiano," I say with barely fake indignation. Cravero is a God-tier affineur who comes from a cheese dynasty that has been around since the 1800s.

"Well, good. You should go by his booth at the end of this alley and just ask if you can go."

David mentions vaguely where Cravero's house, the site of the party, is located in town, and we part ways.

As soon as we say goodbye, I bump into Cristi, from Spring Brook Farm, whom I met in the Parisian cheese cave months ago. At the time we met, she was giving a group of Europeans their first-ever taste of American cheese. Here at the festival, she's basically reliving that same moment every two seconds.

With a medley of milky aromas in the crisp fall air, people continuously grab for sample slivers of Tarentaise, Pleasant Ridge, and Bayley Hazen Blue, all arrayed on cutting boards lining the counters at each booth. If they don't already know that this is American cheese from the enormous sign that reads AMERICAN CHEESE COMPANY just overhead, they find out soon enough.

"Where is it from?" an ashen man with a cruciferous nose asks a woman at the Jasper Hill booth, as he chomps on a cheese sample.

"Vermont."

The man's face sours.

"*That* Vermont?" he says, perhaps confusing the Green Mountain State with some clandestine royal fiefdom of Vermont hinted at on a treasure map. He doesn't seem very happy with the information, but he buys some Alpha Tolman anyway.

Most of the festivalgoers don't have extreme reactions to tasting American artisan cheese for the first time. I don't know what I was expecting to see, exactly: pure glee, rending of garments, a pledge written in blood to only eat Pleasant Ridge Reserve henceforth. Whatever it was, I might have been expecting too much. People come, they nibble, they buy or don't buy, and they move on to the thousand other cheeses they'll consider today. Some of them project a quizzical mix of surprise, confusion, and delight, like they now have a fresh anecdote but don't know who needs to hear it. And others look almost sad to find out the cheese they're enjoying is American, like the time I realized a song I liked was written and performed by the Black Eyed Peas. To those people, tasting fine American cheese might have had the opposite effect the ancient Presidia cheeses had on me: a portal to an uncertain future instead of a glimpse at the distant past.

SOME MOMENTS IN life end up not nearly as excruciating as you dread they'll be.

Others turn out exactly how your inner-catastrophizer advertised, making you want to rip off your own skin.

Attempting to gain access to the Neal's Yard Dairy party turned out to be the second kind.

We had dropped by the Cravero booth, as David suggested, and asked a prim Italian woman in an unzipped motorcycle jacket about the rumored party. She took down my name and number, probably adding *nerd writer* next to it, in a rushed way that was not at all encouraging. Undeterred, a few hours later

Gabi and I headed in the general direction David had given us for Cravero's house. We spotted a flock of fashionable strangers who had too much pregaming energy to be walking away from the festival and started following them. Sure enough, they eventually lead us to the foot of a long driveway on a gated property, where a line has formed in front of a folding table. Gabi and I are ecstatic, until we notice the woman from the Cravero booth playing bouncer at the table, at which point we stare at each other with pre-embarrassment panic.

"Are we really going to do this?" I say.

"Imagine how you'll feel if we went this far and didn't even try," Gabi says.

I put on my most confident face—which is the face I always make, only more effortful—and approach the table. The woman from the booth recognizes me immediately and lets out a deep, low sigh only with her eyes.

"Remember me, from before?" I say meekly.

"So, I think it is going to be full," she says, wincing. "But I can check with Giorgio."

Before I can stop her, she gets up, clipboard in hand, and walks to the gate at the back of the driveway, where a handsome middle-aged man in a silver blazer is standing. She starts talking with him and points at me, and this is the moment that's every bit as bad as I feared. My stomach is in knots, and I contemplate skulking away.

Just then, Mateo Kehler walks up with his family, curly hair dangling at the shoulders of the same *Dark Side of the Moon*–knockoff Jasper Hill T-shirt he's worn almost every time I've met him. I close the few feet between us and introduce him to Gabi.

"How's your festival been?" I ask, straining to appear casual and not in any way like a person who's about to get denied entry into a party.

"It's been awesome," he says. "I thought people would be ragging on us pretty hard here because of the tariffs, but it hasn't been so bad."

The deadline for the proposed tariffs on European cheeses headed to America is in a couple of weeks. Nobody knows what will happen, but most of the cheese people I talk with at the festival seem pessimistic. They've gone from hoping to avoid getting dragged into an intercontinental dispute to hoping it won't be worst-case-scenario bad when the hammer comes down.

While we're talking about tariffs, I notice the man the gate-keeper went to speak with is now walking toward Mateo and me. Giorgio Cravero is trim, but he looks like he's carved from oak. Jordan Edwards told me he once saw him pick up a ninety-pound wheel of Parmigiano-Reggiano with a knife, throw it in the air, and cut it in half before it landed.

"I hear you want to crash my party?" he says, eyebrows raised.

If only there were a way to astral project outside my body and escape from this moment. Just when I'm about to politely and solemnly offer to go fuck myself, Mateo cuts in.

"Let him in, he'll be fine."

Giorgio looks from Mateo to me and then Gabi, who is smiling uneasily, and crosses his arms.

"This man vouches for you," he says, finally. "You should make the most of that."

Gabi and I shake Giorgio's hand vigorously, then we levitate up the long driveway, mouthing silent screams at each other, and slip through the gates into cheese heaven.

An unruly international mix of guests is already spread across the pebbled courtyard, drinking wine and talking cheese. I recognize some of them from ACS, others from visits to Vermont, and others still just from Google-stalking. Clara Díez was Adam Moskowitz's guest at the first Barnyard Collective I attended last year, when he'd just started importing cheese from her Quesería Cultivo in Spain. We're in the middle of talking about how Cultivo has fared in America when Philippe Goux from Marcel Petite, maker of the best Comté in existence, cuts in to say hello to Clara.

The cheese world is very small, and for the moment, it seems like all of it is right here.

Jason Hinds from Neal's Yard Dairy—dapper and scarf-ensconced, not one hair mussed—stands near the entrance to the Cravero cheese cave, speaking through a megaphone because Giorgio apparently misheard his microphone request.

Jason gives a short welcoming speech before declaring: "The cathedral of Parmesan is now open."

Everybody floods in at once, like polite Black Friday shoppers. Just beyond the threshold, an olive-skinned woman greets us with Parmigiano-Reggiano pieces she tongs into a napkin from a freshly cracked wheel, which looks like a tree stump struck by lightning. To the left of the entrance is so many library rows of wooden planks, stacked with honey-gold Parmesan wheels as big as truck tires. I gawk at how high up the shelves seem to go, stretching way further than their actual twenty feet, each wheel another sun of its own universe. Looking through a blank space in one row and seeing the parabolic curve of all the other wheels in the rows beyond, it feels like staring into cheese infinity. I have this inexplicable instinct to do a spider-monkey climb up the shelves and liberate wheel after wheel—Mateo Kehler would take the blame, after all—but I refrain. Instead, I do what everyone else does and try to find the best angle for a photo that could possibly capture the immensity of all the cheese in this cave.

Once we walk past the initial rows of wheels, and turn a corner in the spartan cathedral of Parmesan, there are further rows, along with scattered stations where aproned cheesemakers who sell their wares with Neal's Yard Dairy cut samples of their handiwork. Somebody's kids are playing very short games of hide-and-go-seek in one of the latter rows, not far from a circular stained-glass window over a doorway to the backyard. It's the same pineapple yellow as the Parmesan wheels all around us, painting the sky beyond them the color of cheese.

Gabi and I chat with a man, Mike, from Belfast who makes a Stilton-style blue called Young Buck, the first raw milk cheese in Northern Ireland. Although he isn't sampling here at the party, he is affiliated with Neal's Yard Dairy and has a booth set up at the festival. He mentions that he's going on his first trip to America soon, and asks for recommendations around the Boston area. I recommend Vermont, just in general, as a place to go for cheese, and he laughs.

"You know, in Italy people don't think about America as having good cheese," Mike says, "but Americans are so into making craft beer and things like that. Of course, they're gonna make cheese."

It's a backhanded compliment, but a compliment nonetheless.

"Budweiser is the only beer a lot of Europeans can get from America," Gabi notes. "So, a lot of them never know about all the American craft beer."

"Yeah, a lot of people do associate America with craft," Mike says, moving out of the way of someone's selfie path. "But over here you only get Kraft, like with a big *K*."

There it is, Kraft. The inescapable albatross. The monolith whose shadow American cheese may be doomed to live under forever; whose global reach and mediocrity are so supreme that people seem shocked to hear the country that created it is capable of producing anything better. America's cheese reputation is bound to improve someday, as more people like Mike understand what's happening here, but only gradually. It's a game of inches, the accrued social echo from thousands of microtransactions slowly eroding the bedrock shared belief that the country whose biggest contribution to world cuisine is McDonald's only makes fast-food cheeseburger cheese. The change will happen over time, like affinage, but it will happen.

"Do you remember the first time you had good American cheese?" I ask Mike.

"Yeah, I remember," he says, smiling so big I brace myself for a wild story.

"I mean, it was yesterday."

We chat for a while longer, and then leave through the gates of cheese heaven, back down to Earth. A few days later, we leave Italy for the final destination on our cheese odyssey.

THE DÉSALPE HASN'T yet begun but there are already cows everywhere in the mountain town of Charmey, within the district of Gruyère. Illustrations of happy cows with pink horns adorn the welcoming road signs on the way into town, and they pop up everywhere within as well. Little plush cows sit on grocery store shelves, branded with the Gruyère logo. There's even a friendly cardboard cow standing on the thatched wood awning of the local butcher shop—along with, for reasons only God knows, a cardboard Pumbaa, the warthog from Disney's *The Lion King*.

In a short while, the actual cows will join their inanimate brethren in taking over the town, in a celebration to mark the animals and their herdsman returning from a summer spent making cheese at higher elevation. And I'll be here for it.

This year marks the first time I've actually known to anticipate the cheeses that only arrive with the changing of the seasons. Since I was in Europe anyway, I knew there was a place I could celebrate the slide into winter in a more substantial way than I otherwise might, which would be eating Rush Creek Reserve while drinking apple cider and making Halloween costumes for my cats. Instead, after Cheese in Bra, Gabi and I packed up our rental and headed for Switzerland.

Although the Swiss cheesemakers' summer-ending descent from the mountains has been a Charmey tradition for centuries, the Désalpe festival celebrating transhumance is only forty years old. In that time, it has become the town's flagship event, bringing in residents of the surrounding Fribourg area who want to immerse themselves in their roots, along with up to fifteen thousand tourists from around the world.

How to describe the view in Charmey? You have to physically restrain yourself from doing a *Sound of Music* twirl at all times. No matter where you stand, a panorama of mountains hangs over your head, so big and so close it's like you're standing on them while also seeing them in the distance. You can't escape them, and you wouldn't want to. The shadows from the peaks shift across the thickets of trees, dotted by redwood cottages, all beneath an unending sky the cerulean blue of dreams.

Tour buses arrive and sleep-deprived travelers in matching shirts spill out into a meadow to stretch, as Gabi and I leave our hotel and head to the festival. Accordion music blasts out of speakers mounted on balconies while we walk around town. People are already drinking in bars and singing folk songs, and it's not even 9:00 A.M. The crowds forming around the steel barricades along the streets are still pretty slim, though.

When the accordion music abruptly switches off and a live announcer begins speaking in French, the sparse crowd applauds. Beyond the quaint cafés and houses with flower-enrobed balconies lining the street, the first animals of the Désalpe appear in the distance. The announcer begins narrating their journey, his voice swelling with nasal-voweled excitement as the goats clomp by with clanging bells on leather straps around their necks. Fresh flowers hang from their horns and are woven into garlands circling their entire torsos. Pairs of children lead them on, the girls in plaid dresses with colorful aprons and the boys in woodsy brown vests and matching fedoras, clutching shepherd's crooks. Bringing up the rear are the herdsmen, dressed identical to the young boys, but with bigger crooks and better hats—more like black Stetsons.

The area behind the barricades starts to get packed just as the first sheep come by, a leashed dog with a handsome blue bow around his neck helping to lead them. Very few Americans are here. I recognize a group of cheese people I'd seen in Bra, but that's about it. The townspeople in ceremonial velvet jackets and the ones selling coffee and Bavarian pretzels all seem a little surprised to see Gabi and me here, the same way other people seemed surprised to taste American cheese back in Bra. But even the tourists coming from surrounding areas didn't just come here to check out a cheese-stuffed animal parade they heard about on a podcast; many of them grew up knowing about this. They've always been aware that some Swiss families venture up into the mountains for the whole summer, in order to make food that everyone has feasted on for ages, and they know to appreciate and celebrate the bridge of tradition wending its way through history. Everyone knows that here; whereas, up until just over a year ago, I didn't even know that anyone made cheese in California.

The sun comes out, aggressively, just before the cows finally do. Gabi translates what the announcer is saying, which is that sheep and goat can't do much damage if they get loose, but cows can. I start to wonder whether this is something I should worry about but remember that there are no bulls involved and, in the same way there are very few female serial killers, there are probably not many rampaging cows either.

The cows come trotting down the street to massive cheers, preceded by their own steeply shadows. Black leather straps straddle their necks, embroidered either in the shape of edelweiss or a specific year marking a previous Désalpe. Because they have more cranial real estate than the goats and sheep, the flowers on their heads come in bouquets, like small tornados of roses.

Parents have to restrain their kids from reaching out through the barricades to try and, well, if not touch the cows, get as physically close to their mojo as they can manage. They laugh at the first plops of cow poop, as well as when one cow stops in the street and innocently starts peeing. The more herds of cows pass by—with cheesemakers riding behind them in dusty pickup trucks full of bungee-strapped copper vats and other equipment—the more the poop gets stomped into the ground and covered in fresher poop. The thick, smudgy dividing line in the middle of the street gradually gets thicker throughout the day, and runs the length of the town.

The next wave of cows has Liberty-sized bells beneath their

necks, which make a sound more like coins inside a washer or dryer than a clang. It looks incredibly uncomfortable, like an apparatus a cruel dietician would devise to make it harder for someone to eat cheese, but the herdsmen look back at their cows so tenderly I'm certain they're aware when their cows are in pain. There's a communion between them, and it extends beyond them; an airborne agent hovering over us all. These people—the herdsmen, and the crowds—respect these animals. Even though the cows *are* the parade, the parade is *for* them, too. Appreciation for the cows and for the cheese they make possible, is interwoven in the fabric of these people's lives in a way that borders on spiritual.

There's only so much of this communion you can experience, however, until you have to taste some of the cheese it's created.

After a while, we go further down the road, past cottages that all look like ski lodges, toward the mountain the cows are descending, until we see groups of people walking into a massive white pavilion in the distance. We pass by brass bands, their shiny tubas reflecting the vast sky, and walk through rows of vendors selling wooden cow carvings, those leather straps with bells at the end, and every kind of mountain knickknack. We stop briefly to see a cheesemaking demonstration in an open replica of the cabins the cheesemakers stay in over the summer, about a mile higher up in the mountains. The man doing the demo, in ceremonial garb, is stirring a copper vat that looks like the world's biggest Moscow Mule, but filled with coagulating milk under a layer of froth. It looks so different from all the make rooms I've been in over the past year. But they're all part of the same continuum.

Finally, just in front of the pavilion, which turns out to be a food hall, are little booths topped with colorful awnings, where members of each of the returning cheesemaker families are selling the cheese they made up in the mountains. Gabi and I visit each of the dozen stands and taste samples, trying to decide which ones to buy. Les Groins' Gruyère tastes like all the separate parts of a fully loaded baked potato, fading in and out of each other. Then there's one from a dairy called les Niez, which has a beautiful, faded gold color dappled with crystals. It tastes like a sirloin lightly rubbed in brown sugar. They're all similar—the cows have been eating the same pastures in the same microclimate, and the techniques are largely the same, passed down for generations—but if you taste them one after the other, you can make out little differences. A milky burst of caramel here, a tangy smack of pineapple there. And I can definitely taste the difference between these Gruyères d'Alpage and Gruyères that weren't made on a mountain. I couldn't explain the difference for the life of me, but I can taste it.

Gabi tries a piece of Gruyère from the Vounetz dairy, and her face becomes a mask of licked-finger-in-the-air concentration.

"I get some caramelized banana in this," she concludes, nodding.

How much we've both changed in this past year. I didn't even think about it until now, but as I've slowly turned into the kind of person who has opinions about Gruyère d'Alpage, Gabi has been on her own cheese journey.

"What?" she says. "What is that look?"

I want to tell her how much I love her in this moment. But it feels like a strange response to a description of cheese.

"Imagine how hard you would have rolled your eyes at anyone saying they tasted *notes of caramelized banana* a year ago," I say.

She feigns—or half feigns—being insulted.

"But it does taste like that, right?"

She's right. I don't know whether the Vounetz really does taste like caramelized banana or if she just put that in my head, but what I know for sure is that it doesn't matter.

"I think this is my favorite cheese," I say. "Let's get some."

The inside walls of the food hall tent are covered in blue and white stripes, and kids' abstract paintings of cows. Families in traditional costume are eating fondue at picnic tables in an area separated by a wooden picket fence. Sneaky-drinking teens are lounging in NASA sweatshirts, *Ghostbusters* jackets, and Red Bull hats—cherry-picking American cultural ephemera. Later on, Alex Klein and the Las Vegas Country Band will take the stage wearing cowboy hats and Canadian tuxedos, and get Swiss natives line dancing to bouncy country music. But that's not for a while.

For now, there's a pressing decision to be made.

"We have two options," Gabi says as we stand at the lip of the tent. "A beautiful sunset back there, or we can get some fondue."

The fondue will still be there later; the sunset won't.

We walk over and find the perfect spot in a flower-filled meadow for taking in the view. The rolling hills of lush green grass look, from a distance, as though they're stacked in crooked layers right on top of each other; the mountains cascading behind them, and the sun setting above. A cottony expanse of clouds breaks open in the fading sky and lets a keyhole of tangerine sunshine escape, painting the underside of the clouds the exact shade of inside-eyelid.

The sunset we're looking at may be the best one I've ever seen, just as the cheese we're bringing home may be the best I've ever tasted. These things are impossible to quantify, you just feel them and try to hold on to them. But like a unique flavor, the sunset can't be captured. The camera flattens it, dulls the colors, drains them of their pop, reduces the frame to what is directly ahead without the peripheral backdrop of the surrounding mountains or the slow ballet of cloud tendrils unfurling. Tomorrow's sunset will be completely different. It will be different for me, because I'll be back home. But it will be different here too. And there is something so sad about something so beautiful gracing the world only temporarily. Even after a week of seeing firsthand how centuries-old traditions can be kept alive or brought back from extinction, I'm still as aware as ever that everything is fleeting. All good things come to an end. Even cheese. Even the sun, one day. For now, I watch it slowly set with my wife and I let go of my certainty that the memory won't compare to the experience of being here. I just let it wash over me and appreciate it, hoping that I do remember this feeling when I eat the cheese that I'm bringing home.

While it lasts.

EPILOGUE

Exit Through the Cheese Shop

ABOUT A MONTH AFTER I RETURN HOME FROM EUROPE, THE IMPOSSIBLE happens.

Rogue River Blue takes the top spot at the 2019 World Cheese Awards, the first time ever for an American cheese, beating out 3,803 other entries from 42 other countries. David Gremmels was apparently right when he told me in Bra that his famous seasonal cheese was tasting "really good" this year. For the time being, it was considered the best cheese in the world.

The golden trophy for the award, shaped like a trier piercing the globe, enjoyed a police escort to the executive lounge in Heathrow Airport, before occupying a first-class seat on the flight to Austin, and eventually getting hand-delivered to its rightful place, Rogue Creamery, where the mayor joined David in an unveiling ceremony.

If Rogue River Blue winning best in its category back in 2003 helped kick-start the boom in American artisan cheese, there was no telling what a victory like this could do.

Just after the impossible happens, the unthinkable is thankfully averted. Well, somewhat.

The tariffs on European imports, which had been looming over the industry like a guillotine blade for much of the year, ended up only being around 25 percent, rather than the feared 100 percent. Importers specializing in the marquee Italian cheeses ultimately took a painful hit, and retailers had to reckon with Parmigiano-Reggiano sticker shock, but it wasn't the existential threat it might have been. And while it was cold comfort for producers with friends who were hurting from the outcome, the tariffs provided further incentive for retailers to stock up on more American artisan product.

As for me, a few months later, on the day before Valentine's Day, I realized it had been two full years since my cheese epiphany at Murray's. The date of this cheesiversary occurred to me while I was in line at BKLYN Larder, picking up cheeses for me and Gabi. Not because of any special Valentine's Day plans, but just to celebrate, like, the Feast of St. Thursday.

I carefully chose a mix I thought Gabi would enjoy—an alpine cheese called Challerhocker, Jasper Hill's Bayley Hazen Blue, and a British farmhouse cheddar from Neal's Yard Dairy—and served them on a board with cashews, cornichons, spicy olives, and—eh, why the hell not?—Golden Grahams cereal. Then we sat in our living room watching a *Friday the 13th* movie and exchanging ideas on what to pair with what else. "Challerhocker really brings out the sweetness in these cashews!"

Objectively, we no longer lived basic-ass cheese lives. The same love I had seen in the community that I'd spent well over a year exploring was now evident within our community of two:

mutual enthusiasm and knowledge, and a sense of insatiable curiosity.

My time within that community had also taught me, I now recognized, what it means to truly savor. The best cheeses are reflections of the time that went into making them, and they taste best when you take the time to truly enjoy them. Slowing down in the best way possible for each cheese moment made me think about all the care I could put into every other kind of moment—all the different flavors of experience, all the things I love most about this world. Maybe I would start to milk and ferment all of those things, too, taking the time to savor the cheese of life whenever I was lucky enough to have the chance.

Carpe caseus: seize the cheese!

ACKNOWLEDGMENTS

THIS BOOK WOULD NOT HAVE BEEN POSSIBLE IF THE AMERICAN CHEESE community weren't a warm and welcoming place full of amazing people who are excited to talk about what they do and why they do it. I am so grateful to everyone who talked with me, vouched for me, and of course fed me during the years it took to research and write this book. If you aren't yet convinced you should buy cheese from all of them, I don't know what else to tell you.

Thank you to my agent, Noah Ballard, who didn't laugh when I told him I was thinking of writing a cheese book despite knowing next to nothing about cheese, my editors Stephanie Hitchcock and Sarah Ried, for helping me turn that thought into a book people might actually read, and Suzette Lam, Amy Hawley, Lisa Erickson, Corey Leonard, and everyone else at Harper-Collins who contributed invaluable input and energy.

Thank you to my editors at *Fast Company*, David Lidsky and Missy Schwartz, who let me fly around the world eating cheese for eighteen months on the clock. It would have been hilarious if they had let me do that and it turned out there was no book.

The following people went above and beyond at every point and were incredible ambassadors for their industry: Adam Moskowitz of Columbia Cheese, Andy Hatch of Uplands Dairy,

David Gremmels of Rogue Creamery, Anne Saxelby of Saxelby Cheesemongers, Christian and Ashley Coffey of Folly Cheese Company, Tenaya Darlington aka Madame Fromage, Rory Stamp, Jordan Edwards, Lilith Spencer, Kristina Graeber, Lauren Cunningham, Eris Schack, Doug Jacknick, Jonathan Richardson, Andy and Mateo Kehler, and Zoe Brickley of Jasper Hill Farm.

Thank you to Sue Conley of Cowgirl Creamery, Lisa Gottreich of Bohemian Creamery, Jill Giacomini of Point Reyes Farmstead Creamery, Tamara Hicks of Tomales Farmstead Creamery, Will Studd, Giorgio Cravero, Liz Thorpe, Pascal Vittu and Karim Guedouar at Daniel, Caroline Hesse at Crown Finish Caves, Tia Keenan, Gordon Edgar, Elena Santogade, Emily Schwed, Erika Kubick aka Cheese Sex Death, J. C. Abbruzzi and Cat Wilson of 72andSunny, Kendra Snyder and Carl Mehling of the American Museum of Natural History, Allison Hooper of Vermont Creamery, Peter Dixon and Rachel Fritz Schaal of Parish Hill Creamery, Tom Perry, Elizabeth Davis of Shelburne Farm, Paola Nano of Slow Food, Emmanuelle Porta of La Gruyère Tourisme, Laini Fondiller of Lazy Lady Farm, Carlos Yescas, Andrew Zimmern, Jim Gaffigan, Noah Fecks, Hunter Fike of Di Bruno Bros., Jason Hinds of Neal's Yard Dairy, Grace Singleton of Zingerman's, David Gibbons, Mike Geno, Alex Armstrong, Sarah Dvorak, Ursula Heinzelmann, Tom Bivins, Vivien Straus, Sarah Kaufmann, Hilary Green, Matthew Rubiner, Nitin K. Ahuja, MD, MS, Rebecca Orozco, Ashley Greco, Josh Hendrickson, Nora Weiser of the American Cheese Society, Lizzie Duffey and Rachel Kerr of Dairy Farmers of Wisconsin, Chalet Cheese Co-op, Kiri Endicott, Ruth Fiore, Michelle Hotaling and everyone at Murray's Cheese, Eric Meredith, Yoav Perry, Cristi Menard, John Fischler,

Julian Bach, Stephanie Skinner, Sue Sturman, Lauren Mosness, Kristine Jannuzzi, Marissa Mullen, Martin Johnson, Alissa Barthel, Edgar Villongco, Michaela Grob, Michele Buster of Forever Cheese, Nathan Arnold of Sequatchie Cove, Nick Bayne, Mary Quicke, Kiri Fisher of The Cheese School of San Francisco, Cathy Strange, Rodolph Le Meunier, Paula Homan of Red Barn, Michael Barry, Russell Smith, Gavin Webber, Brian Schlatter of Old Chatham Creamery, Donna Pacheco of Achadinha, Jill Zenoff, Jeff Forlastro, Andy Johnson, Shelby Anderson, Terrance Brennan, Aaron Kirtz, Keith Dresser, Dan Souza, Anna Juhl, Rachel Juhl, Beat Wampfler, Blythe Riske, Samantha Genke and Austin Genke of Boxcarr Handmade Cheese, Renee Baumann of 61 Local, Jessica Sennett, Daniel Angerer, Clark Wolf, Claudia Lucero, Nicole Easterday, Deena Siegelbaum, and Ellie Studd.

I couldn't have written this book without the patience, encouragement, company, and feedback of my wife, Gabi O'Connor, whom I love very much.

Finally, this book owes an incredible debt to New York City.

ABOUT THE AUTHOR

JOE BERKOWITZ is the author of *Away with Words: An Irreverent Tour Through the World of Pun Competitions*, and a staff writer at *Fast Company*, covering entertainment and pop culture. He's also written for *The Awl, Cosmopolitan, Salon, Rolling Stone, Vulture, McSweeney's, GQ*, and the *Village Voice*. He lives in Brooklyn with his wife and two amazing cats.

ALSO BY JOE BERKOWITZ

"Relentlessly hilarious and consistently compassionate, *Away with Words* isn't just a chronicle of competitive punning but also a story about discovering where you belong and claiming your destiny."

—Josh Gondelman, author of *Nice Try*